Seyyed Hossein Nasr

Three Muslim Sages

Avicenna – Suhrawardī – Ibn 'Arabi

CARAVAN BOOKS
ANN ARBOR

For
Shaikh Isa Nur al-Din

Published by Caravan Books
Ann Arbor, Michigan, U.S.A.

Originally published in 1964 by Harvard University Press

Reprint edition published Caravan Books
by arrangement with Harvard University Press
Reprinted in 1976, 1985, 1997, 2004, 2007

Printed on acid-free paper and made in the United States of America

Library of Congress Cataloging-in-Publication Data

Nasr, Seyyed Hossein.

Three Muslim sages : Avicenna, Suhrawardi, Ibn 'Arabi.

Reprint of the 1969 ed. published by Harvard University Press, Cambridge.
Bibliography : p.
ISBN-13: 978-0-88206-500-7 (alk. paper)
ISBN-10: 0-88206-500-9 (alk. paper)
1. Avicenna, 980–1037. 2. Al-Suhrawardi, Yahya ibn Habash, 1152 or 3 –1191. 3. Ibn al-'Arabi, 1165–1240. I. Title.
[BP70.N36 1975]
297'6 [B]

75-14430

List of Transliterations

Arabic characters

ء	'
ب	b
ت	t
ث	*th*
ج	j
ح	ḥ
خ	*kh*
د	d
ذ	*dh*
ر	r
ز	z
س	s
ش	*sh*
ص	ṣ
ض	ḍ
ط	ṭ
ظ	ẓ
ع	ʿ
غ	*gh*
ف	f
ق	q
ك	k
ل	l
م	m
ن	n
ه	h
و	w
ي	y
ة	ah; at (construct state)
ال	(article) al- and 'l- (even before the anteropalatals)

long vowels

ا	ā
و	ū
ي	ī

short vowels

ـَـ	a
ـُـ	u
ـِـ	i

Diphthongs

ـَـو	aw
ـَـي	ai (ay)
ـِيّ	īy (final form ī)
ـُوّ	uww (final form ū)

Persian letters added to the Arabic alphabet

پ	p
چ	*ch*
ژ	*zh*
گ	g

CONTENTS

INTRODUCTION 1

I. AVICENNA (IBN SĪNĀ) AND THE PHILOSOPHER - SCIENTISTS 9

The Predecessors of Avicenna — 9
Avicenna, a Biographical Sketch — 20
The Avicennian Corpus — 23
Ontology — 24
Cosmology and Angelology — 28
The Natural and Mathematical Sciences — 31
Psychology — 38
Religion and Revelation — 40
The Esoteric Philosophy — 43
The School of Avicenna — 45

II. SUHRAWARDĪ AND THE ILLUMINATIONISTS 52

The Background before Suhrawardī — 52
Suhrawardī's Life and Works — 55
Sources of *Ishrāqī* Doctrine — 60
The Meaning of *Ishrāq* — 62
The Classes of Those Who Know — 63
Geographic Symbolism — 64
Ḥikmat al-ishrāq and Its Basic Doctrines — 66
The Significance of the Visionary Recitals — 77
The *Ishrāqī* Tradition — 79

III. IBN 'ARABĪ AND THE ṢŪFĪS 83

The Ṣūfī Tradition — 83
The Significance of Ibn 'Arabī — 90
The Life of the Sage from Murcia — 92
The Works — 97
The "Sources" of Ibn 'Arabī — 100
The Doctrine — 102
Sufism after Ibn 'Arabī — 118

SELECTED BIBLIOGRAPHY 125

NOTES 131

INDEX 171

ACKNOWLEDGMENTS

The three chapters which follow were delivered originally as open lectures at Harvard University during March 1962, under the auspices of the Center for Middle Eastern Studies and the Center for the Study of World Religions. I am particularly indebted to Professor R. H. L. Slater, the director of the Center for the Study of World Religions, for making possible the delivery of these lectures and for helping to have them appear in published form. I am also thankful to Miss M. Kathleen Ahern and to Mrs. Patricia Swanson for preparing the manuscript for publication.

Seyyed Hossein Nasr

Visiting Lecturer
in World Religions,
1961–1962
Harvard University

Cambridge, Massachusetts
1963

Bi ʿawnika yā laṭīf

Introduction

THE "golden age" of Islam, insofar as the intensity of the religious and spiritual life and the realization of its ideals are concerned, must be identified with the lifetime of the Prophet Muḥammad – upon whom be peace – and the first Muslim community at Medina. But just as the seed sown in the ground grows into a tree and finally bears fruit only after the passage of time and the gaining of nourishment from a suitable soil, so did the tree of Islamic civilization bear its intellectual and artistic fruits several centuries after its inception, during which it was nourished by the legacy of the previous civilizations to which Islam became the heir. The arts and sciences, as well as philosophy and metaphysics, reached their zenith of formal perfection and became fully articulated only after Muslim society had become completely consolidated, and only after the tenets of the Islamic revelation had been realized in concrete and tangible forms so as to make the new civilization distinctly Islamic, even when elements of non-Islamic origin had been incorporated into it.

The spread of Islam and the subsequent consolidation of Muslim society is one of the most rapid and decisive events in human history. By the end of the earthly career of the Prophet, under the banner of Islam, the whole of Arabia was united for the first time, and by A.D. 700, that is, less than eighty years after the birth of Islam, the new religion had spread over the whole of the Middle East and North Africa and its domain stretched from the Indus Valley to Andalusia. Moreover, unlike the only other expansion that can be compared in any way to it, namely, the Mongol invasion of Western Asia seven centuries later, the effect of the Islamic conquest was permanent. Except for Andalusia, from which the Muslims were expelled in the fifteenth century, every country into which Islam spread during that short period became Islamicized, and in many cases "Arabicized," and has remained so until the present day.

As might be expected, this sudden expansion and the conquest of such a vast territory by the Muslims needed time before the conquered domain could be transformed into a society constructed upon the Islamic pattern. There was at this moment an urgent need to find administrative codes and rules of government for situations that had never existed in the Arabian Muslim community at the time of the Prophet, and to apply the laws of the Quran and the practices of the Prophet to new circumstances which had never occurred before. So it was that the early caliphs, the four who followed the Prophet immediately and who are usually called *al-khulafā' al-rāshidūn*, as well as the Umayyads, spent most of their energy in solving the immediate problems of creating an Islamic society. They supported and cultivated such sciences as the reading and interpretation of the Quran, assembling the traditions or *ḥadīths* of the Prophet, and systematizing the study of the Arabic language, all of which were of immediate concern to the new community inasmuch as the sacred law of this new society, or the *Sharī'ah*, was based on the Quran and the *ḥadīth*, and its language, unknown to many newly converted non-Arab Muslims, was Arabic.

Preoccupation with such immediate concerns prevented the Umayyads from turning their attention to the vast heritage which the hands of fate had placed in reach of the Muslims, and so, during this early period of Islamic history, there was only an occasional figure like Khālid ibn Yazīd who began to cultivate interest in pre-Islamic sciences, and only very rarely was a book translated from Greek or Syriac into Arabic. Rather, this early period was one in which the traditional religious sciences of Quranic commentary and *ḥadīth* became fully established, and the study and cultivation of the Arabic language reached a high state of accomplishment with the formation of the Kūfa and Baṣra schools of grammar and the appearance of many outstanding grammarians, poets, and literary critics.

It was inevitable, however, that sooner or later the Muslims would turn their attention to the treasury of pre-Islamic sciences that had been stored within the very citadel of Islam. Before the rise of Islam, the writings of many of the masters of the school of Alexandria, which itself was the meeting place of Hellenic, Jewish, Babylonian, and Egyptian cultural currents, were translated into Syriac and transplanted to Antioch, and from there, farther east to such cities as Nisibis and Edessa. This situation, which was of great consequence insofar as it concerned the later Islamic civilization, had been brought about by the schisms that had developed in the eastern Christian churches. This internal division had separated the Nestorians, and later the Monophysites, from the Greek-speaking orthodox church and had forced them to establish their own schools and centers of learning and to cultivate their own language, namely Syriac, in order to be independent of the Greek-speaking church of Alexandria and Byzantium from whom they had separated. Encouraged by the Persian kings, who were naturally opposed to the Byzantines and who therefore favored the opponents of their enemies, Nestorians spread far into the domains of the Persian Empire and had even established churches in Central Asia. Moreover, wherever these churches spread, they carried with them the Hellenistic philosophy and theology which Christianity had made its own, along with a tradition of reading and interpreting the Greek texts which contained the sciences and philosophy.

In addition to the Christian centers of learning, there was also the city of Ḥarrān, home of the Ṣabaeans, who considered themselves the followers of the Prophet Idrīs, or Hermes, and who had preserved and propagated much of the learning of the more esoteric schools of the Hellenistic period, such as Neopythagoreanism and Hermeticism, into the Islamic period. Hermeticism had also entered into Persia even before the rise of Islam, and in some Pahlavi writings, which were later translated into Arabic, such Hellenistic elements along with certain Indian ones were combined with properly speaking Iranian modes of thought.

The Persian kings had also established a school in Jundishāpūr to compete with the Byzantine centers of learning, and here Indian, Christian, and Jewish philosophers and scientists were brought to teach and study. It was at this center that the Indian tradition of medicine was established and combined with that of the Greeks; and here also that Hindu astronomy and astrology became known to the Sassanids, and with the help of the Hindu astronomers the famous astronomical tables called the *Zīj-i shahriyārī* were compiled.

In such cities as Jundīshāpūr, Ḥarrān, Edessa, and Nisibis a great deal of the learning of the Greeks and Babylonians, as well as that of the Hindus and Persians, was preserved as a living tradition of learning well into the Islamic period. Moreover, once the Muslims turned their attention toward the pre-Islamic sciences and sought to integrate them into their civilization, they found within easy reach people who were competent in translating the sources into Arabic. In these centers, all of which lay within the domain of the Muslim world, there were scholars, mostly Christian and Jewish and some Persian, who had a thorough knowledge of the subject with which they were dealing and who also knew Greek, Syriac, Pahlavi, or Sanskrit, as the case might be, as well as the Arabic language into which they were making translations. And so, with the advent of the Abbasids, especially under Hārūn al-Rashīd, al-Ma'mūn, and al-Mu'taṣim, when attention began to turn toward pre-Islamic sciences and a vast effort was made to translate the sources into Arabic, there were qualified translators easily accessible to the seat of the caliphate in Baghdād. Within two centuries, ranging from about A.D. 750 to 1000, an immense corpus of metaphysical, philosophical, and scientific works was translated into Arabic from Greek, Syriac, Pahlavi, and Sanskrit by several schools of translation that differed from each other in competence and aptitude. Mention must be made especially of such masters of translation as the Christian Ḥunain ibn Isḥāq and his son, Isḥāq ibn Ḥunain, who also prepared critical texts before translating them; the Ḥarrānian Thābit ibn Qurrah, and the convert to Islam from Zoroastrianism, Ibn Muqaffa', all of whom enriched the Arabic language immensely through their translations and prepared the ground for the formation of the various schools of philosophy and the sciences. These schools, which followed on the heels of the translation of this vast corpus into Arabic, came into being as a result of the application of Islamic principles to the various forms of knowledge thereby inherited and the integration of these forms of knowledge into the Islamic perspective.

Of course, it may be asked why suddenly the attention of the Muslim community turned toward the pre-Islamic sciences and philosophy to the extent that the caliphs established and financed large centers for the translation of books into Arabic. Perhaps the best answer that can be given to this important question is that by this time, the Muslims had come into contact with Jewish and Christian religious authorities who were defending the tenets of their faith and also attacking those of Islam by appealing to arguments drawn from Aristotelian logic and philosophy of which the Muslims were ignorant. Such debates are known to have taken place in Damascus. Most likely it was in order to supply the Islamic faith with intellectual armor of a similar kind, and thereby to preserve the power of the *Sharī'ah*, upon which their own authority depended, that the caliphs, especially al-Ma'mūn, spent so much effort to have philosophic and scientific works translated into Arabic. This is not to deny the private interest of the early Abbasid caliphs in the pre-Islamic sciences, but there must also have been a more general cause connected with the interest of the Muslim community and the caliphate to which it was connected, to have caused such an unprecedented effort to be made on the part of these rulers to have the "wisdom of the ages" translated into Arabic.

With the philosophy and much of the science of the Greeks, Persians, and Indians at hand, the Muslims began gradually to bring into being the various intellectual perspectives which have dominated the horizon of Islamic civilization ever since. The schools of law and the Ṣūfī brotherhoods became separately established in the third Islamic century, and the revelation which was until that time still close to its origin, and therefore in a state of "fusion," became "crystallized" into its components. In a similar manner, the various intellectual perspectives, after several centuries, absorbed the nourishment provided by the vast heritage of the ancient world, already existing in Arabic, into the Islamic world view, and founded the diverse schools of philosophy and the arts and sciences. We can thereby legitimately refer to these schools as Muslim, since the concepts and formulations used by them were integrated into the Islamic view even if they originated elsewhere.

In the essays that follow we have chosen to discuss three of the most illustrious Muslim sages, Ibn Sīnā (or Avicenna), Suhrawardī, and Ibn 'Arabī, hoping to express through them the point of view of three important schools, namely, the philosopher-scientists, Illuminationists, and Ṣūfīs. In the East it has always been the idea that has dominated over the individual, according to the saying of 'Alī ibn Abī Ṭālib, the representative *par excellence* of Islamic wisdom and of the esoteric message of the Prophet, who taught his disciples to consider as important what is said, not he who has said it. The three personalities whose doctrines form the subject of our present study are of course of great importance in their own right and play a particularly significant role in the school with which they are connected. But, in addition, each speaks for a perspective which has been lived, and a world view which has been contemplated by generations of sages and seers over the centuries. Moreover, although their schools are not the only ones to have existed in Islam, they are among the most important to have come into being after this early period, and they demonstrate in their totality a very significant aspect of Islamic intellectuality, revealing horizons which have determined the intellectual life of many of the great sages of Islam.

I

Avicenna (Ibn Sīnā) and the Philosopher-Scientists

THE PREDECESSORS OF AVICENNA

In traditional Islamic circles it is generally considered that the first philosopher to have appeared in the Muslim world was a Persian by the name of Īrānshahrī who tried to bring philosophy to the East which many a later philosopher from al-Fārābī to Suhrawardī considered as its original home.[1] But of this figure there remains nothing but a name, and no appreciable fragments of his writing have survived to enable us to claim him as the founder of Muslim philosophy. Rather, Peripatetic, or *mashshā'ī*, philosophy, which is only one school among several that have existed in the Islamic world but which is the only one well known in the West and is often identified with Islamic philosophy as such, was founded by Abū Yūsuf Ya' qūb al-Kindī, commonly called the "philosopher of the Arabs."[2]

Al-Kindī must be considered as the founder of that school in which Aristotelian philosophy as interpreted by Alexandrian commentators – especially Alexander Aphrodisias and Themistius – became combined with Neoplatonism, which had reached the Muslims through the translation and paraphrasing of sections of the *Enneads* under the name of the *Theology of Aristotle*, and the pseudo-Aristotelian *Liber de Causis*, which was the epitome of Proclus' *Elements of Theology*.[3] In this school, also, science was combined with philosophy and in fact was considered as a branch of it just as in another sense philosophy began with the classification of the sciences. The great figures of this school, like al-Kindī himself, were philosophers as well as scientists, although in some cases, like that of Abū Sulaimān al-Sijistānī, philosophy dominated over science, and in others, like that of al-Bīrūnī, science prevailed over philosophy.

Al-Kindī the founder of this school of philosopher-scientists, was born in Baṣra around 185/801 of an aristocratic Arab family of the tribe of Kindah, his father having been the governor of Kūfa. He received the best education possible in Baṣra, which had not been left untouched by the influence of the nearby school of Jundīshāpūr, and later in Baghdād, which had become the great center of learning under the Abbasids. He soon came to master the philosophy and the sciences then being made available in Arabic and sought to integrate them into the Islamic perspective. His competence in various fields of learning made him a favorite at the court of the caliphs al-Ma'mūn and al-Mu'taṣim and he even became the tutor of the latter's son, enjoying a position at court which has rarely been equaled by later philosophers and sages. But al-Kindī's lofty position and proximity to the court did not last, and toward the end of his life, during al-Mutawakkil's reign, he fell into disgrace and died obscurely around 252/866.[4]

Although the name of al-Kindī became among the most famous in the annals of Islam, few of his treatises in Arabic were known until thirty years ago when a large number of his works were discovered in Istanbul, enabling scholars to study his ideas directly from his own words. Still, the forty or fifty treatises of his that have survived are only a small fraction of the vast corpus that he must have written if we are to judge by the titles of his works — numbering two hundred and forty — mentioned in the *Fihrist* of Ibn al-Nadīm. The works that have survived include his treatise on metaphysics, various works on logic, his classification of the sciences, discussion of the works of Aristotle, his celebrated treatise on the Intellect – well known in the West as *De Intellectu* – which had such a profound influence upon later philosophers like Avicenna,[5] his prediction of the duration of the Abbasid caliphate, and works on the various natural and mathematical sciences.[6]

The fame of al-Kindī spread also to the Latin West through the translation of some of his philosophic and scientific writings. In fact, he was one of the best known of Muslim figures in the Occident, especially in astrology in which he was highly respected as an indubitable authority. Indeed, he was considered by many as one of the nine judices of astrology. His fame in the medieval period was so great that it carried well into the Renaissance, and we find such a well-known writer of that period as Cardanus ranking al-Kindī as one of the twelve most influential and important intellectual figures of human history.[7]

In al-Kindī most of the traits that are associated with the later philosopher-scientists are already apparent. A man of universal interest, at home in logic, the natural sciences, medicine and music, as well as in theology and metaphysics, he remained a devout Muslim while at the same time he sought the truth in whatever source he might find it. As he himself writes in the oft-quoted introduction to his *Treatise on Metaphysics*, "We should not be ashamed to acknowledge truth and to assimilate it from whatever source it comes to us, even if it is brought to us by former generations and foreign peoples. For him who seeks the truth there is nothing of higher value than truth itself; it never cheapens or abases him who reaches for it, but ennobles and honours him." [8]

But there are also distinguishing features in al-Kindī. In philosophy he was closer to the Athenian school of Neoplatonism than to the Alexandrian one adopted by al-Fārābī, and he preferred hypothetical and disjunctive syllogisms made use of by the Athenian Neoplatonist, Proclus, and criticized later by al-Fārābī who followed Aristotle more closely and considered this form of demonstration as weak. Al-Kindī also exhibited a special interest in the occult sciences not to be seen among most of the later philosopher-scientists.

On the question of religion he sympathized with Muʿtazilite theology to which he sought to give a philosophic structure and conceived of a relation between philosophy and religion, or faith and reason, that is not to be seen in the writings of al-Fārābī and Avicenna. For al-Kindī there are two possible types of knowledge, divine knowledge (*al-ʿilm al-ilāhī*), which is given to prophets by God, and human knowledge (*al-ʿilm al-insānī*), the highest form of which is philosophy. The first is superior to the second for it can arrive at truths that human knowledge can never reach of its own accord. Therefore, such revealed truths as creation *ex-nihilo*, or resurrection of the body, must be accepted even if not demonstrable by philosophy or even contradictory to it. Philosophy and the sciences are thus subordinated to revelation, and al-Kindī finds no incongruence in adopting the Neoplatonic conception of the generation of the intellects and heavens while at the same time asserting that there is creation *ex-nihilo* and that the chain of being depends upon the Act of God.

With al-Kindī, themes and ideas of Hellenistic origin begin to be contemplated in an Islamic background and meditated on in a new language. Plato and Aristotle, the Neoplatonists and Stoics, the Hermeticists and Pythagoreans, the ancient physicians and mathematicians, all contribute some element to the structure of this new school which comes into being with al-Kindī. It is a school which, while remaining faithful to the inner consistency and logical demands of the disciplines with which it deals, also assimilates elements that have a profound connection with the intellectual and psychological needs of certain components of the new Islamic community. It thereby creates an intellectual perspective which corresponds not only to a possibility that must be realized but also to a need that must be fulfilled, a perspective that must be created within the total world view of Islam.

After al-Kindī, many figures appear who have a universal interest in nearly every branch of the sciences and the arts as well as in philosophy and theology, who combine the general interests of a Renaissance scientist and philosopher in the arts and sciences with the special interest of a medieval theologian and philosopher in religion. They become a class of men who, while cultivating to the utmost philosophy and the sciences, find their need for causality fulfilled within Islam and so do not bring about that breach between religion and science that occurred after the Middle Ages in the Western world. Al-Kindī is the first example of this new school of philosopher-scientists in the Islamic world and serves in many ways as a pattern for the sages who followed after him and who shared his vision of the universe.

Of al-Kindī's immediate pupils the most famous is Aḥmad ibn Ṭayyib al-Sarakhsī,[9] the Shī'ah tutor of the caliph al-Mu'taḍid, who later fell into disgrace after divulging the secrets of the caliph and who became notorious among many later authorities as one who had denied prophecy.[10] One may also mention among al-Kindī's students Abū Ma'shar al-Balkhī, the celebrated astrologer known to the medieval West as Albumasar,[11] and Abū Zaid al-Balkhī,[12] the author of *Ṣuwar al-aqālīm* (*The Figure of the Climes*), and *al-Masālik wa'l-mamālik* (*Roads and Kingdoms*), which are among the most important early works of Muslim geography and the source for the later better-known treatises of al-Istakhrī and Ibn Ḥawqal. These men propagated the influence of al-Kindī, particularly in the sciences, bridging the temporal gulf which separates al-Kindī from his real successor as a philosopher-scientist, Abū Naṣr al-Fārābī.

Al-Fārābī, the Alpharabius of the Latins, and the "Second Teacher" (*al-mu'allim al-thānī*) of the later Muslim scholars,[13] was born at Wasīj in Fārāb in the province of Khurāsān around 257/870.[14] As a young man he journeyed to Baghdād to study logic and philosophy with Mattā ibn Yūnus and then to Ḥarrān where he became a student of Yuḥannā ibn Ḥailān. Possessed from the beginning of a keen intelligence and a great gift for mastering nearly every learned subject, he soon became famous as a philosopher and scientist and returned to Baghdad where a group of disciples, including the famous Christian philosopher, Yaḥyā ibn 'Adī, gathered around him. But al-Fārābī's stay at the Abbasid capital was not permanent, for in 330/941 he left that city for the court of Saif al-Dawlah al-Ḥamdānī at Aleppo and stayed there until his death in 339/950.

Al-Fārābī is generally regarded as the great commentator and follower of Aristotle. He wrote commentaries upon the *Categories*, *Hermeneutics*, *Prior* and *Posterior Analytics*, *Sophistics*, *Rhetoric* and *Poetics*, as well as the *Isagoge* of Porphyry in logic, and also upon Aristotle's *Nichomachean Ethics*, *Physics*, *De Caelo* and *Meteorology*. He also composed a commentary upon the *Metaphysics* which, besides its importance as an exposition of al-Fārābī's own solution of metaphysical and ontological questions, had a direct bearing upon Avicenna's understanding of Aristotelian metaphysics.

In logic, especially, al-Fārābī's works were particularly significant because in them Aristotelian logic was expressed in a very appropriate and exact Arabic terminology which henceforth became a heritage of nearly all branches of Islamic learning.[15]

Despite his great loyalty to Aristotelian demonstration, which he considered the key to all discursive forms of science, and despite the fact that he followed the Stagirite closely on the question of psychology, al-Fārābī was not by any means just an Aristotelian. He sought rather to unify the wisdom of Aristotle and Plato and, like nearly all other Muslim sages, considered the wisdom expounded by these men to have come ultimately from Divine revelation, and could not therefore be completely contradictory. He wrote several works to this end, the most famous being *Kitāb al-jam' bain ra' yai al-ḥakīmain Aflāṭūn al-ilāhī wa Arisṭū* (*The Book of Argument between the Ideas of the Two Sages, the Divine Plato and Aristotle*) in which he sought to harmonize the perspectives of these two ancient masters as the Neoplatonists and those whom Proclus called "The Golden Chain of Philosophers" had done before him.[16]

Al-Fārābī was also a political philosopher and must in fact be considered as the founder of political philosophy in Islam.[17] On this question, he followed mostly the doctrines of Plato, whom he calls the *imām* of the philosophers and whose political philosophy became known to him through an unknown commentary upon the *Republic* and the *Laws*.[18] Al-Fārābī sought to identify the figure of the prophet-king of Plato with the prophet and law-giver of the Abrahamic Tradition and described the perfect state in which a single revealed law would reign supreme over the world. His political philosophy contained in such major works as *Ārā' ahl al-madīnat al-fāḍilah* (*Treatise on the Opinions of the Citizens of the Ideal State*),[19] *Kitāb taḥṣīl al-sa'ādah* (*On Attaining Happiness*), and *Kitāb al-siyāsat al-madanīyah* (*On the Government of the City State*) are the most important of their kind in Islam and exercised a significant influence upon Averroes, who in more than one way was closer in spirit to al-Fārābī than to Avicenna who stood closer to him in time.

Al-Fārābī also differed from Aristotle in that he was very musical and had a deep sympathy for the Pythagorean point of view, while the Stagirite, from all accounts, must have had little talent for music. The "Second Teacher" composed treatises on all branches of the Pythagorean *Trivium* and *Quadrivium* but it is essentially in music that he gained special fame, to the extent that many stories have been told of his remarkable musical talents. He was himself an excellent performer in addition to being an expert theoretician. He has in fact left us what is perhaps the most important work on medieval music, *Kitāb al-mūsīqa'l-kabīr* (*The Grand Book of Music*),[20] which exercised considerable influence in the East and the West and became an authoritative reference during later periods. Al-Fārābī's compositions became rapidly disseminated in the East, especially among certain Ṣūfī orders, and are still performed by some of the orders that have preserved the spiritual concert, or *samā'*, to the present day.

This connection with Sufism, or *taṣawwuf*,[21] is not just accidental because al-Fārābī, despite his mastery of logic and political philosophy, lived the life of a Ṣūfī, and the spirit of Sufism and even some technical Ṣūfī terms run throughout his works.[22] He despised the excessively worldly life and had a particular love for virgin nature and the simplicity of life that living in it involves. He even held his classes and discussions in the nearby fields by a river outside of the crowded city. He also often dressed in his Central Asiatic attire with a large fur hat and refused to comply with the regulations for dress when at court. Yet at other times he would appear dressed better than anyone else, perhaps to confound his critics at court.[23]

Al-Fārābī's particular interest in Sufism is manifest most of all in his well-known *Fuṣūṣ al-ḥikam* (*Bezels of Wisdom*),[24] his most continuously influential work in the East, which has been taught and read in the *madrasas* to the present day. Although its authenticity has been recently questioned,[25] the reasons advanced do not seem sufficient, and it appears more than likely that the work is al-Fārābī's, or that it at least belongs to his school. On the surface this work purports to expound the principles of Peripatetic (*mashshā'ī*) metaphysics, but in its symbolic meaning it contains a complete cycle of gnosis (*'irfān*) and it is as such that it is taught in present-day Persia.[26] Many commentaries have been written on this work over the centuries, the most famous being that of Ismā'īl al-Ḥusainī al-Fārānī, bearing witness to the great significance that it has had for the Islamic world at large.[27] We see, therefore, that the "Second Teacher," who is famous for commenting upon and propagating the works of Aristotle and for formulating logic in its totality in the new vehicle of the Arabic language, was also a political philosopher following the example of Plato, a scientist, an especially gifted mathematician and musician, and the author of a work which has come to be known to posterity as a summary of the doctrines of gnosis. He was thus another eminent representative of the school of philosopher-scientists and, even more than al-Kindī, must be considered as the predecessor of Avicenna in whom this school found its most celebrated representative.

Also worthy of special mention as a forerunner of Avicenna is al-Fārābī's contemporary, Muḥammad Zakarīyā' al-Rāzī (d. between 311/923 and 320/932), the Latin Rhazes, who was as well known in the West as in the Islamic world.[28] Although he considered himself a philosopher on a par with the greatest seers of antiquity, and although he expounded a special cosmology based on five eternal principles and related to the *Timaeus* in its later Alexandrian interpretation, he was considered more as a competent physician than as a philosopher by his contemporaries as well as by later generations. His philosophical and religious views, bearing the influence of Platonism and Gnosticism on the one hand and Manichaeanism on the other, came under the severe criticism of such men as al-Fārābī and later al-Bīrūnī,[29] and few of his works dealing with these subjects have survived. But his experimental method in medicine, as seen in his medical masterpiece *Kitāb al-ḥāwī* (*Continens*) and in chemistry, as is evident in the alchemical *Sirr al-asrār* (*Secret of Secrets*),[30] had an important role to play in the natural sciences of his period and also left his mark upon certain aspects of Avicenna's works, especially those concerned with medicine and the natural sciences.

In the general histories of Islamic philosophy, one usually turns from al-Fārābī to Avicenna as the next important figure in this school. There are, however, intermediate philosophers and scientists who are significant in that they provide the immediate background for Avicenna. Not only can one mention such important scientific figures as Abu'l-Wafā', Abū Sahl al-Kūhī, Ibn Yūnus, 'Abd al-Jalīl al-Sijzī, al-Bīrūnī, the Ikhwān al-Ṣafā'[31] and such scientific encyclopedists as al-Khwarazmi, who compiled the *Mafātīḥ al-'ulūm*, and Ibn al-Nadīm, the author of *al-Fihrist*;[32] there are also several significant philosophers and logicians, among them Abu'l-Barakāt al-Baghdādī,[33] Ibn Miskawaih, the contemporary of Avicenna whose ethical writings are so famous, Abū Sulaimān al-Sijistānī, his pupil Abū Ḥayyān al-Tawḥīdī and Abu'l-Ḥasan al-'Āmirī.

Of this group, al-Sijistānī and al-'Āmirī are quite unknown in the Western world, despite their great influence and fame in their own lifetime and among the later followers of Islamic philosophy. Al-Sijistānī, whose life stretched over most of the 4th/10th century, from about 310/922 to 390/999, was a student of Mattā ibn Yūnus and Yaḥyā ibn 'Adī and became the leading philosopher of Baghdād in the period stretching from al-Fārābī to Avicenna. His house became the meeting place for all men of learning, and many discussions were held there which his foremost disciple and student Abū Ḥayyān al-Tawḥīdī has recorded in his *Muqābasāt*. In fact, most of al-Tawḥīdī's very informative writings, such as *al-Imtā' wa'l-mu'ānasah*, are replete with the sayings and opinions of his master. Al-Sijistānī is famous essentially as a logician and also as the author of a famous history of philosophy called *Ṣiwān al-ḥikmah*,[34] of which only fragments have remained, but which was completed by Abu'l-Ḥasan al-Baihaqī in his *Tatimmah ṣiwān al-ḥikmah*.[35] His influence and views on various philosophical subjects can best be discovered through a study of al-Tawḥīdī's works, which also reveal what a dominant place al-Sijistānī held in the intellectual life of Baghdād during the days preceding those of Avicenna.

Abu'l-Ḥasan al-'Āmirī (d. 381/992), who was a contemporary of al-Sijistānī and who met him during a journey to Baghdad, may be considered in many ways as the most important philosopher between al-Fārābī and Avicenna. Born in Naishāpūr, he studied with Abū Zaid al-Balkhī and later met many of the great scholars of his day and even debated with the philosophers of Baghdad, a city which he disliked and soon left for his native Khurāsān.[36] Al-'Āmirī sought to harmonize religion and philosophy and wrote a book on the defense of Islam and its superiority to other religious and political ways called *al-I'lām bi manāqib al-islām* (*Declaration of the Virtues of Islam*).[37] He was attracted to and influenced by the political philosophy of the Sassanids as much as by Greek sources, and in his writings it is possible to discover one of the channels through which Iranian ideas of government and society entered into Muslim speculation.

Many of al-'Āmirī's works have survived. The most important are the ethical treatise *al-Sa'ādah wa'l-is'ād* (*On Seeking and Causing Happiness*) and *al-Amad 'ala'l-abad* (*Time within Eternity*), an important history of philosophy known to later sages, especially Mullā Ṣadrā, who quotes it often in his *Asfār*. Mullā Ṣadrā seems also to have derived his doctrine of the union of the intellect, the intelligible, and intellection, which Avicenna had specifically rejected, from al-'Āmirī, who is the first philosopher known in the Islamic world to have discussed and accepted it. Traditional sources like Ibn Abī Uṣaibi'ah's *'Uyūn al-anbā'* also report a series of letters exchanged between al-'Āmirī and Avicenna but this is most unlikely since at the time of the former's death the young Avicenna was only eleven years old. Rather, one must consider al-'Āmirī as one of the philosophers who prepared the way through his writings and the training of disciples – some of whom, like Ibn Miskawaih, became famous – for the culmination of the school of the philosopher-scientists which took place with the advent of Avicenna.

AVICENNA, A BIOGRAPHICAL SKETCH

Abū 'Alī Sīnā, known to the Western world as Avicenna and entitled "the Prince of Physicians," was born in 370/980 near Bukhārā.[38] The sage who was later to become the most influential of all figures in the Islamic arts and sciences and who was to gain such titles as al-Shaikh al-ra'īs (the Leader among Wise Men) and Ḥujjat al-Ḥaqq (the Proof of God), by which he is still known in the East, displayed a remarkable aptitude for learning from an early age. He was also fortunate in that his father, an Ismā'īlī, took great interest in his education and that his house was a meeting place for scholars from near and far. Avicenna learned the whole of the Quran, as well as grammar, by the age of ten and then undertook to study logic and mathematics, the latter under the direction of Abū 'Abdallāh al-Nātilī. Having rapidly mastered these subjects he then undertook a study of physics, metaphysics, and medicine with Abū Sahl al-Masīḥī. At the age of sixteen he was the master of all the sciences of his day except for metaphysics as contained in the *Metaphysics* of Aristotle which, though he had read it over many times and even memorized it, he could not understand. But even this obstacle was removed when he discovered by chance the commentary of al-Fārābī upon the work which clarified all its difficult points for him. From then on Avicenna had nothing more to learn "in breadth" but needed only to increase his understanding "in depth" of what he had already learned by the time he was eighteen years old. In fact, toward the twilight of his life he once mentioned to his favorite disciple, al-Juzjānī, that in all the intervening years he had learned no more than he knew as a youth of eighteen.

Avicenna's mastery of medicine had already made him a favorite of the ruler. The doors of the palace library were opened to him and he enjoyed a reputable position at court. But the pressure of political turmoil in Central Asia caused by the growing power of Maḥmūd of Ghazna was making life difficult and unstable in his home province and eventually forced Avicenna to abandon Bukhārā for Jurjānīyah and finally leave that region altogether for Jurjān. In 403/1012, amidst great hardships, in which several of his companions perished, Avicenna crossed the desert to Khurāsān. According to most traditional authorities, he visited the famous Ṣūfī saint and poet, Abū Sa'īd ibn Abi'l-Khair, before reaching Jurjān, where he hoped to meet the famous patron of the arts, Qābūs ibn Wushmgīr. But upon arrival he discovered that his would-be patron had already died.

Disappointed by this misfortune, he retired to a village for a few years and then left for Rai sometime between 405/1014 and 406/1015. At this time Persia was under the control of the Buyid dynasty, various members of which ruled over the different provinces of the country. Avicenna spent some time at the court of Fakhr al-Dawlah in Rai and then set out for Hamadān to meet another member of this dynasty, Shams al-Dawlah. This meeting was made easy, for soon after his arrival in that city he was asked to treat the ruler, who had become ill. Shams al-Dawlah recovered, and Avicenna became so great a favorite at court that he was finally made a wazīr, a position whose heavy duties he performed for several years until the ruler's death. Then his political fortunes took a bad turn and upon his refusal to continue as wazīr he was imprisoned and could only escape by taking advantage of a siege of Hamadān, and then incognito in the dress of a dervish.

Having freed himself at last from his involvements in Hamadān, Avicenna set out for Ispahān, which, as a great center of learning, he had wanted to visit for many years. In Ispahān he came to the attention of 'Alā' al-Dawlah and enjoyed a long period of peace in that city which lasted fifteen years. During that time he wrote many important works and even began to study astronomy and to construct an observatory. However, even this peaceful interim in a tumultuous life was interrupted by the invasion of Ispahān by Mas'ūd, the son of Maḥmūd of Ghazna, who had forced Avicenna to leave his original abode in his youth – an invasion which caused many of the sage's works to be lost. Deeply disturbed by these conditions and suffering also from an attack of colic, he returned once again to Hamadān where he died in 428/1037 and where his tomb is to be found today.

Thus ended a life which saw many political upheavals and was itself marked by many difficulties. Avicenna experienced numerous ups and downs in life, numerous happy days, but some difficult and trying ones as well. He acted most often as a physician to various princes and so led a very active social life. On occasion he even had to accept the responsibility of running a state. Yet he lived at the same time an intense intellectual life, as witnessed by the number and nature of his works and the quality of his students. He was a man of great physical power, spending long nights in gay festivities and going on from there to write a treatise on some question of philosophy or science. He was also a man of remarkable concentrative powers, dictating some of his works to a scribe while riding on horseback with the king to a battle. In fact none of the external disturbances of the world seems to have affected his intellectual output. The man who was so immersed in the life of the world in both politics and at court was also able to lay the foundation of medieval scholastic philosophy, to synthesize the Hippocratic and Galenic traditions of medicine, and to influence the Islamic arts and sciences in a way which no other figure has ever been able to do before or after him.

THE AVICENNIAN CORPUS

The writings of Avicenna, of which nearly 250 have survived if we take all his short treatises and letters into account, range over nearly every subject known to the medieval world.[39] These works are mostly in Arabic, but occasionally in Persian, as for example, the *Dānishnāmah-i 'alā'ī* (*The Book of Science Dedicated to 'Alā' al-Dawlah*), which is the first philosophic work in modern Persian.[40] Avicenna's Arabic style in his earlier works is rather difficult and uneven; and it was only during his long sojourn in Ispahan – when under the criticism of certain literary experts he began to study Arabic literature intensely – that his style became polished and perfected. The works written later in life, especially the *Ishārāt wa'l-tanbīhāt*, testify to this change.

Avicenna's philosophical works include his Peripatetic masterpiece *al-Shifā'* (*The Book of the Remedy*), the Latin *Sufficientia*, which is the longest encyclopedia of knowledge ever written by one man,[41] his *Najāt* (*The Book of Deliverance*), which is a summary of the *Shifā'*, *'Uyūn al-ḥikmah* (*Fountains of Wisdom*), and his last and perhaps greatest masterpiece *al-Ishārāt wa'l-tanbīhāt* (*The Book of Directives and Remarks*). In addition he wrote a large number of treatises on logic, psychology, cosmology, and metaphysics.[42] There are also the "esoteric" works pertaining to his "Oriental Philosophy" of which the *Risālah fi'l-'ishq* (*Treatise on Love*), the Trilogy *Ḥayy ibn Yaqẓān* (*The Living Son of the Awake*), *Risālat al-ṭair* (*Treatise of the Bird*) and *Salāmān wa Absāl*, the last three chapters of the *Ishārāt*, and *Manṭiq al-mashriqīyīn* (*The Logic of the Orientals*), which is a part of a larger work now lost, are the most important.[43]

In the sciences, also, Avicenna composed many small treatises dealing with particular problems in physics, meteorology, and so on, as well as sections contained in the larger compendia, especially the *Shifā'*, in which is found the most complete exposition of his views on zoology, botany, and geology, as well as psychology, which in Peripatetic philosophy — and contrary to the view of the later schools like the *Ishrāqīs* — is considered as a branch of physics or natural philosophy. As for medicine, Avicenna composed the famous *Qānūn*, or *Canon*, which is perhaps the most influential single work in the history of medicine and is still taught in the East today,[44] the *Urjūzah fi'l-ṭibb* (*Poem on Medicine*), containing the principles of Islamic medicine in rhyming verses easy to memorize, and a large number of treatises in both Arabic and Persian on various diseases and drugs.

In addition to his philosophical and scientific works, Avicenna wrote several poems in Arabic and Persian of which *al-Qaṣīdat al-'ainīyah* (*Ode on the Soul*) [45] is deservedly the most famous. Moreover, he wrote several religious works which include not only treatises on particular religious subjects, such as the meaning of fate and free will, but also commentaries upon several chapters of the Quran. This latter category is particularly important because it was primarily in these commentaries that Avicenna sought to harmonize reason and revelation along lines already begun by al-Kindī, al-Fārābī, and the Ikhwān al-Ṣafā', continued after him by Suhrawardī, and finally brought to its fruition by Mīr Dāmād and Mullā Ṣadrā. These writings add an important dimension to the already multidimensional corpus of Avicenna's literary output and emphasize the richness of a collection of writings which range from observational and even experimental science to ontology, from mathematics to gnosis and metaphysics, and from logic to commentaries upon the Sacred Book.

ONTOLOGY

The metaphysics of Avicenna is essentially concerned with ontology, and it is the study of being and all the distinctions pertaining to it that occupy the central role in his metaphysical speculations.[46] The reality of a thing depends upon its existence, and the knowledge of an object is ultimately the knowledge of its ontological status in the chain of universal existence which determines all of its attributes and qualities. Everything in the Universe, by the very fact that it exists, is plunged in Being; yet, God, or Pure Being, who is the Origin and Creator of all things, is *not* the first term in a continuous chain and therefore does not have a "substantial" and "horizontal" continuity with the beings of the world.[47] Rather, God is anterior to the Universe and transcendent with respect to it. It is God as conceived in the religions of the Abrahamic Tradition; it is God not only as envisaged by the Muslim Avicenna but also by Jewish and Christian philosophers who shared a common conception of the Supreme Deity and who, like Avicenna, reformulated the tenets of Greek philosophy in monotheistic terms.

Avicenna's study of existence – an existence which is shared by all things without its being reduced simply to a genre common between them – depends upon two fundamental distinctions that characterize the whole of his ontology. These distinctions concern the essence or quiddity (*māhīyah*) of a thing and its existence (*wujūd*) on the one hand and its necessity, possibility, or impossibility on the other.[48] Whenever a person thinks about something, immediately, in the framework of his mind, he can distinguish between two different aspects of that thing: one is its essence or quiddity, which is all that would be included in the answer given to the question, what is it? (*quid est*, or *mā hiya*), and the other is its existence. For example, when a person thinks of a horse, he can distinguish in his mind between the idea of the horse, or its quiddity, which includes the shape, form, color, and everything else that comprises the essence of the horse, and the existence of that horse in the external world. In the mind the quiddity is independent of existence in the sense that one can think of the quiddity of an object without in any way being concerned with whether it exists or not. In the external world, however, the quiddity and existence of each object are the same; they are not two components having each an independent external reality which are added together to form an object, as one would add cream to coffee or water to dough. It is only in the mind, in the analysis made by human reason, that these two elements become distinct and one realizes that every object in the Universe has a quiddity to which existence is added.

Avicenna, after making this basic distinction, emphasizes that although the existence of a thing is added to its essence, it is the existence which gives each essence, or quiddity, its reality and is therefore principial (*aṣīl*). The quiddity of a thing is in fact no more than its ontological limitation abstracted by the mind. It was against this basic tenet of Muslim philosophy that Suhrawardī and Mīr Dāmād spoke in later centuries, claiming on the contrary the principiality of quiddity over existence. And it was in defense of Avicenna's view that Mullā Ṣadrā, seven centuries later, once again championed the principiality of existence over essence, adding, moreover, that the existence of each thing is not a totally separate form of existence but that all existence is a degree of the light of Being; that there is the transcendent unity of Being (*waḥdat al-wujūd*) hidden behind the veil of the multiplicity of quiddities and particular forms of existence.

Closely connected to this fundamental distinction between quiddity and existence is Avicenna's division of being into the impossible (*mumtani'*), possible (*mumkin*), and necessary (*wājib*). This division, which gained acceptance by later Muslim philosophers as well as by Latin scholastics, does not appear in such a formulation in Aristotle but is original with Avicenna. In fact, Avicenna bases the whole of his philosophy upon the distinction among these three divisions and the relation which quiddity and existence have in each case with each other. If one considers the quiddity of an object in the mind and realizes that it could not accept existence in any way, that is, it could not exist, that object is impossible and cannot exist, as in the case of a second Principle for the Universe whose existence would be metaphysically absurd and would lead to contradictions. If the quiddity of an object stands equal vis-à-vis existence and nonexistence – that is, if it could exist or not exist without in either case causing a contradiction or impossibility – that object is a possible being, like all creatures in the Universe whose quiddity could either take on existence or remain nonexistent. Finally, if the quiddity is inseparable from existence, and its nonexistence would involve absurdity and contradiction, it is necessary. In such a case the quiddity and Being are the same, and such a Being is the Necessary Being, or God, who could not not be since His Essence and Being are the same; Being is His essence and His Essence, Being.[49] It is only He that possesses Being in Himself and is self-subsistent; all other existing things have their existence added to their essence as accident and are therefore contingent beings.[50] The being of the whole Universe has no higher status than that of contingency and depends for every moment of its existence upon the Necessary Being that keeps all things in existence by the continued effusion of the light of its Being upon them.

The Universe and all things in it are therefore possible beings and metaphysically contingent upon the Necessary Being. Moreover, the possible beings are themselves of two kinds: (1) those that, although possible in themselves, are made necessary by the Necessary Being, and (2) those that are simply possible without any kind of necessity attached to them. The first class consists of the pure and simple intellectual substances, or the angels, who are the "eternal effects" of God in the sense that they are made necessary by Him. The second comprises the creatures of the world of generation and corruption who already contain the principle of "non-eternity" within themselves, who are thus born only to wither and die away.

Besides this division of possible beings into the "eternal" and temporal, or permanent and transient, Avicenna also divides being according to whether it is substance or accident, applying to the quiddity of existing things the Aristotelian categories as systematized by Porphyry. According to this distinction, quiddities are either accidents or substance, depending on whether they are dependent on something else, like the color on a wall; or independent, like the material of the wall itself. The category of substance is itself divided into three kinds, as follows:

1. Intellect (*'aql*) which is completely divorced from matter and potentiality.
2. Soul (*nafs*) which although divorced from matter has need of a body in order to act.
3. Body (*jism*) which accepts divisibility and has length, depth, and breadth.

The elements of the Universe, therefore, which are contingent and possible in their totality, are also divided into three substances which comprise the various domains of the cosmos and form the constituents from which the Universe is made and in terms of which the sciences of the cosmic domain are understood.[51]

COSMOLOGY AND ANGELOLOGY

It is with full consideration of the fundamental ontological distinction between the Universe and God that Avicenna turns to a study of cosmology and cosmogony and undertakes to show how the many is brought forth from the One, who is at the same time transcendent with respect to all multiplicity. But whereas in metaphysics Avicenna's aim is essentially to demonstrate the contingent character of the Universe, in cosmology and cosmogony his aim is to delineate the continuity that exists between the Principle and Its manifestation.

The process of creation, or manifestation, is closely tied to the function and significance of the angel, for the angel is the instrument through whom the act of creation is achieved. Cosmology, in the philosophy of Avicenna, is closely tied to angelology, and the angel has a soteriological function in both cosmology and the process of spiritual realization and the attainment of knowledge.[52] Relying upon the Plotinian scheme of successive effusions of the angelic hierarchy, but interpreted in the light of their possibility and contingency, Avicenna sets out to describe the process of the generation of the Universe, making use of the principle that from the One, or Unity, only one can come into being (*ex uno non fit nisi unum*) and of the idea that it is through intellection that creation takes place.[53]

The process of creation, or the giving of existence, and that of intellection are the same because it is through the contemplation of higher orders of reality that lower ones come into being.[54] From the One Necessary Being who is the source of all things a single being is brought forth in accordance with the foregoing principle — a being whom Avicenna calls the First Intellect and who is made to correspond to the supreme archangel. This Intellect then contemplates the Necessary Being as necessary, its own essence as necessary by virtue of the Necessary Being, and its own essence as possible being. It has thus three dimensions of knowledge which give rise to the Second Intellect, the Soul of the first heaven and the body of the first heaven, respectively. The Second Intellect generated in this manner contemplates in a similar way the First Intellect, generating thereby the Third Intellect, the soul of the second heaven and its body. This process then continues until the Tenth Intellect and the ninth heaven, which is that of the moon, are generated.[55] From here on the "substance" of the Universe has no longer sufficient purity to generate another heaven. Therefore, from the remaining "cosmic possibilities" the world of generation and corruption comes into being.

In the sublunary world – the world of change that surrounds the terrestrial life of man – the Tenth Intellect performs several basic functions. Not only does it give existence to this world but also issues forth all the forms which in combining with matter bring into being the creatures of this region. When a creature is generated, the Tenth Intellect emanates the form to make its existence possible and when it withers away and dies it takes back the form unto itself. That is why Avicenna also calls it the Giver of Forms (*wāhib al-ṣuwar*). For example, if water solidifies and becomes ice, watery form is taken away by the "Giver of Forms" and the new icy form added to the *materia* of what was previously water to turn it into ice.

The Tenth Intellect also serves as the illuminator of the mind of man. Man abstracts the forms which he finds combined with matter in his mind and is able to elevate it again to the level of a universal through the illumination received from the Tenth Intellect. Universals therefore exist in the "angelic mind"; then they descend to the world of matter to become material form and are particularized only to be raised once more in the mind of man through the illumination of the angel to the level of the universal again. The Tenth Intellect is therefore not only the instrument of creation but also of illumination and, as we shall see later, of revelation to the prophets and in a more limited sense to the saints and gnostics.

Avicennian cosmology is therefore essentially tied to angelology and closely follows Plotinian cosmology, which, however, it interprets in a different light. For Avicenna was fully aware of the Islamic conception of the relation between God and the Universe and always sought to demonstrate the contingent nature of the whole created order before the Creator and thus to remain faithful to a principle which is fundamental to the Islamic point of view. In his *Risālat al-nairūzīyah*[56] Avicenna takes a further step in bringing his cosmology into conformity with the Islamic and "Oriental" point of view, for he describes the generation of the various links in the chain of being in terms of the letters of the Arabic alphabet. The word and the letters which form it are for the Semite the most tangible and eloquent symbols of the divine essences and archetypes from which this world is brought into being. Consequently, for the Jews as well as the Muslims, whose spirituality is that of the Semitic nomad, the science of letters and their symbolic value have much significance whether it be the Kabbala for Judaism or *Jafr* for Islam.[57]

In this treatise, in which Avicenna follows closely certain esoteric schools in Islam, as well as certain branches of Ismā'īlism, he makes use of the *abjad* alphabetic order,[58] with A = 1 symbolizing the Creator; B = 2, the Universal Intellect; C = 3, the Universal Soul, and D = 4, Nature. This attempt at creating a correspondence between the hypostases of philosophical cosmology and the letters of the language of the revelation, which resembles in many ways the works of Jābir ibn Ḥayyān and the Ikhwān al-Ṣafā', is particularly significant in the case of Avicenna. It shows that the master of Peripatetics was seeking for an "Oriental wisdom" which differed from the commonly known Greek philosophy and that he was not simply a follower of the older philosophers. It also reveals an aspect of Avicenna's many-sided genius which is more akin to the "Oriental Philosophy" he sought to expound in the later periods of his life.

THE NATURAL AND MATHEMATICAL SCIENCES

Avicenna was nearly as great a scientist and physician as he was a philosopher. In fact it was mostly as a master in the field of medicine that he was so well remembered in the

West. His picture as the "prince of physicians" adorned the walls of many cathedrals in Europe, and Dante honored him by placing him in Limbo between the two great medical authorities of antiquity, Hippocrates and Galen.[59] In the East, too, his influence as a physician has always been dominant and is still alive today. Avicenna was interested in nearly every field of the natural and mathematical sciences as well as in the philosophy and "methodology" of science, which he discussed at the beginning of his treatment of natural philosophy.[60] He wrote many individual treatises on scientific and medical subjects but his most important works in this field are his medical *Canon*, which contains a wealth of medical and pharmacological information, and the *Shifā'* in whose chapters on natural philosophy and mathematics he discusses meteorology, mineralogy, geology, botany, zoology, and psychology, as well as arithmetic, geometry, astronomy, and music. Some of the subject matter of the *Shifā'* is repeated in a more cursory fashion in the *Najāt* and the *Dānishnāmah.*

In his study of the sciences of nature, Avicenna relied upon every avenue of knowledge open to man, from ratiocination and the interpretation of Sacred Scripture to observation and experiment. He sought, in fact, to place knowledge derived from each of these sources in his over-all vision of reality – a reality which consisted of the Universe or the macrocosm, man or the microcosm, and God as the metacosmic origin of all things, to Whom both man and the Universe are related, man and the Universe also having a correspondance and interrelation with each other.[61] As far as his approach to the particular sciences of nature is concerned, he sought especially to devise a logical method for forming definitions related to experimental procedure and for adopting the Aristotelian syllogism as a means of deriving knowledge of a particular rather than universal nature. To this end he changed the middle term, which in the Aristotelian syllogism is the metaphysical cause, to an empirical one, thereby adapting it to the ends of an inductive science.[62] Also of interest, in view of ideas later developed in physics, is his distinction between primary and secondary qualities which, when applied systematically to all of Nature by Galileo, brought into being modern physics, a physics that considers only the quantitative aspect of Nature. Avicenna also believed in the wave theory of light which he discussed in his study of vision and the anatomy of the eye.

The master of Muslim Peripatetics showed both special interest and acumen in observation and experimentation.[63] This is best shown in his medical works where often both in the diagnosis of an illness and the effect of a particular drug administered for its cure he appealed to his own experience with the patient. His observations, moreover, often carried into the field of psychology which for him, as for other Muslim physicians, was closely associated with medicine. In geology, meteorology, astronomy, and physics he also applied both observation and experiment. In his account of the formation of rocks and the structure of meteorites he writes of his own observations and even of his attempt to analyze and melt a meteorite in Khwārazm, with the result that he was left with only ashes and a green smoke but no dissolved metal. In meteorology he describes many times how he saw a rainbow in a bathhouse or in a garden being watered and compares these phenomena with the large rainbows in the sky.[64] In astronomy, while he found a few years of rest at Ispahān, he set out to make a new instrument for observation and criticized some of those of Ptolemy.[65] And in physics he made observations on projectile motion of heavy and light bodies and made certain fundamental criticisms of the Aristotelian theory of motion.

Avicenna's works in medicine climaxed a series of very important writings which had synthesized Greek, Indian, and Iranian schools of medicine as well as fresh material derived from the experience and practice of the Muslim physicians themselves. Among the most important of his predecessors were Abu'l-Ḥasan ibn 'Alī al-Ṭabarī, the author of the *Firdaws al-ḥikmah* (*The Paradise of Wisdom*); Muḥammad Zakarīyā' al-Rāzī, who wrote the *Kitāb al-ḥāwī* (*Continens*) and *Kitāb al-manṣūrī* (*Liber Almansoris*), and 'Alī ibn 'Abbās al-Ahwāzī, the Latin Haly Abbas, the author of *Kāmil al-ṣinā'ah*, or *Kitāb al-malikī* (*Liber regius, regalis disposito*). The *Canon* of Avicenna itself was based to a large extent on these works and because of its order and perfection came to replace them as the basic text used by medical students and physicians, especially as it was clarified and explained by later commentaries of which the most important is that of Quṭb al-Dīn al-Shīrāzī.[66]

The *Canon*, Avicenna's greatest medical work, is perhaps the most fruitful source for the study of the observational and experimental sides of the author's contribution to the sciences of Nature. The work is divided into five books, each further divided into sections and chapters, the five main parts dealing with such general principles of medicine as the description of the human body, its constitution, temperament, faculties; its diseases, hygiene, death, and so on; then *materia medica;* particular diseases; diseases affecting the whole of the human body rather than a single organ or location; and finally pharmacology, this last section being particularly valuable from an experimental point of view.[67] The *Canon* is a synthesis of the traditions of Hippocrates, Galen, and Dioscorides but it also contains much that is not found in Greek sources, especially in the application of herbs in the treatment of various ailments.

There is much that is new in the *Canon* that is the result of Avicenna's own medical experience and reasoning, such as the use of new herbs, the discovery of the antiseptic value of alcohol, and the discovery of brain tumors and stomach ulcers.[68] In the physiology and anatomy of the eye and in his theory of vision expounded in his psychology or *De*

Anima, according to which light comes from the outside to the eye while at the same time a "psychological act" issues forth from the eye to the object,[69] Avicenna describes theories which had a considerable influence on such eminent Western men of science as Roger Bacon and Robert Grosseteste.[70] Altogether, the *Canon*, much of whose content has not been closely studied, had a profound influence in both the East and West and along with his other medical writings remains as an eloquent testament of Avicenna's mastery in medicine and the reason why for a thousand years he has been called the "Prince of Physicians."

The *Shifā'* presents other aspects of Avicenna's genius, not only as a philosopher but also as a natural historian, physicist, and mathematician. In natural history Avicenna discusses in detail all that was known in his period in the science of the three kingdoms — the animal, plant, and mineral. The section of the *Shifā'* dealing with minerals is of particular interest in that it was translated into Latin by Alfred Sareshel around 1200 under the name of *De Mineralibus* and had a wide influence during the Middle Ages and the Renaissance.[71] In this work Avicenna deals with mineralogy and chemistry as well as geology. He categorically rejects the possibility of transmuting one metal into another while at the same time accepting the cosmological theories underlying alchemy. He also classifies minerals into stones, fusible substances, sulfurs, and salts and discusses the subdivisions and characteristics of each. In geology he describes the formation of sedimentary rocks, the hardening of stones, the formation of mountains through erosion of softer layers of rocks, the change of land masses into sea, and vice versa, and the origin of fossils as remains of marine animals of older epochs. He appeals in many cases to his own observations through his numerous journeys through Persia and presents discoveries of much importance in the history of the earth sciences.

In physics, which he discusses in the *Shifā'* as well as in shorter works, Avicenna's basic contribution is his criticism of the Aristotelian theory of projectile motion which was the Achilles' heel of Peripatetic physics. Avicenna adopts the theory of John Philoponos against Aristotle and asserts that a body in projectile motion has a power within it — given to it by the cause that first put it into motion — to push that which prevents it from moving in any particular direction, namely, the resistance of the medium.[72] Moreover, according to Avicenna, and in contradiction to the view of John Philoponos as well, this force, which he calls *mail qasrī*, is not dissipated in a void but would continue if there were a void in which a body could move. Avicenna also seeks to give a quantitative relation for this form of motion and asserts that a body moved by a given power would have a velocity inversely proportional to its "natural inclination," or weight, and that the distance traversed by such a body moving with constant velocity is directly proportional to its weight. This theory, refined by his contemporary Abu'l Barakāt al-Baghdādī, strongly influenced later Muslim philosophers like Fakhr al-Dīn al-Rāzī and Naṣīr al-Dīn al-Ṭusī. In the West Avicenna's impetus theory was adopted by the Andalusian al-Bitrūjī before it entered the Latin world and had a direct bearing on Peter Olivi's writings, in which the Arabic term *mail qasrī* is translated as *inclinatio violenta.* This expression was in turn renamed by John Buridan as *impetus impressus* and defined as the product of the mass and velocity which is the same as the momentum of modern physics. The *impeto* of Galileo, which was his name for momentum, was none other than this concept brought into being by John Philoponos and Avicenna but no longer having the same connotation as it had among the medieval writers. Whereas, for the medieval scientists, impetus was the efficient cause of motion, for Galileo it became a means of describing motion mathematically, making possible through this new interpretation the creation of a new type of physics while at the same time employing some of the basic concepts of medieval natural philosophy.[73]

As for mathematics, Avicenna did not make as many contributions to its many branches as Khwājah Naṣīr al-Dīn al-Ṭūsī, who in other ways is perhaps, of all Muslim philosopher-scientists, most worthy to be compared with him. Nonetheless, in at least one branch of traditional mathematics or the *Quadrivium*, Avicenna did make highly valuable contributions and that was in music, a subject in which he was well versed both in theory and practice.[74] He wrote many compositions on music, of which three survived, these being the musical sections of the *Shifā'*, *Najāt*, and *Dānishnāmah.* The first two are in Arabic and the third in Persian, in which he gave for the first time the Persian name of the musical modes. In these works Avicenna has described the earliest forms of harmony and also "mensural music" in which there is a system of notation expressing the relative duration as well as pitch of the notes.[75] Avicenna followed al-Fārābī closely in his musical theories; both men based their writings upon music being practiced at that time and were not just transmitters of Greek musical theory. The fact that they used the Pythagorean scale does not mean that they were simply following theories set out by the Greek authorities, for the pentatonic scale was in use in China long before historical contact could have been made with Hellenic civilization and was also to be found in Western Asia independent of any Greek influence. Avicenna was studying and deciphering the theory of music being performed in the Persia of his time, a music which to a large extent has been preserved as a continuous tradition of classical music to the present day in that country.[76] In the performance of present-day Persian music one can hear the actual sounds upon which Avicenna's musical theories are based.

PSYCHOLOGY

The psychology of Avicenna is essentially Peripatetic in that he seeks to describe the faculties of the soul in terms which closely resemble those of Aristotle and his Alexandrian commentators – especially Alexander Aphrodisias and Themistius. Psychology in Peripatetic philosophy is concerned with the moving and animating force in the members of the three kingdoms and so falls under the heading of natural philosophy. Just as there is a descent from the Necessary Being, through the Intelligences and Souls to the four elements, so is there a gradual ascent, the rising or ascending arc of the chain of being, which is brought into existence as a result of the mixture of the four elements in ever more perfect proportions.[77] As the elements mix into ever purer combinations, the vegetative, animal, and finally rational souls are added to them *ad extra* and by way of a nexus by the World Soul. In fact each of these souls may be considered as a faculty of the World Soul which enters the stage of the cosmic drama at a particular moment when conditions are prepared for it, that is, when the elements have combined in such a way as to "attract" that faculty toward themselves.

Since the three kingdoms are connected together, like steps of a ladder, without there being a missing link anywhere between them, the plant kingdom rests upon the mineral, and the animal upon the plant. Moreover, the highest member of the mineral kingdom resembles closely the lowest plant and similarly the highest plant is like the lowest animal. Consequently, the members of each kingdom possess all the faculties and powers of those that stand below them in the chain of being. The plant possesses the mineral "virtues" in addition to the faculties of the vegetative soul, which consist of feeding, growth, and reproduction. The animal in turn has the powers of the minerals and plants in addition to the faculties of the animal soul. These consist of the faculty of motion, which itself is comprised, on the one hand, of the power of desire leading to lust or anger and the power of moving the body; and, on the other, of comprehension consisting of the five internal and external senses.[78] The internal senses are the *sensus communis*, the power of retaining forms or representation, sensitive imagination, estimation and retention, and recollection. These faculties Avicenna locates in various parts of the brain, following the tradition of Galen. As for the five external senses, they consist of touch, smell, taste, hearing, and sight, which appear in an imperfect state in the lower animals and are developed in full only in the higher animals and man.

With man a new faculty of the Universal Soul which Avicenna calls the rational soul or human soul comes into play. It has two faculties, one practical and the other theoretical, which are added to those of the vegetative and the animal souls. The practical faculty is the source of all movements of the body, and with it man directs his practical life. It is the theoretical faculty, however, that is the distinguishing feature of man. Avicenna, following the example of al-Kindī and al-Fārābī, divides this theoretical faculty, or intellect, into four levels, or states. The lowest level is the *intellectus materialis*, which is the given hieratic virtuality and potentiality to acquire knowledge and is possessed by all men. Then as man learns the basic principles of knowledge and correct thinking he reaches the state of *intellectus in habitu*, and if he progresses a step further and becomes able to arrive at knowledge by himself and to generate his own intellectual activity he reaches the level of *intellectus in actu*. Finally, there is the highest stage open to man — excluding the prophets, who enjoy a special state because of the total perfection of their nature — and that is the level of *intellectus adeptus*, or *acquisitus*, in which the Universe of being is realized within man and man becomes a copy of the intelligible world. Above these levels of the intellect stands the

Universal, or Active, Intellect, through whom all knowledge is received by illumination and with whom the human intellect at its most exalted level becomes united.

Although following the Peripatetics in his classification of the faculties of the soul, Avicenna differs from them in his insistence upon the immortality of the individual soul, its incorruptible and immaterial substance, and the fact that it is in a degraded state while in the prison of the senses. In his "esoteric philosophy," as well as in some of his beautiful poems, he writes over and over again of the original celestial abode of the soul and the necessity to remember once again its heavenly dwelling place. In these works he ceases to be a Peripatetic philosopher theoretically interested in the faculties of the soul and becomes, like the Platonists and the later Illuminationists, a spiritual doctor who seeks to cure the disease of forgetfulness and negligence that has befallen the soul and to save it from its pitiful terrestrial state. Nowhere is this concern of Avicenna and this aspect of his psychology better illustrated than in the well-known *Ode on the Soul* which ends with these lines:

> Now why from its perch on high was it cast like this
> To the lowest Nadir's gloomy and drear abyss?
> Was it God who cast it forth for some purpose wise,
> Concealed from the keenest seeker's inquiring eyes?
> Then is its descent a discipline wise but stern,
> That the things that it hath not heard it thus may learn,
> So 'tis she whom Fate doth plunder, until her star
> Setteth at length in a place from its rising far,
> Like a gleam of lightning which over the meadows shone,
> And, as though it ne'er had been, in a moment is gone.[79]

RELIGION AND REVELATION

Avicenna was a devout Muslim and possessed a deep religious nature which manifested itself not only in his poetry and Quranic commentary but also in his philosophical works, where he tried at every turn to conform to the Islamic point of view and was in fact inspired by the teachings and spirit of Islam in many aspects of his doctrines.[80] He was sensitive to the charge of irreligiosity brought against him by some of the excessively exoteric theologians and doctors of the Law and wrote a Persian quatrain in his own defense in which he insists on his faithfulness to Islam:

> It is not so easy and trifling to call me a heretic
> No belief in religion is firmer than mine own.
> I am the unique person in the world and if I am a heretic
> Then there is not a single Musulman anywhere in the world.[81]

Avicenna went to a mosque to pray whenever he was beset with difficulties in a scientific or philosophic problem and in fact wrote several treatises on the efficacy of prayer, the performance of daily rites, pilgrimage to the tombs of saints, and so on.[82] He considered these religious acts beneficial because in his world view there is a sympathy between all orders of reality, and especially between the souls of men and God and the heavenly Souls, a sympathy which is strengthened by the acts of worship prescribed in various religions. The sympathy which pervades the Universe and which gives significance to acts of worship is the result of the love which runs through the veins of the cosmos and which is the motivating force and cause for the existence of the created order. This love in turn derives from the love of God who is the highest object of love and also its highest subject. As Avicenna writes in his *Treatise on Love*:

> That Being which is too exalted to be subject to the governance must be the highest object of love, because It must be the maximum in goodness. And the highest subject of love is identical with the highest object of love, namely, Its [God's] high and sublime Essence. Because the good loves the good through that attainment and penetration whereby it is connected with it, and because the First Good penetrates Itself in eternal actuality, therefore Its love for Itself is the most perfect and complete. And because there is no distinction among the divine qualities of Its

Essence, love is here the essence and the being purely and simply, that is, in the case of the Pure Good.

In all beings, therefore, love is either the cause of their being, or being and love are identical in them. It is thus evident that no being is devoid of love, and this it was our intention to show.[83]

Of special interest in Avicenna's religious philosophy is his theory of prophecy in which he seeks to formulate a philosophical theory in conformity with the teachings of the Quran and consistent at the same time with his general world view.[84] He thereby relates the prophetic consciousness and the revelation received by the prophet to his fourfold division of the intellect and its illumination by the Active Intellect who is thus identified with Gabriel, the angel of revelation. The prophetic consciousness is the perfection of the human state possessing all of the human faculties in their perfection. The prophet fulfills, more specifically, the three conditions of clarity and lucidity of intelligence, perfection of the imagination, and the power of making external matter serve and obey him as the bodies of men obey their commands. If all of these conditions are fulfilled, then the prophet gains the degree of prophetic consciousness, a "sacred intellect," which receives all of knowledge, directly, suddenly and without any previous human instruction, from the Active Intellect and thus comes to know at once all things past, present, and future.

Moreover, not only is the prophet's intellect illuminated by the Tenth Intelligence but his imaginative power also receives illumination so that what he perceives abstractly and universally in the intellect appears as concrete and particular, sensible and verbal, images in the imagination. His mission likewise has two aspects, one theoretical and the other practical. The first orients the soul of man toward its eternal felicity by teaching it the basic tenets of belief in the existence of God, the reality of revelation and prophecy and the after life; and the second teaches such practical aspects of religion as the ritual acts to be performed by the believers. The prophet is thereby distinguished from sages and saints first, because his reception of knowledge from the Divine Intellect is complete and perfect and theirs partial, and, second, because he brings a law into the world and directs the practical lives of men and societies while the sages and saints seek after knowledge and inner perfection and have no law-bringing function. They are therefore subordinated to prophets, although they are themselves the most exalted and worthy of the vast majority of men who are not endowed with the extremely rare nature which is that of a prophet.

THE ESOTERIC PHILOSOPHY

Before concluding this summary study of Avicenna, there is still another aspect of his many-sided genius to consider. Toward the end of his life the master of the Muslim Peripatetics wrote a treatise called *Manṭiq al-mashriqīyīn* (*The Logic of the Orientals*) which is the opening section of a more general work.[85] In it he writes that his famous Peripatetic philosophical works, such as the *Shifā'* and *Najāt*, are only exoteric writings meant for the common people and then proposes to expound the "Oriental Philosophy" which he considers to be for the elite and which, in fact, he calls "the science of the elite." Unfortunately the rest of the work is lost so that there is no direct indication as to what Avicenna had in mind after this startling introduction.

If we glance at the Avicennian corpus, however, we discover that there are certain works which differ in nature from his Peripatetic writings and which give every indication of being the remnants of the treatises in which his "Oriental Philosophy" was expounded. In this group one can name, in addition to the *Logic of the Orientals*, the last three chapters of the *Ishārāt wa'l-tanbīhāt*, his last work, where he has given one of the best formulations of many of the cardinal doctrines of Sufism, his *Risālah fi'l-'ishq*, or *Treatise on Love*, where he employs technical Ṣūfī terminology, some of his poems and orations, and finally the three visionary recitals, or narratives, *Ḥayy ibn Yaqẓān*, *Risālat al-ṭair*, and *Salāmān wa Absāl*.[86] From a study of these works one can discern some of the distinguishing features of Avicenna's "esoteric philosophy." Especially in the visionary recitals, the Orient in its symbolic meaning appears as the world of light or pure forms as the Occident symbolizes the world of shadows or matter. The soul of man is caught as a prisoner in the darkness of matter and must free itself in order to return to the world of lights from which the soul of man originally descended. But in order to accomplish this difficult feat and be delivered from his "Occidental" exile he must find a Guide who will orient him in the cosmos and lead him to his ultimate salvation.

In such a perspective the cosmos becomes an immediate experience for the traveler or adept and ceases to be just a theoretical formulation. It speaks to the adept in the language of symbols and conveys to him a message of the greatest significance, one which is a matter of life and death and concerns the ultimate well-being of his soul. The cosmos is thus interiorized, and the abstract, rationalistic language of the Peripatetic philosophers is transformed into a concrete, symbolic one. The traveler learns from the Guide, whom many later Shī'ah authors came to identify with 'Alī ibn Abī Ṭālib, or the Mahdī — upon whom be peace — what the structure of the cosmic crypt is and what dangers he must face if he undertakes to journey through and beyond it. Then he accepts the challenge and makes the sojourn through the cosmic mountains and valleys until he finally comes out of the world of formal manifestation and meets at the end with death, which symbolizes birth into a new spiritual life and also conveys the irreversibility of the process of spiritual realization. He who has left the cosmos does not become imprisoned in it again.

In these writings which depict the Universe in a beautiful language of often high poetic quality, Avicenna relies heavily upon the role of the angels as the guides of man and the directing forces of the Universe. Angelology is in fact essential to the "Oriental Philosophy" of Avicenna as it is central to the Illuminationists whose views are so close to this aspect of his philosophy. The heavens are filled with angels of various orders corresponding to the Intelligences and the Souls. Also, the intellect of man is illuminated by the angel in its quest for spiritual realization so that the angel becomes his personal guide, the St. Bernard and Beatrice of the *Divine Comedy*. Avicenna does not negate the tenets of Peripatetic philosophy but interprets them in a different light so that the rationalistic Universe of the Aristotelians is transformed into a cosmic cathedral where every symbol concerns man in a real and immediate way and plays a role in his spiritual realization. In this manner Avicenna reached toward an "Oriental Philosophy" which, if not taken seriously by most of his Occidental interpreters, was nonetheless of great significance in the Islamic world and pointed to the direction of the "Illuminationist theosophy" that was to be inaugurated nearly a century and a half later by Suhrawardī.

THE SCHOOL OF AVICENNA

As already mentioned at the beginning of this chapter, Avicenna plays the role of the guardian angel of the Islamic arts and sciences, and his influence is to be seen whenever and wherever philosophy or the sciences have been cultivated in the Islamic world. Of his immediate students the most notable was Abū 'Ubaid al-Juzjānī, his life-long companion, to whom Avicenna dictated his autobiography and who completed several of the master's unfinished works; Abu'l-Ḥasan Bahmanyār, the author of a very important work on philosophy, *Kitāb al-taḥṣīl*,[87] as well as *Kitāb al-ḥujjah*; Ibn Zailah, who wrote a commentary upon *Ḥayy ibn Yaqẓān* and summarized the *Shifā'*; and Abū 'Abdallāh al-Ma'ṣūmī, the author of a treatise on separate substances (*Fī ithbāt al-mufāraqāt*), who was the most learned of his students and who had asked his master to be permitted to answer the questions which al-Bīrūnī had posed to Avicenna.

Outside of the group of his immediate disciples, Avicenna's influence was felt by nearly every important intellectual figure of the next century: 'Umar Khayyām, the incomparable poet and mathematician whose apparent and formal doubt, based on metaphysical certainty and meant as a cure for false and bigoted religiosity, has been mistaken by many modern readers as that lack of certainty and entanglement in essential doubt which characterize the modern mind, had the highest respect for Avicenna and even translated one of his treatises into Persian.[88] Moreover, Nāṣir-i Khusraw, the greatest philosopher of Ismā'īlism, who wrote many important philosophical and religious works, all in Persian, fell under the sway of certain of Avicenna's ideas.[89] And even the mathematician and optician Ibn al-Haitham (the Latin Alhazen) came to know of his writings.

During the next centuries Avicenna came under severe criticism by al-Ghazzālī and Fakhr al-Dīn al-Rāzī, as well as by the Andalusian philosophers – especially Averroes. But one of the greatest geniuses ever to appear in Islamic civilization, Khwājah Naṣīr al-Dīn al-Ṭūsī, came to his defense and set out to re-establish Avicenna's philosophy and refute the arguments of his critics. He wrote a masterly commentary upon the *Ishārāt* and brought the teachings of Avicenna back to life.[90] After him there has continued to the present day, especially in Persia, a school which is distinctly Peripatetic. Naṣīr al-Dīn's own nephew, Afḍal al-Dīn al-Kāshānī, wrote a large number of treatises in exquisite Persian style on the principles of Avicennian philosophy.[91] Quṭb al-Dīn al-Shīrāzī, Naṣīr al-Dīn's student, composed in Persian the large encyclopedia, *Durrat al-tāj*, which resembles the *Shifā'* in some respects. Naṣīr al-Dīn's coworker at the observatory of Marāghah, Dabīrān al-Kātibī al-Qazwīnī, left behind one of the most popular works on Peripatetic philosophy, called *Ḥikmat al-ʿain*, again based mostly on Avicenna's teachings.[92] A generation later Quṭb al-Dīn al-Rāzī wrote his *Muḥākamāt* (*Trials*) in which he attempted to judge the merits of the respective commentaries of Naṣīr al-Dīn and Fakhr al-Dīn al-Rāzī on the *Ishārāt*. In this manner the tradition was carried on by one generation after another, to the Safavid period, and many works were composed in these centuries by such philosophers as Ṣadr al-Dīn al-Dashtakī, Ghiyāth al-Dīn Manṣūr al-Shīrāzī, and Jalāl al-Dīn al-Dawānī, all bearing the imprint of Avicenna's thought. And also during this period Athīr al-Dīn al-Abharī composed his *Kitāb al-hidāyah* which, with its commentaries by Ḥusain al-Maibudī and Mullā Ṣadrā, has become one of the two or three most widely studied texts of Peripatetic philosophy in Persia and India.

During the Safavid period, with the artistic and intellectual renaissance that took place, the philosophy of Avicenna also received special attention from such influential figures as Mīr Dāmād who sought to give it an Illuminationist interpretation; from Sayyid Aḥmad al-ʿAlawī who composed a vast commentary upon the *Shifā'*; and from Mullā Ṣadrā who made the philosophy of Avicenna one of the cornerstones of his vast intellectual synthesis. The tradition has been continued after them by many important figures — men like ʿAbd al-Razzāq al-Lāhījī, the student of Mullā Ṣadrā, who in his *Gawhar murād* and *Shawāriq* sought to follow a Peripatetic line combined with that of *Kalām*, or theology. And the school continues today as exemplified by such men as Mīrzā Ṣāliḥ Ḥā'irī Māzandarānī whose *Ḥikmat-i Bū ʿAlī*[93] is the most exhaustive study made in recent times of Avicenna's metaphysics from a Peripatetic point of view.

In the Occident, also, the influence of Avicenna was a long and enduring one, although more diffuse and less marked than that of Averroes, who was both attacked and defended more passionately than his predecessor. During the twelfth century certain works of Avicenna began to be translated into Latin, among them his autobiography as recorded by al-Juzjānī, sections of the logic and physics of the *Shifā'*, and the entire metaphysics. Most of the translations were made in the school of Toledo, especially by or under the direction of Dominicus Gundissalvus, but many of the works were also rendered into Latin by Joannes Hispalensis, or Avendeuth (Ibn Dāwūd), who became celebrated as a translator of the Avicennian corpus.[94] This early series of translations was soon followed by a new translation of sections of the *Shifā'* and the *Najāt*. Also, the *Canon* was translated into Latin during the last half of the twelfth century by Gerard of Cremona, to be followed in the thirteenth by a rendering of the *Poem on Medicine* by Blaise. In fact, interest in Avicenna's works and their translation continued through the Middle Ages and even into the Renaissance, when, despite a certain amount of reaction against Islam and the Arabic language – so clearly noticeable in attempts to "cleanse" the language from Arabic words – the sixteenth-century Italian savant Andrea Alpago made fresh translations into Latin of some works of Avicenna and Averroes.[95]

The views of Avicenna, both scientific and philosophical, began to influence European centers of learning from the twelfth century onward, Salerno and Montpelier being influenced mostly by his medicine, and Paris and Oxford by his philosophy. The first person to have been distinctly influenced by Avicenna was his translator Gundissalvus. Also, there still exist today the treatise *De causis primis et secundis et de fluxu qui consequitur eas*, attributed to Avicenna but not by him, and a gnostic work on the journey of the soul in the other world,[96] both of which are deeply Avicennian and belong to that school which R. De Vaux has called "Latin Avicennianism." [97]

The influence of Avicenna can also be clearly seen in the writings of William of Auvergne and Roger Bacon, who praised him over Averroes; in Albertus Magnus, in St. Thomas, whose third argument for the proof of the existence of God is essentially that of Avicenna, and in Peter of Spain who later became Pope John XXI. His philosophical and especially his scientific works were also significant in the formation of the views of such figures as Robert Grosseteste, and in the fourteenth century served as the "point of departure" for the theology of Duns Scotus which came to challenge the Thomistic system. In medicine, likewise, his influence reigned everywhere, and it was his books along with those of Galen that Paracelsus burned as a symbol of authority when he tried to defy the authorities of traditional medicine and establish his new school in the sixteenth century. Altogether, Avicenna was influential in nearly every circle of medieval thought and, although not accepted fully by any recognized school, played a role, either scientifically or philosophically, in nearly all of them.[98]

Despite the fact that some doubt has been cast upon the existence of a genuine "Latin Avicennianism," the researches of Etienne Gilson have clearly demonstrated the existence of an "Avicennizing Augustinism" whose most important exponent is perhaps William of Auvergne. In the twelfth century the Avicennian corpus provided a metaphysical cosmology for the Latin world and even enabled the Dionysian angelology, known for centuries to the West, to be interpreted in a new cosmological light. But the gradual "Augustinizing" of the doctrines of Avicenna meant the destruction of that very cosmology and cosmogony which he had provided and which became perhaps the most lasting aspect of his teachings in the East. The "Avicennizing Augustinians" sought to identify the illuminating angel of Avicenna with God himself and gradually destroyed the necessity of the angel in the cosmos. The criticism of William of Auvergne and others of similar point of view was most of all against Avicenna's angelology and the significant role that it played in both cosmology and noetics.[99] With the destruction of this angelology the Universe became "depopulated" of the spiritual beings that sustained it, and therefore secularized, preparing the ground for the Copernican revolution [100] as a result of which the Universe began gradually to lose its spiritual character until in the seventeenth century not only cosmology in the traditional sense but the meaning of the cosmos itself was destroyed.[101]

It is both interesting and significant to contrast this critical reception of Avicenna in the West with his acceptance in the East. In the West it was his angelology and cosmology and his noetics based on illumination and gnosis that were most violently attacked and rejected. And it was the rationalistic aspect of his philosophy and his scientific and medical works that were most appreciated and accepted. In the East a small school has kept all of his philosophy alive to the present day and his medical theories are still practiced in many places. But it was essentially the "esoteric" or "Oriental Philosophy" of Avicenna that had the greatest import in the Orient. It was his cosmology supported by his angelology that was elaborated by Suhrawardī and, after being divorced from the rationalistic and syllogistic mesh in whose matrix it was at first placed, became integrated into certain schools of Sufism. Like a precious jewel glittering in light, the beautiful cosmology expounded by him began to glow in the light of Islamic gnosis and shed a light which extended over the world of Islam wherever the doctrines of gnosis and illumination were propounded and studied. And his theory of noetics through illumination of the human intellect by the angel came to be interpreted in later centuries as affirming the reality of gnosis which has always been held as the highest form of knowledge in Islam.[102]

The study of Avicenna and his influence is therefore not just a historical one. Not only was he given the highest honor by entering into the folk tales of the Islamic people as one of their cultural heroes,[103] and exalted over the centuries as the greatest philosopher-scientist of Islam, but he still lives in the figure of the traditional physician and wise man, or *ḥakīm*, who is usually a curer of the ills of the body as well as a person in whom one can confide spiritually and to whom one can surrender oneself with the certainty that one is psychologically as well as physically in safe hands. Wherever traditional medicine is still practiced in the Islamic world the image of Avicenna stands in the background and wherever the Islamic arts and sciences are studied and elaborated he hovers over it as a guardian angel. Moreover, it is his cosmology, as elaborated and interpreted by Suhrawardī and the Illuminationists, as well as by Ibn 'Arabī and the Ṣūfīs, and as fixed by them completely within the matrix of the Islamic revelation and infused by the spirit of the Quran, that delineates the cosmos in which many contemplatives of Islam have lived over the centuries, and which continues to shed its light on the horizon of the intellectual life of Islam.

II

Suhrawardī and the Illuminationists

THE BACKGROUND BEFORE SUHRAWARDĪ

PERIPATETIC philosophy, which had reached the zenith of its perfection with Avicenna and which was propagated after him by some of his able students and disciples, among them Bahmanyār and Abu'l-'Abbās al-Lūkarī, had been criticized from its inception by some of the jurists, as well as by the Ṣūfīs who opposed the tendency of rationalism inherent in Aristotelian philosophy. In the 4th/10th century a new foe joined the rank of the opposition and became in fact the arch enemy of the Peripatetics. The new adversary was Ash'arite theology, or *Kalām*, which was first formulated by Abu'l-Ḥasan al-Ash'arī and later expounded by such men as Abū Bakr al-Bāqillānī during the 4th/10th and 5th/11th centuries and which gradually began to gain support in Sunnī circles.[1]

During the 4th/10th century, however, the political power of the Abbasid caliphate was rather limited, and the local princes, many of whom were Shī'ah and had a more favorable view toward what the Muslims call the intellectual sciences (*al-'ulūm al-'aqlīyah*), as opposed to the transmitted sciences (*al-'ulūm al-naqlīyah*) derived from the sources of the revelation, ruled over much of the Muslim world.[2] Therefore, the intellectual sciences, which included philosophy, continued to flourish to the extent that the 4th/10th and 5th/11th centuries may be considered as their "golden age." But gradually the political situation altered: in the 5th/11th century the Seljuqs, who were the champions of Sunnism and the supporters of the Abbasid caliphate, succeeded in reuniting the Muslim lands of Western Asia and in establishing a strong central government, politically under the Seljuq sultans and religiously under the aegus of the caliphate in Baghdād.[3]

It was at this moment that the school of Ash'arite theology began to be supported by official circles and centers of learning established to teach its tenets and spread its doctrines. And so the ground was prepared for the celebrated attack of al-Ghazzālī against the philosophers. Al-Ghazzālī was a jurist and theologian who understood philosophy well and having at one point fallen into religious doubt had turned to Sufism for the cure of his spiritual illness and therein had found certainty and ultimate salvation.[4] Consequently, with all the necessary gifts of knowledge, eloquence, and experience he set about breaking the power of rationalism within Islamic society. To this end he first summarized the philosophy of the Peripatetics in his *Maqāṣid al-falāsifah* (*The Purposes of the Philosophers*) which is one of the best summaries of Muslim Peripatetic philosophy,[5] and then went on to attack those tenets of the philosophers which were contrary to the teachings of the Islamic revelation in the well-known *Tahāfut al-falāsifah* (*The Incoherence of the Philosophers*).[6]

But it must be added that the attack of al-Ghazzālī upon rationalistic philosophy was more in his capacity as a Ṣūfī than as an Ash'arite theologian, because in his writings as, for example, *al-Munqidh min al-ḍalāl* (*Our Deliverance from Error*), although he considers the view of the theologians to be more in conformity with the tenets of Islam than that of the philosophers, it is Sufism which he believes to possess the only means to attain certainty and ultimate beatitude.[7] In fact the importance of al-Ghazzālī in Islamic history is not only in curtailing the power of the rationalists but also in making Sufism acceptable and respected in the eyes of the jurists and theologians so that eventually its teachings were taught openly even in the religious schools (*madrasas*). And even if an Ibn Taimīyah and an Ibn al-Jawzī did appear from time to time to attack Sufism, theirs were more or less lonely voices which did not succeed in diminishing the respect of the religious community for the Ṣūfīs. Al-Ghazzālī's writings, in fact, represent in a sense Islamic esotericism exteriorized in order to be able to protect its inner life in the cadre of exotericism.

With the advent of al-Ghazzālī, Peripatetic philosophy began to wane in the eastern lands of Islam and journeyed westward to Andalusia where a series of famous philosophers – Ibn Bājjah, Ibn Ṭufail and Ibn Rushd – cultivated it for a century; and Ibn Rushd, the great champion of pure Aristotelian philosophy in Islam and the commentator *par excellence* of the writings of the Stagirite in the medieval period, attempted to retaliate against charges of al-Ghazzālī in his *Tahāfut al-tahāfut*. But his defense had little effect in the Muslim world and it was primarily in the West that he was heard. Indeed a school called "Latin Averroism" came into being which purported to follow his teachings and apply them to a new setting in the Christian world. Thus, almost at the same time that Aristotelianism was being rejected as a completely rationalistic system in the Islamic world, it began to be known in the West through translations of the works of the Eastern Peripatetics such as Avicenna and al-Fārābī, as well as those of the Andalusians, especially Averroes.

Indeed, the parting of the ways between the two sister civilizations of Christianity and Islam after the 7th/14th century can be explained to a large extent in terms of the role that this rationalistic philosophy was to have in the two civilizations. In the East, through the attacks of al-Ghazzālī and others like Fakhr al-Dīn al-Rāzī,[8] the power of rationalism was curtailed, preparing the ground for the spread of the Illuminationist doctrines of Suhrawardī and the gnosis of the school of Ibn 'Arabī. In the West, however, the advent of Aristotelian rationalism had no small part to play in the destruction of the earlier Augustinian Platonism based on illumination and ultimately in bringing about, as a reaction, the secularized form of rationalism and naturalism which in the Renaissance destroyed the castle of medieval scholasticism itself.

SUHRAWARDĪ'S LIFE AND WORKS

The sage whose doctrines came to a large extent to replace, especially in Persia, that Peripatetic philosophy which al-Ghazzālī had criticized so severely was Shihāb al-Dīn Yaḥyā ibn Ḥabash ibn Amīrak al-Suhrawardī, sometimes called al-Maqtūl, that is, "he who was killed." Generally, however, he is known as Shaikh al-ishrāq, the master of illumination, especially by those who have kept his school alive to the present day.[9] He did not have the honor of being translated into Latin in the medieval period and so has remained nearly unknown in the Western world until recent times when a few scholars – among them, Henry Corbin – began to devote a series of important studies to him and undertook to publish and translate his works.[10] Yet even now Suhrawardī remains nearly unknown outside of his homeland, as can be seen by the fact that the great majority of works on the history of Muslim philosophy continue to view Averroes, or at best Ibn Khaldūn, as the terminal point in the intellectual history of Islam, ignoring completely the school of *Ishrāq* and all the later Illuminationists, or *Ishrāqīs*, that followed Suhrawardī. Moreover, this mistake is repeated by most modern Arab, Pakistani, and Indian scholars, many of whom rely primarily on works of modern orientalists for their knowledge of the history of Islamic philosophy and are unaware of the importance of the *Ishrāqī* school, perhaps because it was primarily in Persia that this form of wisdom found its home and where it has subsisted to the present time.[11]

Actually, the reaction of Sunni and Shī'ah Islam to philosophy was somewhat different. In the Sunni world, after the destruction of the Peripatetics, philosophy as such nearly disappeared and only logic continued to be taught in the *madrasas*; moreover, gnostic doctrines came to the fore and even entered into the curriculum of the schools. In Shī'ah Islam the case was quite different. The theosophy[12] of the school of Suhrawardī became gradually integrated with the philosophy of Avicenna on the one hand and the gnostic doctrines of Ibn 'Arabī on the other — all in the matrix of Shī'ism and in fact serving as an isthmus between philosophy and pure gnosis. It is for this reason that a historian viewing the intellectual life of Persia and the lands where Persian culture was influential — such as India, for example, where *Ishrāqī* doctrines spread even among Sunni circles — would say that Islamic philosophy in its true meaning did not end with Averroes but really commenced after his death, as the teachings of Suhrawardī began to be disseminated in the Eastern lands of Islam.

Suhrawardī was born in 549/1153 in the village of Suhraward near the modern Persian city of Zanjān, a village which has produced its share of great men in Islam.[13] He received his early education with Majd al-Dīn al-Jīlī in Marāghah, the city that was to become world-famous a few years later when Hulagu, the Mongol conqueror, built the well-known observatory near it and assembled the great astronomers of the day under the direction of Khwājah Naṣīr al-Dīn al-Ṭūsī in that city. Later Suhrawardī went to Ispahān, then a leading center of learning in Persia, to continue his studies, and completed his formal training with Ẓahīr al-Dīn al-Qārī. Ironically enough, one of his schoolmates was Fakhr al-Dīn al-Rāzī, the great adversary of philosophy, who many years later, after Suhrawardī's death, when presented with a copy of the *Talwīḥāt,* kissed it and wept in memory of the school friend who had followed a path so different from his own.

Having completed his formal studies, Suhrawardī set out to travel over Persia, meeting various Ṣūfī masters to some of whom he became strongly attracted. In fact it was during this phase of his life that he entered upon the Ṣūfī path and spent long periods in spiritual retreats in invocation and meditation. His journeys gradually expanded to include Anatolia and Syria with whose landscape he became infatuated. On one of these journeys he went from Damascus to Aleppo and there met Malik Ẓāhir, the son of Ṣalāḥ al-Dīn al-Ayyūbī, the famous Saladin. Malik Ẓāhir, who had a special love for Ṣūfīs and scholars, became attracted to the young sage and invited him to stay at his court in Aleppo. Suhrawardī, who had developed a special love for those regions, gladly accepted the offer and remained at the court. But his outspoken manner, his lack of prudence in exposing esoteric doctrines before all kinds of audiences, the keen intelligence which enabled him to overcome all opponents in debate, his mastery in both discursive philosophy and Sufism — all these factors combined to make many enemies for him, especially among some of the doctors of the law (*'ulamā'*). Finally, they asked for his execution on the grounds of propagating doctrines against the tenets of the faith, and when Malik Ẓāhir refused they petitioned Ṣalāḥ al-Dīn directly. At a time when Syria had just been recaptured from the Crusaders and the support of the doctors of the law was essential to maintain his authority, Ṣalāḥ al-Dīn had no choice but to yield to their demand. Pressure was therefore put on Malik Ẓāhir to carry out the wish of the group of religious authorities who opposed the young sage. Suhrawardī was therefore imprisoned and in the year 587/1191 he died, the immediate cause of his death unknown. And so, at the young age of 38, the Master of Illumination met with the same fate as his illustrious Ṣūfī predecessor, Ḥallāj, to whom he had been so much attracted throughout his youth and whose sayings he quotes so often in his works.

Despite this short span of life Suhrawardī wrote nearly fifty works in both Arabic and Persian, most of which have survived. These works are written in an exquisite style and are of great literary merit, the Persian works being among the greatest masterpieces of prose-writing in that language and in fact the model for later narrative and philosophic prose. These writings fall into several distinct types which may be classified under five categories: [14]

1. The four large didactic and doctrinal works, all in Arabic, which form a tetralogy dealing first with Peripatetic philosophy as interpreted and modified by Suhrawardī, and then with *Ishrāqī* theosophy itself which follows upon this earlier doctrinal foundation. The tetralogy consists of the *Talwīḥāt* (*The Book of Intimations*), *Muqāwamāt* (*The Book of Oppositions*), and *Muṭāraḥāt* (*The Book of Conversations*) — all three dealing with modifications of Aristotelian philosophy — and finally his masterpiece *Ḥikmat al-ishrāq* (*The Theosophy of the Orient of Light*), which is concerned with *Ishrāqī* doctrines.

2. Shorter treatises in both Arabic and Persian in which the subject matter of the tetralogy is expounded in simpler language and in briefer form. These works include *Hayākil al-nūr* (*The Temples of Light*), *al-Alwāḥ al-'imādīyah* (*Tablets Dedicated to 'Imād al-Dīn*), *Partaw-nāmah* (*Treatise on Illumination*), *Fī i'tiqād al-ḥukamā'* (*Symbol of Faith of the Philosophers*), *al-Lamaḥāt* (*The Flashes of Light*), *Yazdān Shinākht* (*The Knowledge of God*), and *Bustān al-qulūb* (*The Garden of the Heart*). The last two have also been attributed to 'Ain al-Quḍāt al-Hamadānī [15] and Sayyid Sharīf al-Jurjānī, although it seems much more likely that they are Suhrawardī's.

3. Symbolic and mystical narratives, or novels, depicting the journey of the soul across the cosmos to its ultimate deliverance and illumination. These treatises are nearly all in Persian with a few in Arabic versions also. They include *'Aql-i surkh* (*The Red Archangel* (*or literally Intellect*)), *Āwāz-i par-i Jibra'īl* (*The Chant of the Wing of Gabriel*), *al-Ghurbat al-gharbīyah* (*The Occidental Exile*), *Lughat-i mūrān* (*The Language of Termites*), *Risālah fī ḥālat al-ṭufūlīyah* (*Treatise on the State of Childhood*), *Rūzī bā jamā-'at-i ṣūfīyān* (*A Day with the Community of Ṣūfīs*), *Risālat al-abrāj* (*Treatise on the Nocturnal Journey*), and *Ṣafīr-i sīmurgh* (*The Song of the Griffin*).

4. Transcriptions, translations of and commentaries on earlier philosophic works as well as sacred and religious texts, such as the translation into Persian of Avicenna's *Risālat al-ṭair*; commentary upon his *Ishārāt*; composition of *Risālah fī ḥaqīqat al-'ishq*, which is based on Avicenna's *Risālah fi'l-'ishq*, and commentaries on several verses of the Quran and certain *ḥadīths*.[16]

5. Prayers and supplications in Arabic similar to what in the Middle Ages were called the Books of the Hours and which Shahrazūrī calls *al-Wāridāt wa'l-taqdīsāt*.

It is this corpus, along with the numerous commentaries written upon it over the past seven centuries, that forms the source for the doctrines of the *Ishrāqī* school. It is a vast treasure house of wisdom in which symbols of many traditions, including Zoroastrianism, Pythagoreanism, Platonism, and Hermeticism, have been added to those of Islam, for the sources of Suhrawardī's formulations are numerous. He did not hesitate to incorporate into his world view whatever congenial elements he found in other traditions. But for him, of course, as for Ibn 'Arabī, the Universe is a Muslim one on whose horizons certain pre-Islamic symbols are contemplated, just as the cosmic cathedral of Dante is a Christian one in which certain Muslim and Alexandrian embellishments are to be found.

SOURCES OF ISHRĀQĪ DOCTRINE

The sources from which Suhrawardī drew the elements that he synthesized into *Ishrāqī* theosophy include first and foremost Sufism, especially the writings of Ḥallāj and al-Ghazzālī, whose *Mishkāt al-anwār* had a direct bearing upon the relation between light and the *imām* as understood by Suhrawardī. It also includes Muslim Peripatetic philosophy, especially that of Avicenna,[17] which Suhrawardī criticized in part but considered as a necessary basis for understanding the doctrines of *Ishrāq*. As for pre-Islamic sources, he relied heavily upon Pythagoreanism and Platonism, as well as upon Hermeticism as it had existed in Alexandria and had been later preserved and propagated in the Near East by the Ṣabaeans of Ḥarrān, who considered the Hermetic corpus as their sacred scripture.[18]

Above and beyond these Greek and "Mediterranean" sources, Suhrawardī turned to the wisdom of the ancient Persians whose doctrines he sought to revive and whose sages he considered as the direct inheritors of wisdom as it was revealed to the antediluvian prophet Idrīs, or Ukhnūkh, the Hebrew Enoch, whom the Muslim authors identified with Hermes. He relied upon Zoroastrianism especially in the use of the symbolism of light and darkness and in angelology, in which he relied heavily on its terminology. But Suhrawardī made it clear that he was not in any way a dualist and did not purport to follow the exoteric teachings of the Zoroastrians. Rather, he identified himself with a group of Persian sages who possessed an esoteric doctrine based on the unity of the Divine Principle and who constituted a hidden tradition in the Zoroastrian community. Or, as he writes himself:

> There was among the ancient Persians a community of men who were guides toward the Truth and were guided by Him in the Right Path, ancient sages not like those who are called the Magi. It is their high and illuminated wisdom, that to which the

spiritual experiences of Plato and his predecessors are also witness, that we have again brought to life in our book called *Ḥikmat al-ishrāq*.[19]

It should not be thought, however, that Suhrawardī was seeking some kind of eclecticism in relying upon so many different traditions. Rather, Suhrawardī considered himself as the reunifier of what he calls *al-ḥikmat al-ladunīyah*, or Divine Wisdom, and *al-ḥikmat al-'atīqah*, or ancient wisdom. He believed that this wisdom is universal and perennial, the *philosophia perennis* and *universalis*, which existed in various forms among the ancient Hindus and Persians, Babylonians and Egyptians, and among the Greeks up to the time of Aristotle, who for Suhrawardī was not the beginning but rather the end of philosophy among the Greeks, who terminated this tradition of wisdom by limiting it to its rationalistic aspect.[20]

The concept which Suhrawardī has of the history of philosophy is itself of great interest, for it reveals a basic aspect of *Ishrāqī* wisdom. According to Suhrawardī and many other medieval authors, wisdom, or theosophy, was revealed by God to man through the prophet Idrīs, or Hermes, who was thus considered throughout the Middle Ages, in the East as well as in certain schools in the West, as the founder of philosophy and the sciences. This wisdom then divided into two branches, one of which came to Persia and the other to Egypt. From Egypt it went to Greece and finally from these two sources, namely Persia and Greece, it entered into Islamic civilization. In fact, Suhrawardī considered his most immediate predecessors in the Islamic world to be not the well-known philosophers but the early Ṣūfīs, and writes of a dream in which he saw the author of the *Theology of Aristotle* — whom he thought to be Aristotle, but who in reality is Plotinus — and asked him if the Peripatetics like al-Fārābī and Avicenna were the real philosophers in Islam. Aristotle answered, "Not a degree in a thousand. Rather, the Ṣūfīs Basṭāmī and Tustarī are the real philosophers." [21]

Suhrawardī's view of the transmission of this universal wisdom through the chain of ancient sages — some of whom are mythical Persian wise men and kings — can be summarized as follows:

Hermes

Agathedemon (Seth)

Asclepius	Persian priest-kings
Pythagoras	Kayūmarth
Empedocles	Farīdūn
Plato (and the Neoplatonists)	Kai Khusraw
Dhu'l-nūn al-Miṣrī	Abū Yazīd al-Basṭāmī
Abū Sahl al-Tustarī	Manṣūr al-Ḥallāj
	Abu'l-Ḥasan al-Kharraqānī

Suhrawardī

The Master of *Ishrāq* therefore considered himself as the focal point at which the two traditions of wisdom that had at one time issued forth from the same source were once again unified. He thereby sought to synthesize the wisdom of Zoroaster and Plato as Gemistos Plethon was to attempt to do in the neighboring civilization of Byzantium three centuries later, although the subsequent influence and significance of the two men were of course quite different.

THE MEANING OF ISHRĀQ

Muslim historians and philosophers have differed in their view as to the meaning of this form of knowledge called *Ishrāq*, which Suhrawardī brought into being as a synthesis of the two traditions of wisdom. Al-Jurjānī, in his famous *Ta'rīfāt*, or *Definitions*, calls the *Ishrāqīs* "philosophers whose master was Plato," while 'Abd al-Razzāq al-Kāshānī, in his commentary upon the *Fuṣūṣ al-ḥikam* (*The Bezels of*

Wisdom) of Ibn 'Arabī, calls them the followers of Seth who according to the Muslim sources was the founder of the craft guilds and from whom craft initiation, which was closely connected to Hermeticism, originated. As for Ibn Waḥshīyah, who, as far as it can be determined, is the earliest author in the Islamic world to have used the term *Ishrāqī*, they were a class of Egyptian priests who were the children of the sister of Hermes.[22]

We see from these definitions that they all relate *Ishrāqī* wisdom to the pre-Aristotelian period before philosophy became rationalized and when intellectual intuition was still the way *par excellence* for attaining knowledge. Suhrawardī himself follows a similar definition of *Ishrāqī* wisdom:

> Although before the composition of this book I composed several summary treatises on Aristotelian philosophy, this book differs from them and has a method peculiar to itself. All of its material has not been assembled by thought and reasoning; rather, intellectual intuition, contemplation and ascetic practices have played a large role in it. Since our sayings have not come by means of rational demonstration but by inner vision and contemplation, they cannot be destroyed by the doubts and temptations of the skeptics. Whoever is a traveler on the road to Truth is my companion and aid on this path. The procedure of the master of philosophy and *imām* of wisdom, the Divine Plato, was the same, and the sages who preceded Plato in time like Hermes, the father of philosophy, followed the same path. Since sages of the past, because of the ignorance of the masses, expressed their sayings in secret symbols, the refutations which have been made against them have concerned the exterior of these sayings not their real intentions. And the *Ishrāqī* wisdom, whose foundation and basis are the two principles of light and darkness as established by the Persian sages like Jāmāsp, Farshādshūr and Būzarjumihr, is among these hidden, secret symbols.[23]

THE CLASSES OF THOSE WHO KNOW

From the foregoing words of Suhrawardī it becomes clear that *Ishrāqī* wisdom is based on both discursive reasoning and intellectual intuition, both formal training of the mind and the purification of the soul. Suhrawardī, in fact, divides the grades of those who seek after knowledge according to whether one or both of these faculties have been developed in them. According to him there are four categories to be considered:[24]

1. Those who begin to feel the thirst for knowledge and thus embark upon the path of seeking after it.

2. Those who have attained formal knowledge and perfected discursive philosophy but are strangers to gnosis; among these Suhrawardī names al-Fārābī and Avicenna.

3. Those who have not considered discursive modes of knowledge at all but have purified their souls until, like Ḥallāj, Basṭāmī and Tustarī, they have attained intellectual intuition and inner illumination.

4. Those who have perfected discursive philosophy as well as attained illumination or gnosis. Among this group, whose members he calls *ḥakīm muta'allih* – literally meaning theosopher – he counts Pythagoras, Plato, and, in the Islamic world, himself.[25]

Above these categories stand the celestial, or invisible, hierarchy of spiritual beings at whose head stands the Pole (*Quṭb*), or *imām*, for whom all of the other members of the spiritual hierarchy act as representatives. These spiritual beings in turn are the means by which the souls of men gain illumination and become ultimately united with the Pole.

GEOGRAPHIC SYMBOLISM

Before analyzing the various elements of this *Ishrāqī* wisdom, which is realized through a marriage of ratiocination and intuition, a word must be said about the term *Ishrāq* itself and the geographical symbolism with which it is associated. As we have seen in Chapter I, this term in Arabic is related both to the East and the world of light, or illumination, and it is upon this double meaning and the symbolism of directions inherent in it that Suhrawardī bases his descriptive anatomy of the cosmos as Avicenna had done with less precision before him. The sacred geography upon which *Ishrāqī* doctrine is based converts the horizonal dimension of Orient-Occident to a vertical one; that is, by Orient is meant the world of pure lights or archangels which is devoid of all darkness or matter and therefore invisible to mortal eyes; by the Occident is meant the world of darkness or matter; and by middle Occident, the visible heavens where light is combined with some darkness. The horizontal East and West direction is thus made vertical in the sense that the Occident is considered to be this earthly existence in which matter predominates, the middle Occident the astronomical heavens, and the true Orient above and beyond the visible sky and therefore hidden from mortal eyes. The boundary between the "Orient" and "Occident," therefore, is not, as in the case of Aristotelian philosophy, the sphere of the moon; rather it is the heaven of the fixed stars, the *primum mobile.* The heavens studied by the astronomer are still a part of the Occident, although a purer part of it and therefore closer to the world of lights; but they are still combined with matter and so are devoid of the perfection that belongs only to the Orient of pure angelic substances. Moreover, there is not a sharp distinction between the sublunary regions and the heavens as in the Aristotelian system.

It is against this background of the geography of the cosmos that we must understand the language of Suhrawardī whenever he speaks of the Orient and Occident or the rising and setting Sun. And it is against this background that most of the action of his visionary narratives takes place, especially the *Tale of the Occidental Exile* in which the fall of man into the world of matter is symbolized by his exile in the West, that is, by his having fallen into a well in the city of Qairawān, which is located in the far West of the Muslim world.

And the original home from which he had departed and to which he hopes to return is considered to be the Yemen, the country which stands "on the right side" and is therefore a symbol of the Orient of Lights in which the soul as an angelic substance dwelt before its separation and fall into the world of matter.[26]

ḤIKMAT AL-ISHRĀQ AND ITS BASIC DOCTRINES

In order to understand the basic tenets of the *Ishrāqī* school there is no better source to turn to than the *Ḥikmat al-ishrāq* itself, whose content will now be briefly analyzed. This book, which from the point of view of literary style is one of the most remarkable writings of its genre, was composed in 532/1186 in a period of a few months, revealed suddenly by the Holy Spirit (*rūḥ al-qudus*), according to Suhrawardī's own testimony, at a time when all the seven planets were in conjunction in the sign of the Balance. Its style reveals the fact that it was written rapidly and spontaneously and displays the literary genius of the author the beauty and vividness of whose style is revealed in his Arabic and Persian works alike.

Ḥikmat al-ishrāq does not follow the usual division into logic, mathematics, physics, and metaphysics — though the mathematics section is sometimes deleted — as is the case with most of the other Arabic philosophic texts, such as the *Shifā'* and *Najāt* of Avicenna and the other three large didactic works of Suhrawardī . Rather, this cardinal text of *Ishrāqī* wisdom consists of a prologue and two sections. Beginning with logic, it ends in spiritual union and ecstasy.

Criticism of Peripatetic Philosophy

In the prologue Suhrawardī describes how the work was composed, what its nature is, and what purpose it seeks to accomplish. Having thus defined the general tenure of the work, he then devotes the first section to the study of logic as formulated by Aristotle and Porphyry, without, however, accepting it *in toto.* Rather, he devotes the second part of the first section to a general analysis of some of the aspects of Aristotelian philosophy, including logic. Here he criticizes the Aristotelian definition which he considers to be no more than a tautology and reduces the nine accidents to four, these being relation, quality, quantity and motion.

As for his general criticism of Aristotle and the Muslim Peripatetics, he attacks some of the basic tenets of their philosophy in order to prepare the ground for the formulation of his own *Ishrāqī* doctrines. For example, he does not accept the view of Avicenna and other Aristotelians that in each existing thing, the existence is principial and the essence is dependent for its reality upon existence. For Suhrawardī, at least according to the common interpretation of his words, it is the essence of a thing that possesses reality and is principial, existence playing the subordinate role of an accident added to the essence. This view, which is called the principiality of essence (*iṣālat al-māhīyah*), although accepted later by Mīr Dāmād, was severely criticized by Mullā Ṣadrā, who came to interpret the whole of *Ishrāqī* wisdom according to the view that being is principial (*iṣālat al-wujūd*) and substituted a metaphysics of being for the metaphysics of essence of Suhrawardī.[27]

Suhrawardī also criticizes Aristotle severely for refusing to believe in the world of archetypes, or "Platonic ideas," as his master has done, and for having thereby deprived things of any reality in higher orders of being. Likewise, he rejects the Aristotelian definition of place and prefers a concept of place more akin to that of Plato.

Suhrawardī alters the Aristotelian system by rejecting one of its fundamental tenets, namely, the doctrine of hylomorphism which is the backbone of Peripatetic natural philosophy. For Suhrawardī and the rest of the *Ishrāqī* school the Universe consists of degrees of light and of darkness, which is the absence of light. And bodies, so far as their material aspect is concerned, are no more than this darkness, or obstruction, which does not permit the light to penetrate through it. As for the Aristotelian form, it is identified with the angel which "watches over" and guards each thing, the light that is contained in each body by virtue of which that body is able to exist.

The Master of *Ishrāq* also challenges the Peripatetic argument for the immortality of the soul as being too weak and in fact approaches the question of the study of the soul from a different point of view. Whereas the Aristotelian philosophers are concerned mainly with defining the various faculties of the soul, Suhrawardī is essentially interested in demonstrating the celestial origin of the soul and the misery of its present state, and consequently in seeking a way by which the soul can escape from its terrestrial prison or its "Occidental exile" and return once again to its original abode, where alone it can find felicity and peace.

Finally, mention must be made of Suhrawardī's criticism of the two theories of vision current during the Middle Ages. The Aristotelians generally held to the view that in the act of vision, light coming from the object is impinged upon the pupil of the eye, from which it is transmitted to the *sensus communis* and finally to the soul which thus "sees" the object. The mathematicians, however, held an opposing theory according to which in the act of vision a cone of light leaves the eye with the head of the cone located in the eye and the base on the object to be seen. Suhrawardī, in rejecting both of these views, relates the physical act of vision to illumination, or *Ishrāq*, in which all forms of knowledge partake. One can only have vision of a lighted object. In such a case the soul of the observer surrounds that object and is illuminated by its light. It is this act of illumination which is called "vision," so that even physical vision partakes of the illuminative nature of all knowledge.

Having criticized these and certain other tenets of Peripatetic philosophy, Suhrawardī then turns in the second section of the book to discuss the principles of *Ishrāqī* wisdom itself. He divides this section into several chapters which deal respectively with the meaning of light and its various gradations and ontology based upon light symbolism, the angelic hierarchies, or angelology, physics and psychology, and finally questions of eschatology and spiritual union.

The Light of Lights and Ontology

According to Suhrawardī, all of reality is nothing but light which possesses various degrees of intensity. It needs no definition, for one always defines the obscure by the evident and there is nothing more evident and clear than light, so that there is nothing in terms of which it can be defined. In fact, all things are made evident by it and thus should be defined with reference to it. The Pure Light, which Suhrawardī calls the Light of lights (*nūr al-anwār*), is the Divine Essence whose light is blinding because of its luminosity and intensity. The Supreme Light is the source of all existence, since the Universe in all its planes of reality consists in nothing more than degrees of light and darkness. Or, to quote from Suhrawardī's own words:

> The Essence of the First Absolute Light, God, gives constant illumination, whereby it is manifested and it brings all things into existence, giving life to them by its rays. Everything in the world is derived from the Light of His essence and all beauty and perfection are the gift of His bounty, and to attain fully to this illumination is salvation.[28]

The ontological status of all beings, therefore, depends on the degree in which they approach the Supreme Light and are themselves illuminated. Suhrawardī mentions several ways by which the various realms of the Universe can be so distinguished. For example, one can consider all things from the point of view of whether they are light or darkness. If light, they are either subsistent by themselves, in which case they are called incorporeal light (*nūr mujarrad*), or they depend on something other than themselves, and so are called accidental light (*nūr 'araḍī*). Similarly, darkness is either self-subsistent and then it is called obscurity (*ghasaq*), or it depends on something other than itself, in which case it is called form (*hai'ah*).

Suhrawardī also considers the division of beings according to their degree of comprehension and awareness. A being is either aware of itself or oblivious of itself. If aware, it either subsists by itself, as in the case of the Supreme Light or God, the angels, the human soul, and the archetypes, or it depends on something other than itself in order to become aware of itself, like stars and fire. Likewise, if a being is oblivious of itself, either it subsists by itself and becomes obscurity, such as all natural bodies, or it subsists by other than itself, such as colors and smells. In this way the various stages of the universal hierarchy are differentiated from each other. Ultimately the criterion for distinction is the degree of light each possesses, which is also identified with knowledge and awareness. The Universe therefore issues forth from the Supreme Light – without there being a "substantial" and "material" continuity between the two. Moreover, the Light of lights has its vice-regent and direct symbol in every domain; for example, the Sun in the sky, fire among the elements, and the lordly, or "signeural," light (*al-nūr al-isfahbadī*) within the soul of man, so that everywhere His signs are manifested and all things attest to His Presence.

The Angels

Angelology, which concerns itself with this vast hierarchy of lights, or angelic substances standing between this world of shadows and the Supreme Light, occupies a central position in *Ishrāqī* doctrine. The angel is at once the sustainer of this world, the instrument of knowledge, and that which man seeks to become and after whom he searches in his earthly life.[29] Suhrawardī relies heavily on Mazdean angelology in describing the various orders of angels and uses its terminology, which has survived in the Persian calendar to the present day,[30] to name various angelic lights, while making use also of the traditional Islamic terminology derived from the Quran.[31] It is always the beauty and the dominion of the angel which glitter most in the *Ishrāqī* cosmos and which most dazzles the sight of one who undertakes the task of gaining a vision of it.

Suhrawardī does not limit the angels to any specific number to correspond with the visible heavens, as was done by al-Fārābī and Avicenna; nor does he limit their degree of freedom to the three aspects of intellection enumerated by the Peripatetics.[32] In fact, he criticizes his predecessors for having limited the angelic hierarchy in this manner. For Suhrawardī, the number of angels is equal not to the ten heavens of medieval astronomy, but to the number of fixed stars; that is, it is for all practical purposes indefinite and beyond our ability to enumerate. And the ways in which the angels receive divine irradiation and are illuminated by it is not limited to any preconceived logical pattern.

The hierarchy of the angels is considered by Suhrawardī in terms of two orders, the longitudinal (*ṭūlī*) and the latitudinal (*'arḍī*). Standing at the head of the longitudinal order are the archangels, the highest of whom is called both *Bahman* (the Mazdean *Vohūmen*) and the Greatest Light (*al-nūr al-a'ẓam*), or the Most Proximate Light (*al-nūr al-aqrab*).[33] This supreme archangel brings into being the archangel below, who receives irradiation from it as well as from the Light of lights. This irradiation is transmitted in turn to the next in line until the vertical or longitudinal order, each member of whom is called victorial light (*al-nūr al-qāhir*), is completed. This order is also called the world of mothers (*ummahāt*) [34] since all things in the Universe are generated from it and its members are such that each archangel above has the aspect of domination (*qahr*) to the one below it, and the one below, the aspect of love (*maḥabbah*) for the one above. And each light is an isthmus, or "purgatory" (*barzakh*), between the two luminosities above and below it.[35] It acts as a veil which simultaneously hides and reveals the light of the higher order – hiding it in that it is not transmitted in its full intensity and revealing it in that it allows a certain degree of effusion or irradiation to pass through it to permit the next lower member of the hierarchy to come into being.

From the masculine aspect of this supreme hierarchy – that is, its aspect as dominion and contemplation – there arises the latitudinal order of angels which corresponds to the world of archetypes, or "Platonic ideas." The members of this order do not generate each other – as in the longitudinal order. Rather, they subsist side by side with each other. Everything in the visible Universe is a "theurgy" (*ṭilasm*), or "icon" (*ṣanam*), of one of these archetypes, "containing" its particular "angelic influence," and for that reason Suhrawardī calls these archetypes the masters of the species (*arbāb al-anwā'*), or masters of the theurgies (*arbāb al-ṭilism*), since each dominates over a particular species for which it is the celestial archetype and "Platonic idea." It is here that Suhrawardī makes full use of the names of the Mazdean Amshaspands – the Amesha spentas – to designate the archetypes of various species. For example, the archetype of water he calls *Khurdād*, that of minerals, *Shahrīwar*, of the plants, *Murdād*, and of fire, *Urdībihisht*. Each of these things is thus dominated by a particular latitudinal angel for which it acts as theurgy. In this manner Suhrawardī identifies the Platonic ideas with the separate powers of Ahūrāmazdā in Zoroastrianism.

The angelic orders described thus far are still above the visible cosmos. But now, from the feminine aspect of the longitudinal order of archangels, which is their aspect as love and receptivity to illumination and irradiation, there come into being the fixed stars, and through them the other astronomical heavens. The visible heavens are thus a "materialization" of the angelic substances. They may in fact be considered as the crystallization of that aspect of archangels which is "non-being," or "privation," or separation from the Light of lights, Which alone can be considered to be absolutely Real and therefore without any privation whatsoever.

Finally, the latitudinal order of angels gives rise to an intermediary angelic order which acts as its vice-regent and reigns over the species directly. The members of this intermediate order are called regent lights (*al-anwār al-mudabbirah*) and sometimes lordly lights (*al-anwār al-isfahbadīyah*), this latter name having been given especially to those angels who govern the human soul. These angels move the heavens through love and guard over all the creatures of the earth, from minerals and plants to animals and men.

In the case of man, a "lordly light" exists at the center of each soul and governs each man's activities. As for the human species in its totality, it is Gabriel who is considered as its angel, the archetype of humanity (*rabb al-naw' al-insānī*) whom Suhrawardī identifies with the Holy Spirit and the Spirit of the Prophet Muḥammad — upon whom be peace — and therefore also with the function of revelation, Gabriel being the supreme revealer of all knowledge.[36]

Besides having this guardian angel for the whole of his species, man has also his own guardian angel residing in the angelic world. Suhrawardī considers each soul to have had a previous existence in the angelic domain before descending to the realm of the body. Upon entering the body, the soul, or its inner center which is its immortal, angelic core, divided into two parts, one remaining in heaven and the other descending into the prison or "fort" of the body. That is why the human soul is always unhappy in this world; it is actually searching for its other half, for its celestial "alter ego," and will not gain ultimate felicity and happiness until it has become united with its angelic half and has regained its celestial abode. Man's entelechy is therefore to become once again unified with his spiritual "self," with his angelic prototype which is his real "self" and which he must "become" in order to "be"; that is, he must become what he really "is" and cannot attain peace and bring to an end this wandering as a lost child in the maze of the cosmic labyrinth until he has reunited with his guardian angel which is his real "self." [37]

Physics and Psychology

Having completed his study of the angelic world, Suhrawardī turns to a description of the world of bodies and souls, that is, physics and psychology. His physics, as is to be suspected, is one based on light, not on the form and matter theory of the Aristotelians, which he rejected. All bodies are degrees of light and shadows, and the study of physics is the study of light dimmed in its intensity and subdued by the shadows of the material world. Suhrawardī divides bodies into three classes: those that obstruct light and prevent it from entering; those that are transparent to light and do not obstruct it; and finally those that permit light to enter in varying degrees and so are themselves divided into many classes.[38]

The heavens thus belong to the second category in a luminous state, the earth to the first, water to the second in its normal state, and air to the third category, consisting of many degrees. As for fire, which is the fourth of the traditional elements, Suhrawardī does not consider it to be a terrestrial element like the others but a form of light and a direct vicegerent of the Supreme Light in the terrestrial environment.

With this background, Suhrawardī goes on to discuss various physical phenomena, especially meteorological ones, following the general Peripatetic scheme but with a different emphasis. For example, although he accepts the exhalation and vapor theory, he stresses the importance of light in all meteorological phenomena and changes. In fact, the whole of Suhrawardī's physics is based essentially on the study of bodies as isthmuses (*barzakhs*) between different grades of light which they reflect and transmit in varying degrees. Bodies are governed by the heavens, the heavens by the souls, the souls by the various orders of angels, and the angels by the Light of lights Who has dominion over the whole Universe.

From the mixture of the elements, the three kingdoms come into being, each member of which is the theurgy of a particular angel. For example, in the mineral domain gold and jewels have a particular brilliance and have the effect upon the human soul of bringing it joy and happiness, because the light in them is akin to the light contained within the human soul. Similarly, in the plants and animals the angelic light is dominant and governs the functions of each species.

Suhrawardī follows closely the scheme of Avicenna and the other Peripatetics in enumerating the faculties of the vegetative and animal souls.[39] The vegetative soul, according to the Master of *Ishrāq*, possesses the three basic faculties of feeding, growth, and reproduction; feeding itself consisting of the powers of attraction, retention, digestion, and repulsion. The animal soul has the additional powers of motion – consisting of lust and anger and desire, which are the particular characteristics of the animal soul. But all of these faculties, in the vegetative as well as the animal souls, are merely aspects of the angelic light present in each species, and their functions must be understood with reference to that light.

Man, who is the most perfect of animals, possesses in addition to the above senses and the five external faculties, which he shares with some of the higher animals, five inner faculties which relay impressions received from the external world to the lordly light residing within him. These five senses Suhrawardī enumerates as the *sensus communis*, fantasy, apprehension, imagination,[40] and memory, all crowned by the rational soul (*al-nafs al-nāṭiqah*), which is ultimately the same as the lordly light (*al-nūr al-isfahbadī*) – that spark of angelic light that has become so imprisoned in the fortress of the body that it often forgets its original abode. In fact, Suhrawardī and the *Ishrāqīs* are not so much interested in enumerating the psychological faculties as in showing the pitiful state into which the soul has fallen and the process of remembrance and recollection that it must undergo in order to recall once again the home it has lost and thus try to regain it.

Eschatology and Spiritual Union

The last section of *Ḥikmat al-ishrāq* is devoted to the question of spiritual union and the soul's state after death. Suhrawardī outlines the way in which the soul can become disengaged from its material bonds while still in the body and enjoy the illumination of the angelic lights. This should be the goal of all men, for every soul, in no matter what degree of perfection it may be, is seeking the Supreme Light at every moment of its life even if it is itself unaware of the true object of its search. Joy and felicity come from being illuminated by the heavenly light, and, in fact, Suhrawardī goes so far as to assert that the man who has not tested the joy of being illuminated by the victorial lights does not even know the meaning of joy and what it really is.[41] All the partial and passing joys of this life are no more than reflections of the joy of illumination and gnosis.

The condition of the soul after death depends upon the degree of purity and knowledge it has attained in this life. There are, according to this principle of differentiation, three classes of souls: those who have reached some measure of purity in this life (*su'adā'*); those whose souls have been darkened by evil and ignorance (*ashqiyā'*); and finally those who have already attained sanctity and illumination in this life, that is, the sages or theosophers (*muta'allihūn*). The souls of men belonging to the first group depart after death to the world of archetypes where they enjoy the sounds, tastes, and smells of which the terrestrial ones are but shadows. Those of the second group depart to the world of "suspended," or "hanging" forms, the labyrinth of cosmic imagination which is the dark world of evil forces and the jinn. And finally the souls of the gnostics and saints, after leaving the body, ascend even above the angelic world to enjoy the beatitude of proximity to the Supreme Light.[42]

The condition of the soul after death and whether it suffers pain or enjoys felicity depend upon both its purity and its perfection in the sense of the completion of its possibilities through realization and knowledge. A soul that is both pure and complete, or at least possesses one of these qualities, does not suffer long from being separated from the world, which is the object of love of most men in this life. It is only the soul that is both impure and imperfect, or ignorant, that suffers incessant pain in being separated from the world. The Master of *Ishrāq* consequently suggests that man should be aware of the precious moments of life allotted to him and spend them in purifying his soul, so that it becomes like an angel and similar to its celestial prototype.

THE SIGNIFICANCE OF THE VISIONARY RECITALS

This analysis of the principal doctrines of *Ishrāqī* theosophy as contained in the *Ḥikmat al-ishrāq* brings to light the didactic aspect of Suhrawardī's writings, in which the metaphysical truth is formulated in an objective form. But in order to gain a complete vision of the message of Suhrawardī and the total scope of his writings a study must be made also of the visionary recitals, the short symbolic and mystical treatises, where a particular spiritual experience is told in a rich symbolic language, the symbol itself being an integral aspect of the vision. In these short treatises, which resemble in many ways medieval symbolic tales like *Parsifal*, there is no attempt to present the Truth in all of its aspects. Rather, in each treatise a certain phase of the spiritual life, a certain inner experience, is revealed and a particular set of symbols is unveiled, which gives the reader a glimpse of some aspect of the *Ishrāqī* Universe as well as the soul of Suhrawardī himself.

We cannot examine all of the recitals here, but in order to gain familiarity with their general nature it will be useful to make a brief study of one of them, the *Chant of the Wing of Gabriel*,[43] which presents certain characteristics shared by the others. The initial recital is divided into two parts, in the first of which the disciple, or hero, of the tale has a vision of the sage who is "the prophet within himself," the angel who is to guide him on the road to the realization of the Truth. He asks the sage about his original home and receives the answer that he comes from "the land of nowhere" (*nā kujā ābād*), meaning literally utopia — that is, a land that is not in this world, that is not in any place, that transcends the three dimensions of space. Then the disciple, having discovered where the master comes from, begins to question him on various aspects of the doctrine.

In the second part of the recital the general tone of the work changes. The disciple asks the sage to be taught the Word of God. The sage agrees to his request and first instructs him in the mysteries of *Jafr*, that is, the science of the esoteric meaning of letters and words based on their numerical symbolism. He then tells the disciple that God has created words (in the sense of logos) such as the angels, and a Supreme Word which far transcends the angels, as the Sun outshines the stars. Man is himself a word of God and a chant of the wing of Gabriel. The wings of Gabriel are stretched over the heavens and earth — this world of shadows, or "Occident," being no more than the shadow of his left wing, as the world of angelic lights, or the "Orient," is the reflection of his right wing. All things of this world are therefore brought into being by the chant of the wing of Gabriel. It is by the Word, by the sound of the wing of this archangel, that man came into being and it is by the Word — the Divine Name — that he becomes integrated into his principial state and Divine Origin.

THE ISHRĀQĪ TRADITION

Suhrawardī has sometimes been accused by modern scholars of having had anti-Islamic sentiments and having attempted to revive Zoroastrianism against Islam.[44] But such is not by any means the case. It is true, as has been amply illustrated, that Suhrawardī made use of Zoroastrian symbols, as others like Jābir ibn Ḥayyān had used Hermetic ones, to express his doctrines. But this does not in any way imply that his doctrines were anti-Islamic. It was the universality of Islam which permitted it to integrate many diverse elements into itself and enabled Islamic esotericism to employ the language of previous forms of traditional wisdom. And in Persia, where the school of Suhrawardī found its greatest following, Islamic spirituality served, to quote the words of Massignon, as the light in which "Iran contemplated the visible universe through the illuminated prism of its ancient myths."[45]

The *Ishrāqī* tradition spread most rapidly within Shīʿah circles, although it also had some commentators and followers in the Sunnī world. Suhrawardī's writings served as the main doctrinal corpus and source for the *Ishrāqī* school, and many later sages continued the tradition by adding commentaries and glosses to his writings. The most important commentaries upon the *Ḥikmat al-ishrāq* include that of Shahrazūrī, Suhrawardī's disciple and close associate, and the better-known commentary of Quṭb al-Dīn al-Shīrāzī, who was the celebrated student of both Khwājah Naṣīr al-Dīn al-Ṭūsī and Ṣadr al-Dīn al-Qunawī, the latter being the most important expositor of the doctrines of Ibn 'Arabī in the East.[46] Of these two commentaries, both of which were written in the 7th/13th century, that of Quṭb al-Dīn has been studied more closely over the centuries as the "official" commentary upon the text. The old lithographed edition of *Ḥikmat al-ishrāq*, which has been used by students in the *madrasas* where *Ishrāqī* theosophy is taught ever since its publication during the Qajar period, contains this commentary in the margins along with the glosses added by Mullā Ṣadrā three centuries later.

Among commentators on some of the other works of Suhrawardī one may include Ibn Kammūnah, Shahrazūrī and 'Allāmah Ḥillī, who wrote commentaries upon the *Talwīḥāt* in the 7th/13th and 8th/14th centuries, respectively, and Jalāl al-Dīn al-Dawānī (9th/15th) and 'Abd al-Razzāq al-Lāhījī (11th/17th), who commented on *Hayākil al-nūr.* In addition, one should mention the important philosophers and sages who came under the influence of the teachings of Suhrawardī. In this category the name of Khwājah Naṣīr al-Dīn al-Ṭūsī, the great 7th/13th philosopher and scientist, comes to mind before any other. Although he revived the rival school of Peripatetic philosophy through his masterly commentary upon the *Ishārāt* of Avicenna, he had come under the influence of the Illuminationists on certain questions, such as that of God's knowlege of the world. Here he openly defied the views of Avicenna to follow those of Suhrawardī. Henceforth, Suhrawardī's teachings continued to spread mostly among the Persian philosophers and sages, and in Anatolia and India, until in the Safavid period their influence upon Islamic intellectual life came into full bloom.

During the Safavid period Shī'ism became the official state religion of Persia, and there was not only a renaissance in

Persian art and architecture that is justly famous the world over, but also a revival of the intellectual sciences, which, unlike the art of the period, has remained nearly unknown to the outside world until the present day.[47] The study of philosophy and theosophy was revived by Mīr Dāmād,[48] the great teacher in Ispahān at the time of Shāh 'Abbās, the teacher and master who created an Avicennian school with a Suhrawardian interpretation seen from the Shī'ah point of view. After Mīr Dāmād, his most celebrated pupil, and the figure who is considered in Persia to be the greatest of all Muslim *ḥakīms*, Mullā Ṣadrā, finally integrated the doctrines of Suhrawardī into his own vast synthesis. The doctrines of Mullā Ṣadrā included elements of Peripatetic philosophy as well, and many of the basic principles of gnosis as expounded by the school of Ibn 'Arabī — all in the matrix of the teachings of Shī'ism, especially the metaphysical elements contained in the *Nahj al-balāghah* of 'Alī ibn Abī Ṭālib.[49]

Although the writings of Mullā Ṣadrā came gradually to overshadow the works of Suhrawardī in official schools, it was through them that *Ishrāqī* doctrine continued to be studied. And it was in this way that later sages like Ḥājjī Mullā Hādī Sabziwārī,[50] the most celebrated expositor of the teachings of the Mullā Ṣadrā in the Qajar period, and Shaikh Aḥmad Aḥsā'ī, the founder of the Shaikhī movement, an opponent of some of the doctrines of Mullā Ṣadrā, came under the influence of the Suhrawardī's teachings. In India, too, Suhrawardī has continued to be studied both in his own right and through the works of Mullā Ṣadrā, which have continued to be taught in Muslim schools of the Indian subcontinent until our own day.[51] This is also true of Persia, where traditional philosophy and theosophy is taught today not only in the *madrasas* but also in the Faculty of Religious Sciences, or "Theology," of Tehran University. Indeed, the University has a special chair for *Ishrāqī* theosophy and another for the doctrines of the school of Mullā Ṣadrā.[52]

Furthermore, the influence of Suhrawardī was not confined to the world of Islam. Some of his writings were translated into Sanskrit during the Moghul period in India, as they had been rendered into Hebrew some time earlier, so that his doctrines reached worlds as separate and far apart as the Jewish and the Hindu. His works were also studied closely by the mysterious Zoroastrian priest, Ādhar Kaiwān, and his followers, who during the Safavid period left Shīrāz for India. The perennial wisdom which the Master of *Ishrāq* had sought to establish, or rather to re-establish, in his short terrestrial life thus became not only a dominant intellectual perspective in Shī'ism, and more generally in the eastern lands of Islam, but also overflowed the banks of the Islamic world to reach other traditions. It became in many ways an important element of that Universe of common discourse which Islam shared with its neighboring traditions, a Universe in which was revealed the transcendent unity underlying the different revelations of the truth.

III

Ibn ʿArabī and the Ṣūfīs

THE ṢŪFĪ TRADITION

SUFISM as a way of spiritual realization and the attainment of sanctity and gnosis is an intrinsic aspect of the Islamic Revelation of which it is in fact the heart and inner, or esoteric, dimension.[1] It received its name at a later period and it drew some of its formulations from doctrines of Neoplatonic and Hermetic origin, but the reality of Sufism, its basic doctrines and methods, reach back to the origin of the Revelation and are intimately entwined with the spirit as well as the very form of Islam as it is contained in the Quran, which is its most tangible and concrete embodiment.[2] For a person who participates in Sufism, who lives the life of a "follower of the Path,"[3] the first and most perfect Ṣūfī was the Prophet Muḥammad – upon whom be peace – and after him the representative *par excellence* of Islamic esotericism, ʿAlī ibn Abī Ṭālib.

At the time of the Prophet, when one might say the gates of heaven were open, the very intensity of the spiritual life and proximity to the source of the Revelation did not permit of a total separation of the Tradition into its exoteric and esoteric, or *Sharīʿah* and *Ṭarīqah*, components, although both existed in essence from the beginning. The whole of the Tradition was at first like a molten lava in a state of fusion and did not "congeal" and separate into its various elements until the withering influence of time and the corrupting conditions of this world had gradually "cooled" and "solidified" it. We see, therefore, that during the first two centuries of its life, while the Tradition was extremely strong, as proved by its rapid expansion and power of assimilation, there was neither a definitely codified school of law nor a clearly organized Ṣūfī brotherhood, or order.[4] We also note that in the 3rd/9th century the schools of law, or the *Sharī'ah*, became codified and at the same time Sufism began to manifest itself as a distinct element in the Islamic community, its doctrines and methods being propagated by the brotherhoods, each of which was directed by a master and often named after him.

The spirit that was "in the air" and "everywhere" at the beginning of the Revelation thus became consolidated within various orders so that it could continue as a living spiritual tradition. The later Ṣūfīs did not practice anything which the Prophet and his companions had not practiced before them, especially such companions as 'Alī, Abū Bakr, Abū Dharr, Salmān, Bilāl, and others who received his "esoteric instructions." The Prophet used to make spiritual retreats (*khalwah*) in quiet and faraway places such as the cave on Mount Ḥirā', especially during the middle part of Ramaḍān and also in later life in the mosque of Medina, in all of which he performed the fundamental rite of invocation (*dhikr*). He also called upon his companions to "remember God" and invoke His name in private as well as in gatherings.

It is upon these and other practices of the Prophet and his sayings that the Ṣūfīs have based their methods and practices to the present day. They have always considered themselves as the most ardent followers of the Prophet's teachings and have sought to follow his personal example at every moment of their lives so that we hear a great Ṣūfī master of the 3rd/9th century saying, "All the Paths (of Sufism) are completely closed except to him who follows in the steps of the Apostle."[5] Sufism is thus the inner aspect of the teachings of the Prophet as it gradually took form during the 2nd/8th and 3rd/9th centuries, gaining meanwhile the name Sufism by which the esoteric dimension of Islam has been known ever since.[6]

One cannot properly speak of a history of Sufism because in its essence Sufism has no history. However, since at each epoch it has presented its principles in a language conforming to the general mental and psychological conditions of that age, and since there have developed over the centuries various schools of interpretation, again depending on the "needs" of different types of men, it is possible to speak of the distinct features of the Ṣūfī tradition in each period.[7] One can speak of the early ascetics, readers of the Quran and transmitters of *ḥadīth*, who kept the teachings of the Prophet alive for the generation immediately following that of the Companions and many of whom were among the early saints of Islam. And one must consider that very important figure of the first two Islamic centuries, Ḥasan al-Baṣrī, whose long life, stretching from 21/643 to 110/728, linked three generations of Muslims to the time of the Prophet himself.[8]

Of utmost importance also during the first two centuries are the Shī'ah *Imāms*, of whom the first eight especially, play a cardinal role in the early phase of Sufism. In Shī'ism, which is essentially the "Islam of 'Alī" and is based on supporting 'Alī as the spiritual and temporal successor of the Prophet, the *Imāms*, who include 'Alī himself and his descendants, are the bearers of the prophetic light and the esoteric representatives of the Prophet. Also, many of them had an essential share in the formation of the Ṣūfī orders that have developed in the Sunnī world and figure prominently in their spiritual chain (*silsilah*). Nearly all the Ṣūfī orders trace their origin to the first Shī'ah *Imām*, 'Alī, and many of the later Ṣūfīs were disciples of various *Imāms*, especially the sixth *Imām*, Ja'far al-Ṣādiq (88/702–148/765), and the eighth *Imām*, 'Alī al-Riḍā (around 148/765–203/818). Moreover, several of the *Imāms* have left behind some of the most beautiful and exalted pages of Islamic gnosis of which the *Nahj al-balāghah* of the first Imām and the *Ṣaḥīfat al-sajjādīyah*,[9] by the fourth *Imām*, Zain al-'Ābidīn, are among the most notable.

The third century marks the advent of many famous Ṣūfī figures whose eloquent and penetrating utterances have survived and re-echoed within the soul of the Ṣūfīs of later generations. Among the well-known figures of this century are the Egyptian Dhu'l-Nūn, the saint of Baghdād al-Muḥāsibī,[10] the prince Ibrāhīm ibn Adham, who, like Gautama the Buddha, left the courtly life in order to gain a knowledge of things divine, and the sage from Khurāsān, Bāyazīd al-Basṭāmī,[11] whose antinomial utterance, or "theophanic locutions," based on his experience of ultimate union have made him celebrated as a representative of the most intellectual form of Sufism.

Toward the end of the 3rd/9th century we find the sober school of Baghdād headed by Junaid around whom such figures as Nūrī and Shiblī assembled and with whom the martyr of Sufism, Ḥallāj, associated. This great Ṣūfī, who is quite well known in the Western world, thanks to the many studies that Massignon devoted to him, represents in many ways the spiritual type of Christ within the Islamic tradition and his "passion," as Massignon calls it, presents certain similarities to that of Christ. It was the vocation of Ḥallāj to divulge esoteric doctrines before the common crowd and to be witness to the conscience of the Islamic community as it stood before the reality of the spiritual life contained within Sufism. Ḥallāj left some beautiful Arabic poems behind; he also uttered certain phrases which have never ceased to dominate the horizon of Sufism. His *ana'l-ḥaqq* (I am the Truth) has become perennial witness to the fact that Sufism is essentially gnosis and that ultimately it is God within us who utters "I" once the veil of otherness has been removed.

During the 4th/10th century, at the same time that the Islamic arts and sciences reached their zenith,[12] the Ṣūfī tradition began to express itself in large didactic works as well as in the new vehicle of Persian poetry which henceforth became one of its main forms of expression. In this century appeared such classical manuals of Sufism as the *Kitāb al-luma'* (*The Book of Flashes*) of Abū Naṣr al-Sarrāj,[13] *Kitāb al-ta'arruf* (*Doctrine of the Ṣūfīs*) of Kalābādhī,[14] *Kashf al-maḥjūb* (*The Unveiling of the Hidden*) of Hujwīrī, the first Ṣūfī prose work in Persian, *Qūt al-qulūb* (*The Nourishment of the Heart*) of Abū Ṭālib al-Makkī, and the celebrated *Risālat al-qushairīyah* (*The Treatise of Qushairī*). All of these works are studied still by adepts of Sufism, especially the last, which is the most widely read didactic work on the practical aspect of Sufism. The beautiful locutions, the ecstatic utterances, the wise aphorisms of the earlier Ṣūfīs, were collected and the rules and conditions for following the "Path" delineated.

In this century, also, the first Ṣūfī quatrain in Persian was composed by Abū Sa'īd ibn Abi'l-Khair, the contemporary of Avicenna.[15] And one of the most important of all Ṣūfī authors, Khwājah 'Abdallāh al-Anṣārī, whose *Manāzil al-sā'irīn* (*The Stations of the Travelers*) has been the subject of so much study and so many commentaries over the centuries, wrote several important treatises in Persian. His *Munājāt* (*Supplications*)[16] is now among the best-known classics in that language. Thus Persian became, in addition to Arabic, a major vehicle for the expression of Ṣūfī doctrine, preparing the ground for Sanā'ī, 'Aṭṭār, the incomparable Rūmī, Shabistarī, Sa'dī, and Ḥāfiẓ, with whom the "alchemical" usage of Ṣūfī poetry reaches its culmination. Through these eloquent poets the doctrines of Sufism were expounded in the eastern provinces of the Islamic world — in Persia, Central Asia, and India, as well as in Java and Sumatra —

and it was through the translation of some of these works that the attention of such Europeans as Goethe and Herder was first attracted to Sufism.

During this same century Sufism began to have some contact as well as friction with the tenets of philosophy, theology, and jurisprudence. We have seen how the master of Peripatetic philosophers, Avicenna, was attracted to certain elements of Sufism as was his contemporary Abū Ḥayyān al-Tawḥīdī. Likewise, the *Epistles* of the Brethren of Purity, even when treating of the sciences, present certain similarities to Ṣūfī doctrines as does the Jābirian corpus, attributed to Jābir ibn Ḥayyān, who was a Ṣūfī and who in all likelihood did write some of the works in the vast corpus bearing his name. But there was also the reverse tendency of certain Ṣūfīs' adopting cosmological doctrines to be found in the writings of Avicenna, the Brethren of Purity, and others and integrating them into their metaphysical perspective. Of special interest in this connection is the Andalusian sage, Ibn Masarrah, whose cosmological doctrines foreshadowed those of Ibn 'Arabī, who drew much from his teachings.[17]

There was opposition as well, however, among both theologians and jurists, an opposition which made itself felt more strongly during the 5th/11th century as the domination of the Seljuqs and the establishment of the new universities changed the less organized and more unrestricted atmosphere of the previous century. And it was against this background that Abū Ḥāmid al-Ghazzālī appeared upon the scene to "legitimize" Sufism in official juridical circles and bring about a concordance between the esoteric and exoteric aspects of Islam, in both of which he participated actively. As we mentioned in the previous chapter, al-Ghazzālī essentially exteriorized certain teachings of Sufism in order to give it freedom to carry on its inner life in the bosom of the Muslim community. Thus, his defense of Sufism served an important function in determining the status granted to the orders and their doctrines and practices in the general religious community. Moreover, in some of his more esoteric treatises, like *Mishkāt al-anwār* (*The Niche for Lights*) [18] and *al-Risālat al-ladunīyah* (*Treatise on Divine Knowledge*), he began to discuss the doctrines of Sufism in a manner which foreshadowed the works of Ibn 'Arabī.

Between al-Ghazzālī and Ibn 'Arabī there are still many significant Ṣūfī figures who must not be overlooked. In Persia there were Aḥmad al-Ghazzālī (the brother of the more famous Abū Ḥāmid), who wrote a famous treatise on Divine love called the *Sawāniḥ al-'ushshāq* (*Auspices of Divine Lovers*),[19] and 'Ain al-Quḍāt, who also discussed Ṣūfī doctrines in a manner reminiscent of Ibn 'Arabī. As for the Maghrib, or the West of the Islamic world, one may recall the figure of Ibn al-'Arīf, the author of the well-known *Maḥāsin al-majālis* (*The Virtues of Ṣūfī Gatherings*) [20] of Abū Madyan, the master of Ibn 'Arabī, mentioned so often in his works; and of Ibn Qasyī, the founder of the "Monastic state" of the Murīdīn (or "adepts") in Algarbes in southern Portugal, with whom Ibn 'Arabī had intimate contact.

Also, returning once again to the Orient of Islam, we meet, just before the time of Ibn 'Arabī, not only with the originator of the school of Illumination, Suhrawardī, but also with the founders of some of the most important Ṣūfī orders. In this category we may include Aḥmad al-Rifā'ī, after whom the Rifā'īyah order is named; 'Abd al-Qādir al-Jīlānī, the most universal saint in Islam, whose Qādirīyah order stretches today from Morocco to the Pacific islands; and Najm al-Dīn al-Kubrā, the founder of the Kubrawīyah order.[21] When Ibn 'Arabī came upon the stage of Islamic history the tradition of Sufism was a well-established one, possessing, through the orders, an effective means of preserving and transmitting its spiritual methods and doctrines. It possessed, too, a rich heritage of works, both prose and poetry, in Persian as well as Arabic, in which the illuminations and insights, the experiences and "observations," of the Ṣūfī saints, going back generation by generation to the time of the Prophet, had been preserved.

THE SIGNIFICANCE OF IBN 'ARABĪ

With Ibn 'Arabī we suddenly encounter a complete metaphysical and cosmological, as well as psychological and anthropological, doctrine of monumental dimensions which seems at first to indicate a break or turning point within the tradition of Sufism. It is true that certain earlier Ṣūfī like Ḥakīm al-Tirmidhī and Bāyazīd al-Basṭāmī treat of metaphysical questions and that the writings of 'Aṭṭār or Ibn Masarrah contain cosmological doctrines, but not in the same dimension and proportion as is to be found in Ibn 'Arabī. The earlier Ṣūfī writings are for the most part either practical guides for the followers of the Path or utterances of various Ṣūfīs expressing the state of realization each has attained. There is little theoretical exposition of metaphysics aiming in any way to be total and complete. There are only flashes of light which illuminate a particular aspect of reality with which the Ṣūfī is concerned at a particular moment.

With Muḥyī al-Dīn the doctrines of Sufism, which up to his time had been contained implicitly in the sayings of various masters, became explicitly formulated. He thus became the expositor *par excellence* of gnosis in Islam.[22] Through him the esoteric dimension of Islam expressed itself openly and brought to light the contours of its spiritual universe in such a manner that in its theoretical aspect, at least, it was open to anyone having sufficient intelligence to contemplate, so that he could in this way be guided toward the Path in which he could come to realize the metaphysical theories in an "operative" manner. We encounter in the writings of Ibn 'Arabī such formulations as the transcendent unity of Being (*waḥdat al-wujūd*) and the Universal Man (*al-insān al-kāmil*), which are given this designation for the first time although their reality had existed from the beginning of the Tradition.

The importance of Ibn 'Arabī consists, therefore, in his formulation of the doctrines of Sufism and in his making them explicit. His advent marks neither a "progress" in Sufism by its becoming more articulated and theoretical, nor a deterioration from a love of God to a form of pantheism, as has been so often asserted against Ibn 'Arabī. Actually, the explicit formulation of Ṣūfī doctrines by Muḥyī al-Dīn signifies a need on the part of the milieu to which they were addressed for further explanation and greater clarification. Now, the need for explanation does not increase with one's knowledge; rather, it becomes necessary to the extent that one is ignorant and has lost the immediate grasp of things through a dimming of the faculty of intuition and insight. As Islamic civilization drew away gradually from its source of revelation, the need for explanation increased to the degree that the spiritual insight and the perspicacity of men diminished. The early generations needed only a hint or directive (*ishārah*) to understand the inner meaning of things; men of later centuries needed a full-fledged explanation. Through Ibn 'Arabī Islamic esotericism provided the doctrines which alone could guarantee the preservation of the Tradition among men who were always in danger of being led astray by incorrect reasoning and in most of whom the power of intellectual intuition was not strong enough to reign supreme over other human tendencies and to prevent the mind from falling into error. Through Ibn 'Arabī, what had always been the inner truth of Sufism was formulated in such a manner that it has dominated the spiritual and intellectual life of Islam ever since.

THE LIFE OF THE SAGE FROM MURCIA

Ibn 'Arabī, whose complete name is Abū Bakr Muḥammad ibn al-'Arabī al-Ḥātimī al-Ṭā'ī, was born in Murcia in southern Spain in 560/1165 in a family of pure Arab blood of the tribe of Ṭā'ī. He is best known in the Islamic world as Ibn 'Arabī and was entitled by posterity al-Shaikh al-akbar (Doctor Maximus) and surnamed Muḥyī al-Dīn (The Revivifier of Religion). Like other great saints and sages, his greatest "masterpiece" was his own life, a most unusual life in which prayer, invocation, contemplation, and visits to various Ṣūfī saints were combined with the theophanic vision of the spiritual world in which the invisible hierarchy was revealed to him.[23] In studying his life, therefore, we gain a glimpse of the spiritual character and stature of the sage whose intellectual activity is visible in his many metaphysical works.

After spending his early years in Murcia, Ibn 'Arabī went to Seville where he grew up and received his early education and where his well-to-do family could provide a comfortable and leisurely life for him in which he was left free to pursue his natural inclination toward things spiritual. He met at this early period of his life two women saints, Yāsamīn of Marshena and Fāṭimah of Cordova, who had a strong influence upon the orientation of his life. This was especially true of Fāṭimah of Cordova, who was a very old woman, yet possessed of a radiance and beauty which Ibn 'Arabī compared to that of a young girl of sixteen. She acted as his spiritual guide for two years and considered herself as his spiritual mother.

As a young man of twenty, with great intelligence and already possessed of profound spiritual insights, Ibn 'Arabī began to travel about various cities of Andalusia, meeting saintly men and women wherever he could find them. It was during one of these trips, while he was staying at Cordova, that he met Averroes, the master interpreter of Aristotle, in an encounter which is full of significance, for in it two personalities meet who symbolize the paths to be followed in the future by the Christian and the Islamic worlds. In this meeting two men faced each other, one of whom was a follower of the edicts of reason and who became the most influential of all Muslim thinkers in the Latin West, and the other a gnostic for whom knowledge meant essentially "vision," who became the dominant figure in Sufism, towering like a giant over the subsequent intellectual life of Islam. Since the meeting of two such figures is of so much general interest, we give Ibn 'Arabī's own account of this memorable event, an account which also reveals a great deal of the spiritual personality of its author: [24]

I went one fine day to the house of Abu'l-Walīd ibn Rushd [Averroes] in Cordova. He had expressed the desire to meet me personally because he had heard of the revelations which God had accorded me in the course of my spiritual retreat and had not hidden his astonishment concerning what he had been told. That is why my father, who was one of his intimate friends, sent me one day to his house under the pretext of having to perform some kind of commission but in reality in order for Averroes to be able to have a talk with me. At this time I was still a beardless young man.

Upon my entering [the house] the philosopher rose from his place and came to meet me, showering upon me signs that demonstrated his friendship and consideration and finally embraced me. Then he told me, "Yes." And I in turn told him: "Yes." Upon this his joy increased in noting the fact that I had understood him. Then, becoming myself conscious of what had provoked his joy I added: "No." Immediately Averroes shrank, the color of his features changed; he seemed to doubt that about which he was thinking. He asked me this question: "What kind of solution have you found through illumination and Divine inspiration?" I answered him: "Yes and no. Between the yes and the no souls take their flight from their matter and the necks become detached from their bodies." Averroes became pale; I saw him trembling. He murmured the ritual phrase: "There is no force but in God," because he had understood that to which I had alluded.

Later, after our interview, he interrogated my father concerning me, in order to compare the view he had reached about me and to know if it coincided with that of my father, or that on the contrary, it differed from his view. It is certain that Averroes was a great master of reflection and philosophic meditation. He had thanked God, I have been told, to have lived at a time when he could have seen someone who had entered into spiritual retreat ignorant and had left it as I had done. He said: 'It was a case whose possibility I had affirmed myself without however as yet encountering someone who had in fact experienced it. Glory be to God that I have been able to live at a time when there exists a master of this experience, one of those who open the locks of His doors. Glory be to God to have made me the personal favor of seeing one of them with my own eyes.'

I wanted to have at another time a new interview with Averroes. Divine Mercy made him appear to me in a state of ecstasy in such a form that between his person and myself there was a light veil. I saw him across this veil without his seeing me or knowing that I was there. He was in fact too absorbed in his meditation to take notice of me. Then I said to myself: "His deliberation does not lead him where I am myself."

I had no more occasion to meet him until his death which occurred in the year 595 of the Hegira [A.D. 1198] at Marrākush. His remains were transferred to Cordova, where his tomb is located. While his coffin, which contained his remains, had been loaded on the side of a beast of burden, his works had been placed on the other side in order to counterbalance it. I was there standing motionless; there was with me the jurist and man of letters Abu'l-Ḥusain Muḥammad ibn Jubair, secretary of Sayyid Abū Sa'īd [an Almohade prince] as well as my companion Abu'l-Ḥakam 'Amr ibn Sarrāj, the copyist. Then Abu'l-Ḥakam turned toward us and said: "Do you not see what is serving as the counterweight of the Master Averroes on his mount? On one side the master, and on the other his works, the books composed by him?" Then Ibn Jubair answered: "You say that I do not see my child? But of course I do. May your tongue be blessed!" Then I gathered within myself (this phrase of Abu'l-Ḥakam) since it is for me a theme of meditation and remembrance. I am now the only survivor of this group of friends — may God keep them in his mercy — and I tell myself regarding this subject: On one side the master, on the other his works. Oh! how I would like to know if his hopes have been fulfilled!

Until 595/1198 Ibn 'Arabī spent his life in various cities of Andalusia and North Africa meeting Ṣūfīs and scholars and occasionally holding debates with such diverse groups as the Mu'tazilites who had made a rationalistic interpretation of Islam. During this period he traveled as far away as Tunis where he made a study of the *Khal' al-na'lain* (*Taking off of the Sandals*) [25] of Ibn Qasyī, and wrote a commentary upon it. He also visited Almeria, which had been the center of the school of Ibn Masarrah and later of Ibn al-'Arīf, and where, according to Asin Palacios, Ibn 'Arabī had received his formal initiation into Sufism.[26]

During these years the Shaikh continued to have his theophanic visions. He had already had a vision of the invisible hierarchy ruling the Universe, consisting of the Supreme Pole (*Quṭb*); the two *imāms*; the four "pillars" (*awtād*) governing the four cardinal points; the seven "substitutes" (*abdāl*) the influence of each of whom reigns over one of the climates; the twelve chiefs (*nuqabā'*), dominating the twelve signs of the Zodiac; and the eight nobles (*nujabā'*) corresponding to the eight heavenly spheres.[27] He also had a vision of all the spiritual poles of the revelations anteceding Islam, and realized the transcendent unity of all the traditions revealed by God to man. And it was also in a vision, which he received in 595/1198 in Murcia, that he saw the Divine Throne held up by pillars of light with a bird flying around it who ordered Ibn 'Arabī to depart from his homeland and set out for the Orient of the Islamic world where he was to pass the rest of his days.[28]

With this pilgrimage to the East a new period commenced in Ibn 'Arabī's life. In 598/1201 he visited Mecca for the first time, where he was "commanded" to begin the composition of his *magnum opus*, *al-Futūḥāt al-makkīyah* (*The Meccan*

Revelations) and where in a family of Persian Ṣūfīs from Ispahān he met a young girl of great devoutness and beauty who henceforth became the embodiment of the eternal *sophia* for him and fulfilled a role in his life which resembles that of Beatrice in the life of Dante.

From Mecca, Ibn 'Arabī traveled to different cities and was at this time initiated into the Divine mysteries by Khiḍr,[29] or al-Khaḍir, the prophet who initiates men directly into the spiritual life without their becoming attached to a regular initiatic chain. He thus became a "disciple of Khiḍr" as he had been of various Ṣūfī masters belonging to regular initiatic lines. His initiation into the "line" of Khiḍr is shown most clearly of all in 601/1204 when in Mosul he received the mantle (*khirqah*) of Khiḍr from 'Alī ibn Jāmi' who himself had directly 'received' it from the "Green Prophet."

During these years also, Ibn 'Arabī came into occasional conflict with some of the jurists, as in 604/1207 when he was threatened with mortal danger in Cairo and had to take refuge in Mecca. After spending some time in the holy city, he set out for Anatolia, where in Quniya he met Ṣadr al-Dīn al-Qunawī, his most celebrated disciple, who later became the most important commentator and propagator of his works in the East. From Quniya he traveled eastward toward Armenia and then south to the Euphrates Valley and Baghdād where in 609/1211 he met the famous Ṣūfī master, Shihāb al-Dīn 'Umar al-Suhrawardī, the namesake of the Master of Illumination, with whom he is often mistaken.[30] Ibn 'Arabī also visited Aleppo where he was warmly received by Malik Ẓāhir, who a generation before had been the patron and friend of Suhrawardī, and whose death he had tried in vain to prevent.

Finally, in 621/1223, Ibn 'Arabī decided to settle in Damascus, after he had become famous over the whole of the Islamic world and was invited and wooed by wisdom-loving rulers and princes from lands near and far. But now, after a life spent in traveling, he wished to spend the last years of his terrestrial existence in quiet and peace, and also in intense work. During this period he completed the *Futūḥāt* which contains the spiritual diary of thirty years of the most fruitful period of his life. And it was in Damascus that the great Shaikh died in 638/1240, leaving an indelible mark upon the whole spiritual life of Islam. He was buried at Ṣāliḥīyah, at the foot of Mt. Qāsiyūn north of Damascus, in a spot that was already venerated, before he was interred there, as a place sanctified by all the prophets. After his burial it became an even greater center of pilgrimage. In the sixteenth century Sultan Salīm II built a mausoleum upon it which still stands, and the tomb continues as a place of pilgrimage, especially for the Ṣūfīs. One finds interred next to the greatest master of Islamic gnosis, not only his two sons, but also the famous Algerian patriot 'Abd al-Qādir who, after being exiled by Napoleon III, spent the rest of his life in editing the works of Muḥyī al-Dīn, whose ardent disciple he was. Now he lies buried next to the "Most Grand Shaikh" to whom he was so devoted and for the publication of whose works he is to some degree responsible.

THE WORKS

The very large number of works written by Ibn 'Arabī seems almost sufficient proof of their "supernatural" inspiration. Various traditional sources have attributed several hundred works of which a very large number survive, most of them still as manuscripts in various libraries in the Islamic world and Europe.[31] These works range from short treatises and letters of a few pages to the monumental *Futūḥāt;* from abstract metaphysical tracts to Ṣūfī poems in which the realized aspect of gnosis appears in the language of love. The subject matter of these works also varies widely, covering metaphysics, cosmology, psychology, Quranic commentary, and nearly every other field of knowledge, all approached with the aim of bringing to light their inner meaning.

The largest and most encyclopedic of Ibn ʿArabī's works is the *Futūḥāt* which consists of 560 chapters treating of the principles of metaphysics, the various sacred sciences as well as Muḥyī al-Dīn's own spiritual experiences. It is a veritable compendium of the esoteric sciences in Islam which surpasses in scope and depth anything of its kind that has been composed before or since. Ibn ʿArabī asserts in the work more than once that it was written under Divine inspiration, as, for example, when he says: "Know that the composition of the chapters of the *Futūḥāt* is not the result of free choice on my part nor of deliberate reflection. Actually, God dictated to me everything that I have written through the angel of inspiration." [32]

The *Futūḥāt* contains, in addition to the doctrines of Sufism, much about the lives and sayings of the earlier Ṣūfīs, cosmological doctrines of Hermetic and Neoplatonic origin integrated into Ṣūfī metaphysics, esoteric sciences like *Jafr*, alchemical and astrological symbolism,[33] and practically everything else of an esoteric nature which in one way or another has found a place in the Islamic scheme of things. Thus it has constantly been the main source book of the sacred sciences of Islam, and each of its chapters has been studied and contemplated by generations of Ṣūfīs who have written many treatises that are in reality commentaries upon various threads from which the vast tapestry of the *Futūḥāt* is woven.

Without doubt Muḥyī al-Dīn's most widely read work and his spiritual testament is the *Fuṣūṣ al-ḥikam*, the *Bezels of Wisdom*,[34] which has twenty-seven chapters, each devoted to the basic doctrines of Islamic esotericism. The work was composed in 627/1229, and according to Ibn ʿArabī's own words, stated in the introduction, it was inspired by a vision of the Prophet holding a book in his hand which he ordered the Shaikh to "take" and to transmit to the world so that men might benefit by it.[35] The very title, *Bezels of Wisdom*, symbolizes the content of the book in that each "bezel" contains a precious jewel which symbolizes an aspect of Divine wisdom revealed to one of the prophets. Metaphorically speaking, each bezel is the human and spiritual nature of a prophet which serves as a vehicle for the particular aspect of Divine wisdom revealed to that prophet.

The human and individual nature of each prophet is in turn contained in the logos, or word (*kalimah*), which is his essential reality and which is a determination of the Supreme Word, or the "primordial enunciation of God." [36] That is why the chapters are entitled "The Bezel of Divine Wisdom in the Adamic Word," "The Bezel of the Wisdom of Inspiration in the Word of Seth," and so on, until it ends with the "Bezel of the Wisdom of Singularity in the Word of Muḥammad." Whereas, humanly speaking, the human and individual aspects of the prophets seem to "contain" their essential and universal aspects as the bezel "englobes" the precious jewel, in reality the relation is reversed. It is the inner reality, the supra-individual aspect of the prophet that contains and determines the bezel. The divine revelation is "colored" by its recipient while from a universal point of view the recipient itself is a divine possibility determined from above and contained by its celestial prototype.

The vast corpus left by Ibn 'Arabī includes, besides these two major works, numerous treatises on cosmology, such as *Inshā' al-dawā'ir* (*The Creation of the Spheres*), *'Uqlat al-mustawfiz* (*The Spell of the Obedient Servant*), and *al-Tadbīrāt al-ilāhīyah* (*The Divine Directions*) [37]; on practical methods to be followed by adepts traveling on the Path, such as *Risālat al-khalwah* (*Treatise on the Spiritual Retreat*) and *al-Waṣāyā* (*Spiritual Counsels*); on various aspects of the Quran,[38] including the symbolism of some of its letters, on the Divine Names and Qualities, on law and *ḥadīth* and practically every other question connected with matters religious and spiritual.[39] His writings include also some exquisite Ṣūfī poetry, as, for example, the *Tarjumān al-ashwāq* (*The Interpreter of Desires*[40]) and his *Dīwān*. Indeed, he is considered by many to be the best of the Ṣūfī poets in the Arabic language after Ibn al-Fāriḍ.[41]

Altogether, the scope of Ibn 'Arabī's writings is so vast that it is difficult to describe their contents. Books and treatises poured forth from his pen like waves from the ocean, covering nearly everything in sight. In this large body of writings in Arabic his style is sometimes poetic and at other times laborious. Some of his works, like those concerned with method, are clear and simple and others on metaphysics highly condensed and elliptical. In fact, he had a language of his own and brought into being a technical vocabulary, based partly on that of the earlier Ṣūfīs, a knowledge of which is indispensable to an understanding of his writings.[42] The reader must learn not only the precise meaning of his words but all the nuances and images connected with them. In other words, with him, as with other Muslim authors, one has to learn to read "between the lines" in order to discover the treasures hidden beneath his elliptical and antinomian formulations and his dazzling, and at times complex, symbolic language.

THE "SOURCES" OF IBN 'ARABĪ

One cannot speak in an ordinary historical sense about the origins and sources of the works of any Ṣūfī writer because the Ṣūfī who has realized the goal of the Path receives inspiration directly and "vertically" and is not dependent upon "horizontal" influences. He receives his knowledge through the illumination of his heart by Divine theophanies and only in the expression and formulation of his inner experiences may he depend upon the writings of others. In the case of Ibn 'Arabī, also, his primary source is his gnostic knowledge received in states of contemplation and made possible through the grace (*barakah*) of the Prophet which he received through his initiation into the Ṣūfī Path.

But on the level of interpretation of ideas and formulations we may speak of the "historical sources" of Ibn 'Arabī in the sense that the doctrines of many schools found their profoundest interpretation in the writings of the Shaikh. Within the tradition of Islam, Ibn 'Arabī followed, most of all, the earlier Ṣūfīs, especially Ḥallāj, many of whose utterances he discussed in his works; Ḥakīm al-Tirmidhī, whose *Khatm al-awlīyā'* (*The Seal of Sanctity*) became the subject of the Shaikh's special study; Bāyazīd al-Basṭāmī, whose gnostic utterances he often quoted; and al-Ghazzālī whose later works he followed and whose themes he expanded in many ways. He also adopted certain cosmological ideas found among the philosophers, especially Avicenna – not to speak of the "Neo-Empedoclean" schemes of Ibn Masarrah – and made frequent use of the dialectic of the theologians. In addition, the influence of earlier Islamic Hermetic writings, such as those of the Jābirian corpus, as well as the *Epistles* of the Brethern of Purity with their Neopythagorean tendencies, and other writings associated with Ismā'īlism, are to be discovered in Ibn 'Arabī's works.[43]

As for doctrines of pre-Islamic origin, we find in Muḥyī al-Dīn the interpretation of Alexandrian Hermeticism at its most elevated level of meaning, where the concept of Nature itself takes on a significance transcending the order of formal cosmic manifestation.[44] We also find doctrines belonging to the Stoics, Philo, the Neoplatonists, and other schools of antiquity which are interpreted metaphysically and integrated into the vast panorama of Ibn 'Arabī's theosophy. It is through the prism of his mind that not only gnostic doctrines but also cosmological, psychological, physical, and logical ideas gain a metaphysical dimension and a transparency which reveal the nexus that all forms of knowledge have with the *sapientia* possessed by the saints and sages, just as the root of all things, of all orders of reality, is plunged in the Divine.

THE DOCTRINE

It would be more than pretentious to seek to present even a bare outline of the doctrines of Ibn 'Arabī, doctrines which generations of seers and sages have contemplated and in the comprehension of which men have spent the greater part of their earthly life.[45] Our aim is no more than to give an indication of the general characteristics and language of the doctrines and to mention a few of the principles which are dominant themes in his vision of the Universe, a vision so vast that it is difficult to trace in it even a single theme in all of its amplifications and dimensions. In the case of Ibn 'Arabī we are not dealing with a philosopher either in the modern or the Aristotelian sense, and his doctrines should not be treated as philosophy.

The resemblance between metaphysical and gnostic doctrines of this order and philosophy are more apparent than real. Muḥyī al-Dīn, unlike a philosopher, does not try to encompass all of "reality" in a system and to give a systematic exposition of its various domains. He writes under immediate and direct inspiration so that his writings do not possess the coherence one expects of ordinary works of purely human inspiration.[46] What he shares with the philosophers is the use of human language and the treatment of ultimate questions, but his purpose is different as is the manner in which he makes use of language.[47] His aim is not to give an explanation that is mentally satisfying and rationally acceptable, but a real *theoria*, or vision of reality, the attainment of which depends upon the practice of the appropriate methods of realization. With Ibn 'Arabī, as with other masters of traditional wisdom, doctrine and method are the two legs which must be coordinated in order to be able to climb the spiritual mountain.[48] Method without doctrine may become a blind travail and doctrine without method may develop into a mental trifling with concepts, giving one an agility which is as far removed from traditional wisdom as the acrobatics of a monkey from the soaring flight of an eagle.[49]

The Language of Symbolism

The language of Ibn 'Arabī, although at times abstract, is essentially a symbolic one and he makes use of all forms of symbolism ranging from the poetical to the geometrical and mathematical. The principle involved in the use of symbols is a basic one. It is what Ibn 'Arabī, like the Shī'ah for whom it is also fundamental, calls *ta'wīl,* meaning literally to take something back to its origin or beginning. In the Universe nothing is just what it appears to be – that is, its reality is not exhausted by its exterior. Every phenomenon implies a noumenon, or, in Islamic terms, every exterior (*ẓāhir*) must have an interior (*bāṭin*). The process of *ta'wīl,* or of spiritual hermeneutics, means going from the *ẓāhir* to the *bāṭin,* from the outward reality to the inner one.

For Ibn 'Arabī, as for other Ṣūfīs, symbolism is of vital importance, to the extent that the Universe speaks to them in the language of symbols and that everything, besides its external value, has a symbolic significance as well.[50] The Ṣūfīs have always kept alive the "symbolic spirit," a spirit which was once shared by mankind in general but which has been lost in the modern world and can only be found among the ethnic and racial groups that have not been too deeply affected by the transformations of the past few centuries.[51] For Muḥyī al-Dīn the process of *ta'wīl* can be applied to all phenomena of Nature and all that surrounds man in his terrestrial life. Moreover, the tenets of religion and the events occurring within the soul of man are also subject to this fundamental process of inner penetration and symbolic interpretation.

In Arabic the phenomena of Nature, the verses of the Quran in which the Revelation is contained, and the inner states of the soul are all called *āyāt*, that is, portents, or signs, because their inner meanings, as discovered through *ta'wīl*, are related. The Ṣūfī penetrates into the inner meaning of the manifestations of Nature, then into the rites and beliefs of religion, and finally into his own soul, and discovers within all of them the same spiritual essences for which these diverse realities are so many symbols. The writings of Ibn 'Arabī clearly depict the application of the method of symbolic hermeneutics to the revealed text – the Quran – as well as to the Universe whose creation is based upon the prototype of the "macrocosmic Quran," and to his soul which as the microcosm contains all of the realities of the Universe within itself. There is thus a macrocosmic as well as a microcosmic aspect to Revelation, as there is a "revealed aspect" to both the macrocosm and the microcosm, to both the Universe and man. To all of these domains Ibn 'Arabī applies the method of symbolic exegesis, the process of *ta'wīl*. Moreover, his own works express the realities that he has thus discovered in a symbolic language and must in turn be penetrated "in depth" in order to reveal the inner meaning (*ramz*) hidden behind the veil of the external forms of words and letters.

The Unity of Being

The basic doctrine of Sufism, especially as interpreted by Muḥyī al-Dīn and his school, is that of the transcendent unity of Being (*waḥdat al-wujūd*) for which he has been accused by many modern scholars of being a pantheist, a panentheist, and an existential monist; and more recently a follower of what is called natural mysticism. All of these accusations are false, however, because they mistake the metaphysical doctrines of Ibn 'Arabī for philosophy and do not take into consideration the fact that the way of gnosis is not separate from grace and sanctity. The pantheistic accusations against the Ṣūfīs are doubly false because, first of all, pantheism is a philosophical system, whereas Muḥyī al-Dīn and others like him never claimed to follow or create any "system" whatsoever; and, secondly, because pantheism implies a substantial continuity between God and the Universe, whereas the Shaikh would be the first to claim God's absolute transcendence over every category, including that of substance.[52] What is overlooked by the critics who accuse the Ṣūfīs of pantheism is the basic difference between the *essential* identification of the manifested order with its ontological Principle and their *substantial* identity and continuity. The latter concept is metaphysically absurd and contradicts everything that Muḥyī al-Dīn and other Ṣūfīs have said regarding the Divine Essence.

The term "panentheism," used by Nicholson and several other scholars who knew only too well that pantheism could not be applied to the Ṣūfīs, appears somewhat less distasteful. It is true that God dwells in things but the world does not "contain" God, and any term implying such a meaning is not appropriate as a description of the doctrine of *waḥdat al-wujūd*. Nor is the term "existential monism" a suitable one, for here again monism implies a philosophical and rationalistic system, opposed, let us say, to dualism, and the adjective "existential" again mistakes the essential continuity of all things with their Principle for the substantial one, or the "vertical" for the "horizontal." The unity of the Ṣūfīs is the integration of paradoxes and ontological contrasts; it is the union of all the diverse qualities which characterize the order of multiplicity and has nothing to do with philosophical monism of which Ibn 'Arabī and others have been accused.

Nor can natural mysticism be attributed to Ibn 'Arabī with any justification. This term was created by certain Catholic authors to classify essentially gnostic forms of spirituality that they contrast with "supernatural mysticism" found mostly in Christianity.[53] There is no absolute break between the natural and the supernatural. The supernatural has a "natural aspect" because its "trace" can be found in the very existence of things; and the natural has a supernatural aspect because the "vestiges" of the supernatural are to be found in the created order, and because grace, or *barakah*, flows through the "arteries" of the Universe.[54] Moreover, to consider "mysticism" [55] in one religion to be supernatural and in other religions to be natural, or to be supernatural only in certain cases and then only "accidentally," is to limit the mercy of God. It is to fall into a dangerous provincialism which one can ill afford at a moment when the understanding of other forms of spirituality has become a matter of "urgency" and of immediate concern.

The doctrine of the transcendent unity of Being or "the unicity of Reality," as expounded by Muḥyī al-Dīn and other Ṣūfīs is, then, neither pantheism, nor panentheism, nor existential monism. Nor is it the fruit of a natural mysticism which fails to transcend the created order and which is devoid of the salutary guidance of revealed wisdom and grace. It means, rather, that while God is absolutely transcendent with respect to the Universe, the Universe is not completely separated from Him; that the "Universe is mysteriously plunged in God." It signifies that to believe in any order of reality as autonomous apart from the Absolute Reality is to fall into the cardinal sin of Islam, namely, polytheism (*shirk*), and to deny the *Shadādah* (*Lā ilāha ill'-Allāh*) – there is no divinity but the Divine – which means ultimately that there is no reality other than Absolute Reality. The formula begins with a negation in order not to imprison the Principle in any affirmation whatsoever. The world and the things in it are not God but their reality is none other than His; otherwise they would be completely independent realities, which is the same as considering them to be deities along with Allah.

Ibn 'Arabī, who is so often accused of pantheism, goes as far as the human language allows to affirm the transcendence and Unity of God. As is written in the *Risālat al-aḥadīyah* (*Treatise on Unity*): [56]

> He is, and there is with Him no after nor before, nor above nor below, nor far nor near, nor union nor division, nor how nor where nor when, nor time nor moment nor age, nor being nor place. And He is now as He was. He is the One without oneness and the Single without singleness. He is not composed of name and named, for His name is He and His named is He. . .
>
> Understand therefore . . . He is not in a thing nor a thing in Him, whether entering in or proceeding forth. It is necessary that thou know Him after this fashion, not by knowledge, nor by intellect, nor by understanding, nor by imagination, nor by sense, nor by perception. There does not see Him, save Himself; nor perceive Him, save Himself. By Himself He sees Himself, and by Himself He knows Himself. None sees Him other than He, and none perceives Him other than He. His veil is [only a "consequence" and effect of] His oneness; nothing veils other than He. His veil is [only] the concealment of His existence in His oneness, without any quality. None sees Him other than He — no sent prophet, nor saint made perfect, nor angel brought nigh know Him. His Prophet is He, and His sending is He, and His Word is He. He sent Himself with Himself to Himself.[57]

It seems difficult to accuse one of pantheism who goes to such extremes in asserting the transcendence of God. What Ibn 'Arabī wishes to assert is that the Divine Reality is distinguished from its manifestations and is transcendent with respect to them, but that the manifestations are not in every respect separate from the Divine Reality which somehow encompasses them. As with the symbol of the bezel and the precious stones discussed above, the recipient of a Divine manifestation, or revelation, seems to "color" the revelation it receives; or, in other words, the revelation conforms itself to the nature of its recipient. But from a more profound point of view the recipient itself is determined from "on high" by the spirit or the Divine revelation so that both the "container" and the "contained" are encircled by the Divine Reality which transcends them.[58]

This principle applies to knowledge as well as to being, to the contemplation of the celestial essences in the heart as well as to the consideration of the Universe as a Divine theophany. In both cases the recipient of the theophany "determines" and "colors" the mode of the theophany; but also it is itself in reality determined by the Divine Essence from which the theophany originates and which is a unity encompassing complementary and opposing terms; a center in which all oppositions are united and which transcends all the polarizations and contradictions in the world of multiplicity. It is the center of the circle in which all is unified and before which the mind stands in bewilderment for it involves a *coincidentia oppositorum* which cannot be reduced to categories of human reason and cannot be explained away as a monism which annihilates ontological distinctions and which overlooks the transcendent position the center occupies vis-à-vis all the oppositions that are resolved in it.[59] The Exterior (*ẓāhir*) and the Interior (*bāṭin*), the First (*awwal*) and the Last (*ākhir*),[60] the Truth (*ḥaqq*) and the creature (*khalq*), the Lover (*'āshiq*) and the Beloved (*ma'shūq*), the intellect (*'āqil*) and the intelligible (*ma'qūl*), are all apparent oppositions that are resolved in the Divine Essence which encompasses and contains all these polarities without being reduced to them.

The Names and Qualities

Although the Divine Essence (*al-dhāt*) is absolutely transcendent and above all differentiation and distinction, it has certain modalities on the plane of its first self-determination. In His state of absolute Unity, God is above all qualities, and so this plane is called that of indivisible and unconditional Unity (*aḥadīyah*). But on the plane of unicity, or "oneness" (*wāḥidīyah*), there are principial modalities, or qualities, from which all qualities of being and all modalities of knowledge derive.[61] God is thus above all qualities and yet is not devoid of them, as is implied by the famous Ṣūfī adage that the Divine Qualities "are neither He nor other than He." [62]

The *Shahādah* (*Lā ilāha ill'-Allāh*) implies also the same apparently contradictory relations. On the one hand every quality, every form of "divinity," is negated from God so that he is absolutely transcendent, this being the view of *tanzīh*; on the other hand the same formula implies that there cannot be any quality completely separate from the Divine Quality, so that it must be a reflection of a Divine Reality with which it is compared (*tashbīh*).[63] Ibn 'Arabī's view of the relation between the Qualities and the Divine Essence lies between *tanzīh* and *tashbīh*, positing at the same time God's transcendence and His possessing Qualities of which all cosmic qualities are reflections and images.

Although the Divine Qualities are beyond number, in the Islamic revelation they are summarized in a definite set of Names by which God is described in the Quran.[64] These Names are the Divine possibilities immanent in the Universe; they are the means by which God manifests Himself in the world just as He describes Himself in the Quran through them. The Names are thus the pathways leading toward God and the means by which one can ascend to the unitive knowledge of the Divine Reality. And since they are fundamental aspects of knowledge as well as of being, they manifest themselves in the Universe and in the spiritual life in which they become the object of contemplation. It is through them that Ibn 'Arabī, like other Ṣūfīs, envisages the process of creation as well as that of spiritual realization so that the Names and Qualities play a fundamental role in every aspect of his world view and provide the "language," based on the terminology of the Quran, with which he expounds the doctrines of Sufism.

The Universal Man or the Logos

One of the basic esoteric doctrines of Islam, again formulated for the first time in its present terminology by Ibn 'Arabī, is that of the Universal Man (*al-insān al-kāmil*), which is so dominant in the Ṣūfī perspective that it has been called the "privileged myth" of Sufism.[65] The Universal Man, who is also the Logos, is the total theophany of the Divine Names; he is the whole of the Universe in its oneness as "seen" by the Divine Essence. He is the prototype of the Universe as well as of man by virtue of which man, the microcosm, contains within himself all the possibilities found in the Universe. The microcosm and the macrocosm face each other as two mirrors in each of which the other is reflected, while both "echo" in themselves their common prototype, who is the Universal Man. The Universal Man is also essentially the Spirit, or First Intellect, which "contains" all the Platonic "ideas" within itself, like the Logos in the doctrines of Philo who is "the first born of God" and in whom all the "ideas" are assembled.

In Ibn 'Arabī's doctrine, the Universal Man has essentially three different aspects, namely, the cosmological, the prophetic, and the initiatic.[66] Cosmologically and cosmogonically, he is the prototype of creation containing all the archetypes of Universal Existence within himself so that all of the levels of cosmic existence are no more than so many branches of the "Tree of being" which has its roots in heaven, in the Divine Essence, and its arms, or branches, spread throughout the cosmos. From the point of view of revelation and prophecy, the Universal Man is the Word, the eternal Act of God, each particular "dimension" of which is identified with one of the prophets. As such, each chapter of the *Fuṣūṣ* is dedicated to an aspect of the Universal Man, to a prophet who reveals to the world an aspect of the Divine Wisdom whose embodiment he is in his inner reality. Seen in this light, the Universal Man is the Reality of Muḥammad (*al-ḥaqīqat al-muḥammadīyah*), which found its terrestrial realization in the Prophet of Islam. Just as a seed when sown in the ground first shoots out a stem, then branches, then leaves, then flowers, and finally a fruit which again contains that seed, so did the Universal Man, or the Reality of Muḥammad, who was "the first creature of God," manifest itself fully on earth in Muḥammad, the last of the prophets of the present cycle of humanity.

From the point of view of spiritual realization, the Universal Man is the model of the spiritual life for he is the person who has realized all the possibilities, all the states of being, inherent within the human state and has come to know, in all its fullness, what it means to be a man. As such, the Universal Man is, first of all, the prophets, especially the Prophet of Islam; and secondly the great saints, and especially "Poles" (*Quṭb*) of each age whose outer reality is that of other men but whose inner reality includes all the possibilities inherent within the Universe because they have realized in themselves all the possibilities inherent in the state of man as the microcosm and center who reflects all the universal qualities. Potentially every man is Universal Man but in actuality only the prophets and the saints can be called by such a title and can be followed as prototypes of the spiritual life and guides on the path of realization.

Creation and Cosmology

Creation in the school of Ibn 'Arabī is envisaged as the effusion of Being upon the heavenly archetypes, thus bringing them from their state of non-being or that of a "hidden treasure" into externalized existence.[67] Being may be symbolized by light, and the archetypes, or the universal Names and Qualities, as so many colored pieces of glass through which the light shines, reflecting various colors upon the "mirror of non-being." The cosmos is essentially a set of mirrors in which the Divine realities are reflected; it is a theophany of the Divine Names and Qualities contained in the Universal Man.[68] And from another point of view it is an ever-flowing river whose water is renewed at every moment but which preserves its general form determined by the structure of its bed. The water is a symbol of the light of Being which emanates at every moment throughout the Universe, and the bed of the river symbolizes the archetypes which determine the general direction of the flow.

Creation is also compared by Ibn 'Arabī to the articulation of sound from the human mouth. Just as through the human breath words which are in an undifferentiated state become distinct and articulate, so does the "Breath of the Compassionate" (*nafas al-raḥmān*), the "Breath" of God, considered in His aspect of Mercy and Compassion, bring the principial possibilities, symbolized by the letters of the alphabet, into existence.[69] Moreover, in the same manner that the human breath goes through the cycle of contraction and expansion, the Universe undergoes the two complementary phases of the same cycle. It is annihilated at every moment and re-created at the next, without there being a temporal separation between the two phases. It returns back to the Divine Essence at every moment while in the phase of contraction and is remanifested and externalized in that of expansion. The Universe is thus a theophany of the Divine Essence, which is renewed at every moment without being repeated "identically," for, as the Ṣūfīs say, "There is no repetition in theophany."[70] Creation is renewed at every instant, and its apparent "horizontal" continuity is pierced by the "Vertical Cause" which integrates every moment of existence into its transcendent Origin.

With this concept of creation as the background, Ibn 'Arabī describes several different cosmological schemes in each of which diverse aspects of the cosmic realities are depicted. Sometimes he conceives of the cosmic order as a tree whose branches symbolize various degrees of cosmic existence and at other times he envisages the Universe in terms of the Quranic concepts of the Pen and the Guarded Tablet, the traditional Quranic angelology, and the four natures and qualities of Hermetic cosmology.[71] There is no question here of being limited by necessity to only one cosmological scheme because the cosmic domain can be envisaged in different lights, each of which reveals an aspect of the cosmic realities. But in nearly all of these forms of cosmology, Ibn 'Arabī, although often making use of elements drawn from such pre-Islamic schools as Hermeticism, bases his views essentially on the Quran and specifically Islamic concepts tied closely to the very forms of Islamic revelation and the letters and sounds of the Arabic language.[72]

The cosmological scheme seeks basically to relate the various cosmic orders to their principle and to show how the different worlds are so many determinations (*ta'ayyun*) of the Principle. These determinations can be considered in any number of ways: they may be thought of as the traditional seventy-two thousand veils of light and darkness which cover the "face of the Beloved"; or they can be reduced to a few principal states which contain within themselves the main levels of cosmic existence. They can be summarized in ascending orders as the world of human and bodily forms (*al-nāsūt*); the world of subtle lights or psychic substance (*al-malakūt*), which is also envisaged as the world of imagination or similitudes (*'ālam al-mithāl*); the world of spiritual existence beyond form (*al-jabarūt*); and the world of the Divine Nature revealing Itself in Its perfect qualities (*al-lāhūt*). Above these stands the Divine Essence (*al-hāhūt*) which transcends all determinations.[73] These worlds, which are also "presences" if considered from the point of view of realization and the attainment of knowledge, comprise the main levels of cosmic existence consisting of the corporeal, psychic, and spiritual manifestation as such. The Ṣūfī delineates these worlds and outlines a science of the Universe based on them in order to be able to realize all these states and finally pass beyond these determinations to attain the state of union with God who is the goal of his journey through all the realms of cosmic manifestation.

Union

The aim of all Sufism is union with the Divine which comes as a result of the love created in man for Divine Beauty. This union is generally conceived in terms of a gradual purification of the heart and the attainment of various spiritual virtues leading finally to the state of "annihilation" (*fanā'*) and "subsistence" (*baqā'*) in the Divine. Ibn 'Arabī envisages the state of union, the supreme experience which is impossible to describe in any adequate formulation, in terms somewhat different from that of other Ṣūfī masters. According to him, knowledge of God and union with Him in the supreme state of contemplation does not mean a ceasing to exist individually (*fanā'*), or a ceasing of that ceasing (*baqā'*), as most gnostics have asserted. Rather, it means to realize that our existence from the beginning belonged to God, that we had no existence to start with which could cease to be. It means the realization that all existence as such is a ray of the Divine Being and that nothing else possesses any existence whatsoever. Or, as it is expressed in the *Treatise on Unity*:

> Most of those who know God made a ceasing of existence and a ceasing of that ceasing a condition of attaining the knowledge of God and that is an error and a clear oversight. For the knowledge of God does not presuppose the ceasing of existence nor the ceasing of that ceasing. For things have no existence, and what does not exist cannot cease to exist. For the ceasing implies the positing of existence, and that is polytheism. Then if thou know thyself without existence or ceasing to be, then thou knowest God; and if not, then not.[74]

From the "operative" point of view, spiritual union, brought about through the force of love for the Divine

Beauty, implies that the Divine Nature becomes the content of human nature, and human nature becomes surrounded and immersed in the Divine. Since this state is considered from the point of view of spiritual experience rather than theory, each relation must be said to present an aspect of the total experience whose essence is ineffable. That is to say, God is present in man, and man is immersed in God. Envisaged in the first mode, union implies that God becomes the Subject who "sees" through the eyes of man and "hears" through his "ears." In the second mode, man is plunged in God so that he "sees" through God and "hears" through Him according to the well-known sacred *ḥadīth*: "He who adores Me never ceases to approach Me until I love him, and when I love him, I am the hearing by which he hears, the sight by which he sees, the hand with which he grasps, and the foot with which he walks." [75]

In the state of union the individuality of man is illuminated and so becomes immersed in the Divine light. The world and man are like the shadow of God; it is this shadow in the spiritual man that becomes transparent and luminous through the presence of the Divine in him. Or, as Ibn 'Arabī states in the *Fuṣūṣ* regarding the relation of the individual to God:

> It is like light that is projected through shadow, a shadow which is nothing but the screen [for light] and which is itself luminous by its transparence. Such also is the man who has realized the Truth; in him the form of the Truth, *ṣūrat al-ḥaqq* [the Divine Qualities], is more directly manifested than in the case of others. For there are among us those for whom God is his hearing, his sight, his faculties and organs according to signs given by the Prophet in his message proceeding from God.[76]

This supreme state of union, which is the ultimate goal of the gnostic and the perfection of human life, is the fruit of the practice of spiritual methods, beginning with the canonical prayers and culminating in the prayer of the heart or the creative prayer,[77] in which the innermost center of the Ṣūfī reverberates in the rhythm of the invocation of the Divine Name which is the epitome of all prayer. Muḥyī al-Dīn asserts over and over again the vital importance of the prayer of the heart and of the inner purification which gradually attracts the Divine unto Itself by that "sympathy" which draws all theophanies toward their source and origin.[78]

In the prayer of the saint, man prays to God and God "prays man" and the prayer fashions man's soul. In the state of pure contemplation, which is the fruit and at the same time the most perfect mode of interior prayer, in which the heart is purified of all its dross and loses all its opaqueness, man realizes that "God is the mirror in which you see yourself, as you are His mirror in which He contemplates His Names and their principles; Now His Names are not other than Himself, so that the reality [or the analogy of relations] is an inversion." [79] Ultimately, therefore, the Lord (*rabb*) remains the Lord and the servant (*marbūb*), the servant, but at the same time God becomes the mirror in which the spiritual man contemplates his own reality and man in turn becomes the mirror in which God contemplates His Names and Qualities, so that in the heart of the saint the purpose of creation is achieved in that God comes to "know" the essences which had been in the "hidden treasure," a knowledge for the sake of which the Universe was created.

The Unity of Religions

Of great interest in the doctrines of Ibn 'Arabī is his belief in the unity of the inner contents of all religions, a principle generally accepted by the Ṣūfīs but rarely explored in as great detail as was done by the Andalusian sage.[80] As already observed, early in life he had the theophanic vision of the Supreme Center from which all revelations have been brought forth and in his later years wrote often of the "spiritual poles" of the traditions preceding Islam. His doctrine of the logos, in fact, contains implicitly the principle of the universality of revelation by asserting that every prophet is an aspect of the Supreme Logos and is himself "a logos," or a word of God. Moreover, Ibn 'Arabī sought to study the specific details of the other religions and to separate the universal meaning hidden in their outer structures as far as it was possible and feasible for him to do so.[81] All attempts at a profound *rapprochement* with the other religions made by Muslims today can and should be based on the rich foundations prepared by Ibn 'Arabī and Rūmī.

Ibn 'Arabī's attempt to transcend the external forms of revelation in order to reach their inner meaning did not in any way imply a rejection of them "from below"; that is, a refusal to accept the outward ritual and dogmatic forms of religion. Rather, he sought to transcend the exoteric level by penetrating into the heart of the exoteric rites and practices which themselves are an integral aspect of religion and are revealed by "Heaven," and to which man must conform if his quest of the spiritual life is to be really fruitful. It was through these formal, or exoteric, aspects of religion and not is spite of them that Ibn 'Arabī, like other Ṣūfīs, sought to reach the inner and universal meaning of the Revelation.

Essentially, the "burning of images," or the rejection of the external and formal aspects of religion, means that one must first possess these images and formal aspects. One cannot reject what one does not possess. And it must be remembered that when Muḥyī al-Dīn and the other Ṣūfīs declared their independence of religious forms and rites, they addressed a collectivity in which the observance of religious practices of all kinds was taken for granted and not a world like that of the present day in which the possibility of rejecting the formal aspects of religion, without having ever practiced and lived them, looms very large on the horizon of the reader's consciousness. Ibn 'Arabī spent much of his life in praying the traditional Islamic prayers, in repenting before God for his sins, in reading the Quran, in invoking the Divine Name, and it was by means of these practices and not in spite of them that he came to realize that the divinely revealed paths lead to the same summit and that to have lived one religion fully is to have lived them all. It was at the very heart of the revealed forms that he found the formless and the Universal so that he could sing in his famous and oft-quoted poem:

> My heart has become capable of every form: it is a pasture for gazelles and a convent for Christian monks,
> And a temple for idols and the pilgrim's Ka'ba and the tables of the Torah, and the book of the Koran.
> I follow the religion of Love: whatever way Love's camels take, that is my religion and my faith.[82]

SUFISM AFTER IBN 'ARABĪ

It is not possible to describe the extent of the influence of Ibn 'Arabī upon the life of Sufism except to say that after him there was practically no exposition of Ṣūfī doctrine which did not come in one way or another under the influence of the works of the great Andalusian sage, even if certain later schools did disagree with some of his formulations.[83] His writings spread immediately over the whole of the Islamic world; his prose works began to be studied by the devotees of Sufism and his poems chanted in the centers (*zāwiyah*) of the various orders, and they continue to be studied and chanted today as they were seven centuries ago.

The spread of Ibn 'Arabī's doctrines in the East is due most of all to Ṣadr al-Dīn al-Qunawī, himself one of the great masters of Sufism, who commented on the Shaikh's works and wrote many of his own to elucidate his master's doctrines.[84] It is essentially through him that several important "lines of influence" of Ibn 'Arabī's doctrines in the East can be traced. Ṣadr al-Dīn was the close associate of Jalāl al-Dīn Rūmī, whose *Mathnawī* many a later Persian Ṣūfī has called the *Futūḥāt* of Persian poetry, and in fact served as Rūmī's *imām* during the daily prayers. It is through Ṣadr al-

Dīn that one must trace the link between Muḥyī al-Dīn and Rūmī, who stands as the other great mountain of Islamic spirituality dominating the landscape of Sufism wherever the Persian language is known and spoken. Ṣadr al-Dīn was also the teacher of Quṭb al-Dīn al-Shīrāzī, who, as we noted in Chapter II, wrote the most famous commentary upon the *Ḥikmat al-ishrāq* of Suhrawardī, and corresponded with Quṭb al-Dīn's teacher, Naṣīr al-Dīn al-Ṭūsī, regarding essential questions of metaphysics.[85] Also, it was due to the inspiration received at one of the sessions of Ṣadr al-Dīn's class on the doctrines of Ibn 'Arabī that Fakhr al-Dīn al-'Arāqī, one of the great Ṣūfī poets, or *fedeli d'amore*, of Persia, composed his *Lama'āt* (*Divine Gleams*) which more than any other work helped to introduce Ibn 'Arabī into the Persian-speaking world.

Included among the disciples of Muḥyī al-Dīn's school are all the famous commentators – al-Nāblusī, al-Kāshānī, al-Qayṣarī, Bālī Afandī, and the great Persian poet Jāmī, who wrote several commentaries on Ibn 'Arabī's works as well as on the *Lama'āt* of 'Arāqī, the latter being called *Ashi''at al-lama'āt* (*Rays of Divine Gleams*). This work continues to be studied today in Persia as a "handbook" of Ṣūfī doctrine. One may also name 'Abd al-Karīm al-Jīlī, whose *Universal Man* is a systematic exposition of the *Fuṣūṣ*; and Maḥmūd Shabistarī whose *Secret Rose Garden* summarizes the doctrines of Sufism as expounded by Ibn 'Arabī in Persian verses of celestial beauty and dazzling lucidity. Also of special interest is the group of Shī'ah gnostics, among them Ibn Turkah, Sayyid Ḥaidar Āmulī and Ibn Abī Jumhūr,[86] who gradually introduced the doctrines of the Andalusian sage into Shī'ism so that it soon became one of the main props of Shī'ah spirituality and played a dominant role in the doctrinal formulations of later Persian sages like Mullā Ṣadrā, who relied heavily upon the teachings of the master from Murcia.[87] In other Muslim countries, also, students and disciples of Ibn 'Arabī's doctrines flourished over the centuries, as seen by the large number of commentaries upon his works that have appeared in India, Anatolia, Syria, and Egypt, where such writers as al-Sha'rānī devoted many large volumes to the exposition and clarification of his writings.

Similarly, in the West, Ibn 'Arabī was not without influence although his works were not known in official circles. But in a more hidden and profound way he left his imprint upon the *fedeli d'amore* of the West and especially upon Dante, the great Florentine poet, who reveals many profound similarities with the Ṣūfīs, not only because of a certain historical contact with them through the Order of the Temple, but primarily because he depicts fundamentally the same spiritual experiences and a similar version of the Universe in the context of the Christian tradition.[88] Muḥyī al-Dīn's direct influence can also be discerned in Raymond Lull and in some of the other Christian esotericists belonging to that period of history when the Christian West and the Islamic East lived in two similar types of civilization, sharing ultimately the same views about man and the Universe even if formal differences of various kinds existed on the theological, social, and political plane.

In modern times the influence of Ibn 'Arabī can be seen wherever Sufism continues to flourish. In the East his writings are still taught and read in India, Pakistan, Afghanistan, and Persia, and commentaries continue to be written on them.[89] In Damascus his tomb is the meeting-place of the Ṣūfīs, and in Egypt and the rest of North Africa his odes are chanted in the weekly gathering of the brotherhoods. And the well-known Ṣūfī masters of this century, like the Moroccan Shaikh Muḥammad al-Tādilī[90] and the Algerian Shaikh al-'Alawī,[91] one of the greatest and most influential saints of Islam during this century, have essentially followed the teachings of Muḥyī al-Dīn.

It is true that the essence of Sufism is the spiritual experience attainable through the means of grace contained within the various methods of realization, compared to which all metaphysical formulations are relative. But to the extent that the inner fire of Sufism has given off sparks and has expressed its ineffable hidden treasures in doctrines that lead other men toward the truth, the spirit of Ibn 'Arabī has hovered over it. He has provided over the centuries the precious doctrinal language in terms of which Ṣūfī masters have sought to expound the mysteries of gnosis, the mysteries of an inner illumination that issues forth from the imponderable dimensions of the Divine Name. Their hearts reverberate in the light and grace of the Name by which they are illuminated as Ibn 'Arabī was before them, and the older masters, before him, reaching back to the source of the Revelation which gave the method of Sufism its spiritual efficacy and the inner life which has permitted it to survive as a spiritual tradition to the present day. *Wa'llāhu a'lam.*

SELECTED BIBLIOGRAPHY

NOTES

INDEX

Selected Bibliography

GENERAL

de Boer, Tj., *The History of Philosophy in Islam*, trans. E. R. Jones, London, 1961.

Brockelmann, C., *Geschichte der arabischen Litteratur*, 2 vols., Weimar, 1898–1902; *Supplement*, 3 vols., Leiden, 1937–1942.

Browne, E. G., *Literary History of Persia*, 4 vols., London, 1902–1930.

Carra de Vaux, B., *Les Penseurs de l'Islam*, 5 vols., Paris, 1921–1926.

Delacy-O'Leary, D. D., *Arabic Thought and Its Place in History*, London, 1922.

Dermenghem, E., *Muhammad and the Islamic Tradition*, New York, 1958.

Duhem, P., *Le Système du monde*, 10 vols., Paris, 1913–1959.

Encyclopaedia of Islam (both old and new editions: Leiden, 1913–1934; Leiden, 1954–).

Gardet, L., "Le Problème de la 'philosophie musulmane,'" in *Mélanges offerts à Etienne Gilson*, Paris, 1959, pp. 261–284.

Gauthier, L., *Introduction à l'étude de la philosophie musulmane*, Paris, 1900.

Gibb, H. A. R., *Mohammadanism*, New York, 1958.

Gilson, E., *History of Christian Philosophy in the Middle Ages*, New York, 1955.

Gobineau, Comte de, *Les Religions et les philosophies dans l'Asie centrale*, Paris, 1923.

von Horten, M., *Die Philosophie des Islam*, Munich, 1923.

Ibn Khaldūn, *The Muqaddimah*, trans. F. Rosenthal, 3 vols., New York, 1958.

Iqbal, M., *The Development of Metaphysics in Persia*, London, 1908.

Kraus, P., *Jābir ibn Ḥayyān*, 2 vols., Cairo, 1942–1943.

Massignon, L., *La Passion d'al-Hallāj*, Paris, 1914–1921.

Mieli, A., *La Science arabe et son rôle dans l'évolution scientifique mondiale*, Leiden, 1938.

Munk, S., *Mélanges de philosophie juive et arabe*, Paris, 1859.

Nallino, C. A., *Raccolta di scritti editi e inediti*, Rome, 1944–1948.

Quadri, G., *La Philosophie arabe dans l'Europe médiévale*, Paris, 1947.

Sarton, G., *Introduction to the History of Science*, vols. I and II, Baltimore, 1927–1931.

AVICENNA AND THE PHILOSOPHER-SCIENTISTS

Afnan, S., *Avicenna, His Life and Works*, London, 1958.
Anawati, G. C., *Essai de bibliographie avicennienne*, Cairo, 1950.
Avicenna Commemoration Volume, Calcutta, 1956.
Avicenna, *Avicenna on Theology*, trans. A. J. Arberry, London, 1951.
——— *Le Livre de science*, trans. M. Achena and H. Massé, 2 vols., Paris, 1955–58.
——— *Le Livre des directives et remarques*, trans. with introduction and notes by A. M. Goichon, Beirut, 1951.
——— *Psychologie Jehe dile aš-Šhifā*, 2 vols., ed. and trans. J. Bakoš, Prague, 1956.
——— *Risālah fi'l-'ishq*, trans. E. L. Fackenheim, *Medieval Studies* (Toronto), 7: 208–228, 1945.
——— *A Treatise on the Canon of Medicine, Incorporating a Translation of the First Book*, by O. C. Gruner, London, 1930.
Carra de Vaux, *Avicenne*, Paris, 1900.
Corbin, H., *Avicenna and the Visionary Recital*, trans. W. Trask, New York, 1960.
Cruz Hernandez, M., *La metafisica de Avicenna*, Granada, 1940.
Gardet, L., *La Pensée religieuse d'Avicenne (Ibn Sīnā)*, Paris, 1951.
Goichon, A. M., *La Distinction de l'essence et de l'existence d'après Ibn Sina (Avicenna)* Paris, 1933.
——— *La Philosophie d'Avicenne et son influence en Europe médiévale*, Paris, 1944.
Holmyard, E. J., *Avicennae de congelatione et conglutinatione Lepidum*, Paris, 1927.
von Horten, M., *Die Metaphysik Avicennas*, Halle, 1909.
von Mehren, A. F., *Les Traités mystiques d'Avicenne*, Leiden, 1889–91.
Sharif, M. M. (ed.), *History of Muslim Philosophy*, 2 vols., Wiesbaden, 1963–66.
Wickens, G. M. (ed.), *Avicenna, Scientist and Philosopher: A Millenary Symposium*, London, 1952.

SUHRAWARDĪ AND THE ILLUMINATIONISTS

Carra de Vaux, "La Philosophie illuminative d'après Suhrawardī maqtoul," *Journal Asiatique* (Paris) 19:63–94 (1902).
Corbin, H., *Les Motifs zoroastriens dans la philosophie de Suhrawardī*, Tehran, 1946.
——— *Suhrawardī d'Alep fondateur de la doctrine illuminative (ishrāqī)*, Paris, 1939.

Horten, M., *Die Philosophie der Erleuchtung nach Suhrawardī*, Halle, 1912.

Mullā Ṣadrā Commemoration Volume, Tehran, 1961.

Nasr, S. H., "Ṣadr al-Dīn Shīrāzī, His Life, Doctrines and Significance," *Indo-Iranica* (Calcutta), 14:6–16 (December 1961).

Ritter, H., "Philologika, IX, Die vier Suhrawardī; I. Shihāb al-Dīn . . . al-Suhrawardī al-Maqtūl," *Der Islam* (Berlin), 24:270–286 (pts. 3–4), 1937.

Suhrawardī, "Le Bruissement de l'aile de Gabriel," trans. with introduction by H. Corbin and P. Kraus, *Journal Asiatique* (Paris), 52:1–82 (July–September, 1935).

——— "Epître de la modulation de Sîmôrgh," trans. H. Corbin, in *Hermes* (Brussels–Paris), November 1939, pp. 7–50.

——— *The Lover's Friend*, ed. O. Spies, Delhi, 1934.

——— *Opera Metaphysica et Mystica*, ed. H. Corbin, vol. I (Istanbul, 1945); vol. II (Tehran, 1952).

——— *Three Treatises on Mysticism*, ed. and trans. O. Spies and S. K. Khattak, Stuttgart, 1935.

IBN ARABĪ AND THE ṢŪFĪS

'Abd al-Karim al-Jīlī, *De l'homme universel*, trans. T. Burckhardt, Lyon, 1953.

'Abd al-Raḥmān Jāmī, *Lawā'iḥ, a Treatise on Sufism*, trans. E. H. Whinfield and M. M. Ḳazvīnī, London, 1914.

Abu Bakr Siraj al-Din, "The Origins of Sufism," *Islamic Quarterly* (London), 3:53–64 (April 1956).

Affifi, A., *The Mystical Philosophy of Muhyīd-Dīn Ibn al-'Arabī*, Cambridge, England, 1939.

Anawati, G. C., and L. Gardet, *La Mystique musulmane*, Paris, 1961.

Asin Palacios, M., *El Islam cristianizado*, Madrid, 1931.

——— "El místico murciano Abenarabi," *Boletin de la Real Academia de la Historia* (Madrid), I, 87:96–173 (1925); II, 87:512–611; III, 87:582–637 (1926); IV, 92:654–751 (1928).

——— *Islam and the Divine Comedy*, trans. H. Sunderland, London, 1926.

——— *Vidas de Santones Andaluces*, Madrid, 1933.

——— "La Psicología según Mohidin Abenarabi," *Actes du XIV Congrès Inter. des Orient. Alger, 1905*, vol. III, Paris, 1907.

——— "Mohidin," in *Homenaje a Menendez y Pelayo*, Madrid, 1899, II, 217–256.

——— "La Psicología, del éxtasis en dos grandes místicos musulmanes:

Algazel y Mohidin Abenarabi," in *Cultura Española*, Madrid, 1906, pp. 209–235.
Burckhardt, T., *Clé spirituelle de l'astrologie musulmane d'après Moyhiddin Ibn Arabī*, Paris, 1950.
——— *An Introduction to Sufi Doctrine*, trans. D. M. Matheson, Lahore, 1959.
Corbin, H., *L'Imagination créatrice dans le soufisme d'Ibn 'Arabī*, Paris, 1958.
Horton, M., "Mystische texte aus dem Islam. Drei Gedichte des Arabi 1240. Aus dern arabischen übersetzt und erläutert" in *Kleine Texte für Vorlesungen und Übungen*, Bonn, 1912 (trans. and commentary on three poems).
Ibn 'Arabī, "Les étapes divines dans la voie du perfectionnement du règne humain," trans. Othman Laïba and R. Maridort, *Etudes Traditionnelles* (Paris), 50:76–90 (March 1949).
——— "Oraisons métaphysiques," trans. M. Vâlsan, *Etudes Traditionnelles* (Paris), 50:251–266 (September 1949).
——— "La Parure des Abdal," trans. with notes by M. Vâlsan, *Etudes Traditionnelles* (Paris), 51:248–258 (September 1950); 51:297–307 (October–November 1950).
——— *La Sagesse des prophètes*, trans. T. Burckhardt, Paris, 1955.
——— *Tarjumān al-ashwāq*, trans. R. A. Nicholson, London, 1911.
——— "Textes sur la Connaissance suprême," trans. and annotated by M. Vâlsan, *Etudes Traditionnelles* (Paris), 53:125–133 (April–May 1952); 53:182–188 (June 1952).
——— *The Treatise on Unity (Risālat al-aḥadīyah)*, trans. T. H. Weir as "Translation of an Arabic Manuscript in the Hunterian Collection, Glasgow University," *Journal of the Royal Asiatic Society* (Malayan Branch), October 1901, pp. 809–825.
Jeffery, A., "Ibn al-Arabī's Shajarat al-Kawn," *Studia Islamica*, (Leiden), 10:43–77 (1959); 11:113–160 (1959).
Lings, M., *A Moslem Saint of the Twentieth Century*, London, 1961.
Massignon, L., *Essai sur les origines du lexique technique de la mystique musulmane*, Paris, 1954.
——— *Recueil de textes inédits concernant l'histoire de la mystique en pays d'Islam*, Paris, 1929.
Mir Valiuddin, *The Quranic Sufism*, Delhi, 1959.
Nicholson, R. A., "An Historical Inquiry Concerning the Origin and Development of Sūfism," *Journal of the Royal Asiatic Society*, (London, 1906), pp. 303–348.

——— *Studies in Islamic Mysticism*, Cambridge, England, 1921.
Nyberg, H. S., *Kleinere Schriften des Ibn al-'Arabī*, Leiden, 1919.
Schuon, F., *Understanding Islam*, trans. D. M. Matheson, London, 1963.
——— *Spiritual Perspectives and Human Facts*, trans. D. M. Matheson, London, 1955.
——— *The Transcendent Unity of Religions*, trans. P. Townsend, London, 1953.
Zaehner, R. C., *Mysticism Sacred and Profane*, Oxford, 1957.

Notes

CHAPTER I: AVICENNA (IBN SĪNĀ) AND THE PHILOSOPHER-SCIENTISTS

1. The famous scientist, scholar, and compiler of the 4th/11th century, al-Bīrūnī, mentions Abu'l-'Abbās al-Īrānshahrī's name many times and shows much respect for him; see, for example, his *India*, trans. E. Sachau (London, 1887), I, 6, et passim, as well as his *Chronology of Ancient Nations* and *Picture of the World*. Still, nothing is left of this mysterious figure who is considered as the first philosopher in Islam, except a name and a few scattered views and sayings.

2. For the life, works, and philosophy of al-Kindī, see M. Abū Rīdah, *Al-Kindī wa falsafatuhu* (Cairo, 1950); his *Rasā'il al-Kindī al-falsafīyah*, 2 vols. (Cairo, 1950–1953); Mustafā 'Abd al-Rāziq, *Failasūf al-'arab wa'l-mu'allim al-thānī* (Cairo, 1945); M. Guido and R. Walzer, "Studi su al-Kindī, 1. Uno scritto introduttivo all studio di Aristotele," *Memorie R. Accademia dei Lincei*, ser. 6, pt. 5, vol. VI (1940), pp. 375–419; H. Ritter and R. Walzer, "Studi su al-Kindī, 2. Uno scritto morale inedito di al-Kindī," *Memorie R. Academia dei Lincei*, ser. 6, pt. 1, vol. VIII (1938), pp. 63ff; R. Walzer, "New Studies on Al-Kindī," *Oriens*, 10:203–232 (2, 1957); A. Nagy, "Die philosophischen Abhandlungen des al-Kindī," *Beiträge zur Geschichte der Philosophie des Mittelalters* (Münster, 1897), II, 5; and Tj. de Boer, "Zur Kindi und seiner Schule," in *Arch. für Gesch. der Philos.* 13:153ff (1900).

The general histories of Islamic philosophy, which are nearly all confined to the history of Peripatetic philosophy, have chapters devoted to al-Kindī, as well as to al-Fārābī and Avicenna. See, for example, Tj. de Boer, *History of Philosophy in Islam*, trans. E. R. Jones (London, 1961); G. Quadri, *La Philosophie arabe dans l'Europe médiévale* (Paris, 1947); S. Munk, *Mélanges de philosophie juive et arabe* (Paris, 1859); I. Goldziher, *Die islamische und jüdische Philosophie des Mittelalters* in *Die Kultur der Gegenwort*, I, 5 (Leipzig, 1909; 2nd ed., 1913); Carra de Vaux, *Les Penseurs de l'Islam* (Paris, 1923), vol. IV; L. Gauthier, *Introduction à l'étude de la philosophie musulmane* (Paris, 1923); R. Walzer, "Islamic Philosophy" in the *History of Philosophy East and West* (London, 1953), II, 120–148; and L. Gardet, "Le Problème de la 'philosophie musulmane,' " in *Mélanges offerts à Etienne Gilson* (Paris, 1959), pp. 261–284.

See also G. Sarton, *Introduction to the History of Science* (Baltimore, 1927–1931), vols. I–II, and A. Mieli, *La Science arabe* (Leiden, 1939).

For bibliographical studies on Islamic philosophy see P. J. De

Menasce, *Arabische Philosophie* in *Bibliographische Einführungen in das Studium der Philosophie* (Bern, 1948) and R. Walzer, "A Survey of Works on Medieval Philosophy, 1945–1952. Part I: Medieval Islamic Philosophy," in *Philosophical Quarterly*, 3:175–181 (April, 1953).

3. Most of the well-known critical translations of Greek works were made by Ḥunain ibn Isḥāq, a contemporary of al-Kindī and his school so that they could not have been used by al-Kindī himself. It is known, however, that by al-Kindī's time a translation of the *Metaphysics* of Aristotle had been made into Arabic and that "the Philosopher of the Arabs" possessed a translation of the *Theology of Aristotle* which had been expressly made for him. See R. Walzer, "Islamic Philosophy," p. 125; and his "New lights on the Arabic translations of Aristotle," *Oriens*, 6:91ff (1953).

4. There is no certainty about the exact date of the death — and even less about the birth — of al-Kindī. L. Massignon, in his *Recueil de textes inédits concernant l'historie de la mystique en pays d'Islam* (Paris, 1929), p. 175, considers the date of his death as 246/860, while C. A. Nallino in his *Kitāb ta'rīkh 'ilm al-falak 'ind al-'arab* (Rome, 1911), p. 117, writes that al-Kindī died in 260/873. But the result of the research of Abū Rīdah and Shaikh Muṣṭafā 'Abd al-Rāziq, in works cited above, shows that the date 252/866 is the most accurate.

5. In the *Risālat al-'aql*, whose Latin translation was edited by A. Nagy in "Die philosophischen Abhandlungen des Ja'qūb ben Isḥāq al-Kindī" in *Beiträge zur Geschichte der Philosophie des Mittelalters*, al-Kindī divides the intellect into four categories, following for the most part the commentary of Alexander Aphrodisias upon Aristotle's *De Anima*. This fourfold division was adopted by al-Fārābī and Avicenna and became a stable element in the psychological theories of the Muslim philosophers down to Mullā Ṣadrā and Sabziwārī.

6. Al-Kindī's scientific works, which establish him as an important scientific, as well as philosophical, figure, include his popular work on optics, based on Theon's recension of the *Optics* of Euclid, many treatises on particular optical problems such as the well-known one on why the sky is blue, works on mathematics, especially arithmetic, in which he inclined toward Neo-Pythagorean interpretation of numbers, writings on astronomy as well as on geography and even history. His interest in geography was so great that the *Geography* of Ptolemy was specifically translated for him and some of his students became famous geographers. Moreover, al-Kindī wrote many works on occult sciences — especially astrology — but curiously enough was opposed to alchemy. One of his most famous astrological works is his prediction of the duration of the Abbasid caliphate based on astrological calculations which he then tried to correlate with the results he

had derived from interpreting the esoteric meaning of the opening letters of the chapters of the Quran.

7. This reference is found in Book XVI of his *De Subtilitate*, dealing with the sciences (*De Scientiis*), where Cardanus mentions the name of al-Kindī along with those of Archimedes, Aristotle, Euclid, and others as one of the great intellectual figures of human history and writes of him in these words: "Decimus Alchindus, & ipse Arabs, editorum libroru, quorum Averroes n minit, exemplum est, qui superest libellus de ratione sex quantitarum, que in nos excudendum trademus, exhibet, cum nihil fit ingeniosius." (The 1554 printed edition, p. 445.)

8. Abū Rīdah, *Rasā'il al-Kindī al-falsafiyah*, pp. 102–103; the present translation is that of R. Walzer, "Islamic Philosophy," p. 131; see also A. J. Arberry, *Reason and Revelation in Islam* (London, 1957), pp. 34–35.

9. Although famous in the annals of Islamic history, al-Sarakhsī's life and personality can be reconstructed only from fragments that can be found among such later historians as al-Mas'ūdī and Yāqūt. From information brought together in the detailed study of F. Rosenthal, *Aḥmad B. aṭ-Ṭayyib as-Sarakhsī* (New Haven, 1943), which is the most important work on this neglected figure, it can be concluded that al-Sarakhsī lived from about 218/833 to 286/899, although both of these dates are uncertain. Rosenthal has also assembled the name of his certain and doubtful works which, like those of al-Kindī, cover all branches of philosophy, as well as physics, meteorology, geology, geography and history, astronomy and astrology, mathematics and music, and medicine as well as literature and cultural history. Al-Sarakhsī was particularly significant as a geographer, having written the first of several works in Islamic geography bearing the name *Kitāb al-masālik wa'l-mamālik*. But it was primarily as an astrologer that he became celebrated among later generations.

10. No less a figure than al-Bīrūnī writes: "And shrewd people, when they were not in a position to show their heresy openly and to reveal their opposition, pretended outwardly to consider the prophets as true, but secretly they had their share at the watering place. They were enemies when they pretended to bring salvation. One of them was A. B. aṭ-Ṭayyib al Sarakhsī." Al-Bīrūnī, *Chronology of Ancient Nations*, MS. 'Umūmī, pp. 212–214, quoted and translated by F. Rosenthal in his *Aḥmad B. aṭ-Ṭayyib as-Sarakhsī*, p. 122.

11. Abū Ma'shar (d. 272/886), who turned late in life to the study of astrology, is one of the most influential of Muslim astrologers, in the East as well as in the West where his influence carried on well into the Renaissance. (See W. Hartner, "Tycho Brahe et Albumasar," in *La Science au seizième siècle* [Paris, 1960], pp. 137–148.) He wrote several major works on astrology, revealing strong Iranian and Indian,

as well as Hellenistic, influence. One of the most important of his works is *al-Madkhal al-kabīr*, translated twice into Latin and known in the West as *Introductorium in astronomiam Albumasaris Abalachii octo continens libros partiales*. Concerning Abū Ma'shar and his influence see Sarton, *Introduction*, I, 568–569; P. Duhem, *Le Système du monde* (Paris, 1914), II, 369–386, 503–504; L. Thorndike, *A History of Magic and Experimental Science* (New York, 1923), I, 649–652; J. M. Faddegon, "Notice sur un petit traité d'astrologie attribué à Albumasar: (Abū-Ma'sar)," *Journal Asiatique*, 213:150–158 (1928); and the article on him by J. M. Millás-Vallicrosa in the new *Encyclopaedia of Islam* (Leiden, 1954–).

12. Abū Zaid al-Balkhī, who was born about 236/850, was celebrated as both philosopher and geographer and had many important students, including the philosopher Abu'l-Ḥasan al-'Āmirī. But his influence and significance reside most of all in his geographical studies. He was without doubt a Shī'ah and spent much of his life in Baghdād where he studied with al-Kindī and where he died about 322/934. See M. J. de Goeje, "Die Istakhrī-Balkhī Frage," in *Zeitschrift der Deutschen morgenländischen Gesellschaft*, 25:42–58 (1871); *Ḥudūd al-'ālam* (London, 1937) with preface by V. Minorsky, pp. 15–23; and the article of D. M. Dunlop on al-Balkhī in the new *Encyclopaedia of Islam*.

13. The term "teacher" or *mu'allim* as used in this context does not mean one who teaches or is a master of the sciences. Rather, it means one who defines, for the first time, the boundaries and limits of each branch of knowledge and formulates each science in a systematic fashion. That is why Aristotle, who was the first in Greece to have classified, defined, and formulated the various sciences, is called "The First Teacher," and Mīr Dāmād, who performed the same task on a smaller scale within the consolidated Twelve-imām Shī'ah world of the Safavids is referred to by many in Persia as the Third Teacher.

As for al-Fārābī, it was because his *Iḥṣā' al-'ulūm*, the Latin *De Scientiis* (see the edition of O. Amīn, Cairo, 1350) was the first classification widely known to the Muslims — the effort of al-Kindī in this direction not being generally recognized by later generations — and because he really molded and formulated the various branches of knowledge in a complete and permanent form within Islamic civilization that he gained the title of "The Second Teacher."

14. Regarding the life, works, and philosophy of al-Fārābī, of whom a large number of studies have been made in European as well as Eastern languages, see the still valuable *al-Fārābī des arabischen Philosophen Leben und Schriften*, by M. Steinschneider (Saint Petersburg, 1869); I. Madkour, *La Place d'al-Farabi dans l'école philosophique musulmane* (Paris, 1934); F. Dieterici, *al-Farabi's philosophische Abhandlungen, aus dem Arabischen übersetzt* (Leiden,

1892); F. Rosenthal and R. Walzer, *al-Farabius De Platonis Philosophia, Plato Arabus*, vol. II (London, 1942); F. Gabrieli, *al-Farabius De Platonis Legibus, Plato Arabus*, vol. III (London, 1952); R. Walzer, "al-Farabi's theory of prophecy and divination," *Journal of Hellenic Studies*, 57:142ff (1957); E. I. J. Rosenthal, "The Place of Politics in the Philosophy of al-Fārābī," *Islamic Culture*, 29:178ff (1955); also his *Political Thought in Medieval Islam* (Cambridge, England, 1958), pp. 122–142; and al-Fārābī, *Fuṣūl al-madanī*, trans. D. M. Dunlop (Cambridge, England, 1961). A good bibliography of European works on al-Fārābī as well as other Muslim Peripatetic philosophers and theologians can be found in E. Gilson, *History of Christian Philosophy in the Middle Ages* (New York, 1955), pp. 638–639.

15. Concerning al-Fārābī's logic, see I. Madkour's *La Place d'al-Farabi . . .* and his *L'Organon d'Aristote dans le monde arabe* (Paris, 1934); and D. M. Dunlop, "al-Fārābī's introductory sections on logic," *Islamic Quarterly*, 2:264–282 (1955).

16. It must be remembered, however, that for al-Fārābī, as for other Muslim philosopher-scientists, with the exception of al-Kindī, the *Theology of Aristotle*, that modified version of the *Enneads* which had such a significant influence upon the members of this school, was considered as a work of Aristotle so that the relation between Plato and Aristotle appeared to these medieval philosophers in a completely different light from what it does to a modern historian of philosophy. Also, the principle of the primacy of the Idea over the individual who is its expositor must be kept in mind when considering this question, as in so many other instances.

17. Regarding this question, see the writings of E. I. J. Rosenthal cited in n. 14 above; and also H. K. Sherwani, "Al-Fārābī's political philosophy," *Proc. 9th All-India Oriental Conference*, 1937, pp. 337–360.

18. See R. Walzer, "Islamic Philosophy" in *History of Philosophy East and West*, pp. 136–140.

19. This work was translated by F. Dieterici as *Al-Farabi's Abhandlung der Musterstaat* (Leiden, 1895), and is al-Fārābī's most important political work.

20. See Baron R. d'Erlanger, *La Musique arabe* (Paris, 1930–1935), vols. I and II.

Besides Avicenna, the only other theoretician whose significance compares with that of al-Fārābī, though he is not so well known in the Occident, is the Persian musician and scholar of the 7th/13th century, Ṣafī al-Dīn al-Urmawī, the author of *Kitāb al-adwār* and *Risālat al-sharafiyah*, in which his musical theories are expounded. See *La Musique arabe* (Paris, 1938), vol. III, where these works are translated into French.

21. In order to escape from the danger of considering Sufism as a philosophical system and therefore another "ism," it would be more correct to use the Arabic term *taṣawwuf* but since the term Sufism is quite prevalent in European languages, in a work such as this, which is based on a series of public lectures, we have made use of the more familiar European form rather than the original Arabic term.

22. This point, although denied by many later scholars, was fully recognized by Carra de Vaux in his article on al-Fārābī in the *Encyclopaedia of Islam*.

23. The practice of alternating between simple and highly ornate dress was carried on also by a number of well-known Ṣūfīs like Abu'l-Ḥasan al-Shādhilī, the founder of the famous Shādhilīyah order, perhaps to show their independence not only of the world but also of renunciation of the world, or what Rūmī calls "renunciation of renunciation" (*tark-i tark*).

24. This work should not be confused with the more famous treatise by Ibn 'Arabī bearing the same title.

25. See S. Pines, "Ibn Sīnā et l'auteur de la Risālat al-fuṣūṣ fi'l-ḥikma," *Rev. des études islamiques* (1951), pp. 122–124, in which he argues for its Avicennian origin mostly because in certain manuscripts it has been attributed to Avicenna. But there are many other works, especially of this nature, by various authors attributed during later periods to the Peripatetic master. The arguments given in this article, although coming from the pen of such a reliable scholar, are not altogether sufficient to make the *Fuṣūṣ* a work of Avicenna rather than al-Fārābī, even if one denies its Fārābīan origin. Mention should be made also of the article by Khalīl Georr, "Fārābī est-il l'auteur des 'Fuçûç al-hikam' "?, *Rev. des études islamiques* (1941–1946), pp. 31–39, where he argues against the authenticity of this treatise by showing that some of the terms and concepts used in it, especially those concerning the faculties of the soul, are not the same as those mentioned in some of his other works. But here again it could be added that al-Fārābī is not always systematic on every point of his doctrine and one can often find ideas expressed one way in one work and another in the next.

Whatever the final results of research on the authorship of the *Fuṣūṣ* may be, whether it be actually by al-Fārābī or by one of his disciples as Georr suggests, there is no doubt that it forms one of the basic aspects of al-Fārābī's writings and of the personality and stature of al-Fārābī himself as he has been understood and studied in the East over the centuries. The doctrines described in it, and the tone which it has, however, are by no means unique in al-Fārābī's works but are found in one form or another in his other writings, which thus bear testimony to the possibility of a gnostic, as well as a philosophical, interpretation of him made during later centuries.

26. An important commentary has been written on this work by one of the leading contemporary *ḥakīms* and gnostics of Persia, Ilāhī Qumshahī, who explains and teaches this text as a complete cycle of *'irfān*, such as one would find explicitly in the writings of Ibn 'Arabī, Ṣadr al-Dīn al-Qunawī, 'Abd al-Karīm al-Jīlī, and Maḥmūd Shabistarī.

27. The *Fuṣūṣ* and this commentary have been translated into German by M. Horten, *Das Buch der Ringsteine Farabis, mit dem Kommentare des Emir Isma'il el-Hoseini el-Farani* (Münster, 1906).

28. Concerning al-Rāzī, see S. Pines, *Beiträge zur islamischen Atomenlehre* (Berlin, 1938), chap. ii, pp. 34–93; M. Meyerhof, "The Philosophy of the Physician al-Razi," *Islamic Culture*, 15:45–58 (January 1941); P. Kraus, "Raziana," trans. A. J. Arberry, *Asiatic Review* (1949), pp. 703–713; and R. Walzer, "Islamic Philosophy," pp. 133–136.

29. Al-Bīrūnī was much interested in the writings of al-Rāzī, which he sought for many years and against some of which he expressed his severe criticism. He even wrote a bibliography of the works of al-Rāzī; see *Epître de Beruni contenant le répertoire des ouvrages de Muḥammad b. Zakariya al-Razi*, ed. P. Kraus (Paris, 1936).

30. This important work has been edited and translated into German by J. Ruska, *al-Razi's Buch Geheimnis der Geheimnisse* (Berlin, 1937).

31. The Ikhwān al-Ṣafā' were also particularly significant for their propagation of Pythagorean and Hermetic ideas which were used later by the Ismā'īlīs. See Seyyed Hossein Nasr, *Introduction to Islamic Cosmological Doctrines* (Cambridge, 1968), chap. 1.

32. Concerning the significance of this period in the cultivation of the Islamic arts and sciences see the prologue to Nasr, *Introduction* . . . (n. 31 above).

33. The importance of Abu'l-Barakāt, especially with respect to his criticism of the Aristotelian theory of projectile motion and his relation to Avicenna's theory, has become well known through the studies of S. Pines, especially his *Nouvelles études sur Awḥad al-Zamān Abu'l-Barakāt al-Baghdādī* (Paris, 1955).

34. Concerning this work and its author, see M. Muḥammad Khān Qazvīnī, *Abū Sulaimān Manṭiqī Sidjistānī* (Paris, 1933).

35. This history, which is especially valuable for the figures of the 4th/10th and 5th/11th centuries, has been edited and published by M. Shafī' (Lahore, 1935).

36. Concerning his life and writings see M. Minovi, "Les bibliothèques de la Turquie," *Revue de la Faculté des Lettres*, Université de Téhéran, 4:59–84 (March 1957); Abū Ḥayyān al-Tawḥīdī, *al-Imtā' wa'l-mu'ānasah* (Cairo, 1373), I, 35–36, 222–223; II, 84, 86, 88; III, 94; and his *Muqābasāt* (Cairo, 1929), pp. 165, 202, et passim.

37. See F. Rosenthal, "State and Religion according to Abu'l-Ḥasan al-'Āmirī," *Islamic Quarterly*, III:42–52 (April 1956).

38. The most authoritative account of the life of Avicenna is that of his lifelong disciple, Abū 'Ubaid al-Juzjānī; it is upon this that later accounts found in Ibn Abī Uṣaibi'ah, Ibn al-Qifṭī, and other traditional authors are based. For modern sources about his life, see S. S. Gawharīn, *Ḥujjat al-ḥaqq Abū 'Alī Sīnā* (Tehran, 1331); *Avicenna Commemoration Volume* (Calcutta, 1956), introduction; G. M. Wickens, ed., *Avicenna: Philosopher and Scientist* (London, 1952), chap. I; S. M. Afnan, *Avicenna, His Life and Works* (London, 1958), chap. II; and Nasr, *Introduction . . .* , chap. 11.

A bibliography of works on Avicenna in European languages is given by S. Naficy, *Bibliographie des principaux travaux européens sur Avicenne* (Tehran, 1333); Y. Mahdavi, *Bibliographie d'Ibn Sīnā* (Tehran, 1332); and G. C. Anawati, *Essai de bibliographie avicennienne* (Cairo, 1950); and regarding works in German concerning him, see O. Spies, "Der deutsche Beitrag zur Erforschung Avicennas," *Avicenna Commemoration Volume*, pp. 92–103.

Works on Avicenna in European languages are numerous, each approaching him from a particular point of view. Among these one may mention, besides the writings cited above, the still useful B. Carra de Vaux, *Avicenne* (Paris, 1900); the several well-known studies of A. M. Goichon, especially *La Distinction de l'essence et de l'existence d'après Ibn Sīnā (Avicenna)* (Paris, 1937); *La Philosophie d'Avicenne et son influence en Europe médiévale* (Paris, 1944); *Lexique de la langue philosophique d'Ibn Sīnā (Avicenna)* (Paris, 1938); and *Vocabulaires comparés d'Aristote et d'Ibn Sina* (Paris, 1939); the penetrating articles and books of L. Gardet, especially *La Pensée religieuse d'Avicenne (Ibn Sīnā)*, Paris, 1951; and H. Corbin, *Avicenna and the Visionary Recital* (New York, 1960), which is the most lucid exposition of Avicenna's esoteric philosophy and the influence of this school in the East. Also, special mention should be made of the researches of H. A. Wolfson and E. Gilson which cover many aspects of Avicenna's philosophy and their relation to the general questions of medieval philosophy; see especially Wolfson, *Crescas' Critique of Aristotle* (Cambridge, Mass., 1929), and Gilson, *History of Christian Philosophy in the Middle Ages*.

39. The most thorough bibliographical studies of Avicenna are those of Y. Mahdavi and G. C. Anawati mentioned in n. 38 above.

40. This work has been translated into French by M. Achena and H. Massé as *Le Livre de science*, 2 vols. (Paris, 1955–1958).

41. The original Arabic text of the *Shifā'* has still to be printed in full. A lithographed edition of the *Metaphysics* and *Physics* was published in Tehran in 1303 A.H. and a complete edition is now being published under the direction of I. Madkour of which the logic and

certain parts concerned with mathematics and metaphysics have already appeared. Sections of the *Shifā'* have also been translated into European languages, as, for example, the psychology by J. Bakoš (Prague, 1956) and the part on music by Baron d'Erlanger in his *La Musique arabe*, II, 105ff. For many years M. D'Alverny has been preparing critical editions of the translations of Avicenna in Latin which will appear soon in a series devoted to Latin Avicennianism.

42. Many of these treatises deal with individual problems already dealt with in the larger compendia, but some, like *Risālat al-aḍḥawīyah* (*Treatise on the Day of Splendor*), dealing with questions of eschatology, and the glosses upon the *Theology of Aristotle*, discuss fundamental issues not found, at least in the same light, in other works.

43. See Nasr, *Introduction* . . . , chap. 11, pt. 1.

44. The first book of the *Canon* has been rendered into English with interesting comparisons with later medical ideas by a contemporary physician, O. Gruner, under the title, *A Treatise on the Canon of Medicine, Incorporating a Translation of the First Book* (London, 1930).

45. This poem has been commented upon by many later writers, among them, Dāwūd al-Anṭākī and Sayyid Sharīf al-Jurjānī, and had also been translated several times into European languages; see A. J. Arberry's translation in Wickens, *Avicenna* . . . , p. 28.

46. Avicenna, who has often been called the first Scholastic, is in reality the founder of medieval philosophy which, in both the Islamic and Christian worlds, is concerned essentially with the question of being. He has, therefore, been sometimes called "a philosopher of being"; see A. M. Goichon, "L'Unité de la pensée avicennienne," *Archives Internationales d'Histoire des Sciences*, no. 20–21 (1952), pp. 290–308.

47. See S. H. Nasr, "Polarization of Being," *Pakistan Philosophical Journal*, 3:8–13 (October 1959).

48. Concerning the metaphysical aspects of Avicenna's philosophy and especially this question, see E. Gilson, *Avicenne et le point de départ de Duns Scotus* (Paris, 1927); A. M. Goichon, *La Distinction de l'essence et de l'existence d'après Ibn Sīnā (Avicenna)*; Dj. Saliba, *Etude sur la métaphysique d'Avicenne* (Paris, 1926); and the study of L. Gardet, *La Pensée religieuse d'Avicenne (Ibn Sīnā)* (see n. 38 above), which discusses also his conception of creation, prophecy, and attitude toward various other religious questions; see also Nasr, "The Anatomy of Being," in *Introduction* . . . , chap. 12.

As for Avicenna's own works, the section on metaphysics of the *Shifā'* and *Najāt*, as well as the *Dānishnāmah*, treats fully all the divisions and distinctions of being.

49. Ṣūfī metaphysics would add at this point that the Divine Essence (*dhāt*) transcends even Being which is its first self-determina-

tion or affirmation and is at the same time the Principle of the Universe. See F. Schuon, *The Transcendent Unity of Religions* (New York, 1953), pp. 53ff.

50. The argument of St. Thomas based on the contingency of the Universe derives from this basic distinction of Avicenna between the Necessary Being and possible beings.

51. Page references have not been given for Avicenna's own writings where these questions are discussed. I have mentioned simply the metaphysical section (*Ilāhīyāt*) of his various philosophical works where he discusses these questions. Detailed references to his works, as well as secondary sources, regarding each problem have been given in Nasr, *Introduction . . .*, chap. 12.

52. See H. Corbin, *Avicenna and the Visionary Recital*, sec. II, "Avicennism and Angelology," in which he has made a profound study of Avicennian angelology and its relation to cosmology. It is especially in Avicenna's later "esoteric" works that the significance of the angel as the inner guide of man and the source of illumination becomes central.

53. The ideas of Avicenna concerning cosmogony and cosmology have been summarized in a Persian treatise called *Dar ḥaqīqat wa kaifīyat-i silsilah-i mawjūdāt wa tasalsul-i musabbabāt* (*On the Chain of Being*), ed. M. 'Amīd (Tehran, 1952), which although of somewhat doubtful authenticity gives a good synopsis of concepts described in greater detail in the *Shifā'* and the *Najāt*; see also L. Gardet, *La Pensee religieuse d'Avicenne*, p. 48.

The hierarchies of intelligences and souls and general questions of cosmology are discussed with the greatest detail in the *Metaphysics* of the *Shifā'* (Tehran, 1303), pp. 618ff.

54. See A. M. Goichon, *La Philosophie d'Avicenne et son influence en Europe médiévale*, p. 41.

55. According to traditional Islamic astronomy, the heavens above the moon are, in order, Mercury, Venus, Sun, Mars, Jupiter, Saturn, Heaven of the Zodiacal signs, and the *Primum mobile*. Many authorities, among them L. Gardet (see n. 54 above) believe that the limiting of the intelligences to ten is purely *a posteriori*. However, the numerical symbolism of the nine heavens corresponding to the ten intelligences cannot be ignored inasmuch as the number ten by bringing to a close the cycle of numbers also symbolizes the termination of the totality of the intelligible order.

56. It is of special significance that in this treatise Avicenna attempts to deal with the letters at the beginning of the chapters of the Quran and that the complete title of the treatise is *Fī ma'āni'l-ḥurūf al-hijā'īy'-allatī fī fawātiḥ ba'ḍ al-suwar al-furqānīyah*, that is, on the meaning of the letters of the alphabet which appear at the opening of some of the chapters of the Quran.

57. In his study on this treatise of Avicenna ("La Philosophie orientale d'Ibn Sina et son alphabet philosophique," *Mémorial Avicenne,* Cairo, 1954, IV, 1–18), L. Massignon, who more than any other orientalist has discovered the difference between the Semitic and Greek attitude toward language and the psychological effect of the spoken word upon the soul of the Muslim, points to the triple value for the Semites of the primitive alphabet, which is at once phonetic, semantic (and thus closely related to the basic "ideas" of their world view), and finally arithmetical, having, as it does, a definite numerical value.

The Greek alphabet, which was used by certain esoteric circles in the Near East before the rise of Islam, as P. Kraus has shown in his *Jābir ibn Ḥayyān* (Cairo, 1942, II, 236ff), was itself of Semitic origin, and the numerical values which each letter symbolized was also Semitic.

58. There are several orders of letters commonly in use in the *Jafr* system, of which the *abjad,* namely the one which begins with *alif, bā', jīm* and *dāl* is the most common. Avicenna's order of letters does not, however, follow the traditional Islamic scheme completely.

59. Euclide geomètra et Tolomeo
Ipocrate Avicenna e Galïeno
Averrois, che'l gran comento feo.
(*Inferno,* IV, verses 142–144)

60. Avicenna calls this science *fann al-samā' al-ṭabī'ī,* that is, the first thing which one "hears" when studying natural philosophy or the principles of natural philosophy.

61. These questions have been dealt with fully in Nasr, *Introduction . . . ,* chaps. 12–14.

62. See A. M. Goichon, "La Nouveauté de la logique d'Ibn Sina," *Millénaire d'Avicenne. Congrès de Bagdad* (Cairo, 1952), pp. 41–58. Although Goichon's analysis of this type of syllogism used by Avicenna is an illuminating one, her arguments that it is this attraction for experimental science that constitutes for Avicenna his "Oriental Philosophy" is, to say the least, not very convincing. One cannot dismiss so lightly something which has had so much meaning to many generations of Persian sages, for whom "the Oriental Philosophy" has had deep metaphysical import.

63. See A. Sayili, "Rawish-i 'ilmī-i Abū 'Alī Sīnā," *Le Livre du millénaire d'Avicenne* (Tehran, 1953), II, 403–412.

64. See M. Horten and E. Wiedemann, "Avicenne's Lehre von Regenbogen nach seinem werk al-Shifā'," *Meterologische Zeitschrift,* 11:533–544 (1913).

65. See E. Wiedemann, "Über ein von Ibn Sīnā (Avicenna) hergestelltes Beobachtungsinstrument," *Zeitschrift für Instrumentkunde,* 6:269–375 (1925).

66. Regarding the medical history of Islam leading to Avicenna, see M. Meyerhof, "Science and Medicine," in the *Legacy of Islam* (Oxford, 1931), pp. 311–355; E. G. Browne: *Arabian Medicine* (Cambridge, 1921); C. Elgood, *A Medical History of Persia and the Eastern Caliphate* (London, 1951).

67. See E. Kremers and G. Udang, *History of Pharmacy* (Philadelphia, 1940), pp. 19ff.

68. Book I (chaps. 3, 4, and 5) and Book IV of the *Canon* present Avicenna as a competent surgeon with exact observations on many types of surgery, including that of cancer. See K. I. Gurkan, "Les Conceptions chirugicales d'Avicenne," *Millénaire d'Avicenne*, pp. 17–22.

69. E. Wiedemann, "Zur Geschichte der Lehre von Sehen," *Annalen der Physic und Chemie* (Leipzig), 39:470ff (1890).

70. For the influence of Avicenna on the scientific tradition of the West, see A. C. Crombie, "Avicenna's Influence on the Medieval Scientific Tradition," in G. M. Wickens, ed., *Avicenna . . .*, pp. 84–107.

71. See E. J. Holmyard, *Avicennae de congelatione et conglutinatione lepidum* (Paris, 1927).

72. See S. Pines, "Les Précurseurs musulmans de la théorie de l'impétus," *Archeion*, 21:298–306 (1938); and also his *Nouvelles études sur Awḥad al-Zamān Abu'l-Barakāt al-Baghdādī.*

73. It was P. Duhem who first recognized the medieval origin of many ideas present in seventeenth-century physics and studied them in such works as *Etudes sur Léonard de Vinci*, 3 vols. (Paris, 1906–1913); *Le Système du monde*, 10 vols. (Paris, 1913–1959); *Les Origines de la statique* (Paris, 1905–1906). His research has been followed by a series of important studies in this field such as those of A. Koyré, *Études galiléennes* (Paris, 1939); A. Maier, *An der Grenze von Scholastik und Naturwissenchaft*, vol. I (Essen, 1943), vol. II (Rome, 1952); M. Claggett, *The Science of Mechanics in the Middle Ages* (Madison, 1959); also E. A. Moody, "Galileo and Avempace," *Journal of the History of Ideas*, 12:163–193 (April 1951) and 12:375–422 (June 1951) which have clarified and in most cases substantiated Duhem's theories and assertions.

74. For Avicenna's theories and views on music and his influences in this field, see the many studies of H. G. Farmer, especially his *History of Arabian Music* (London, 1929); "Clues for the Arabic influence on European musical theory," *Journal of the Royal Asiatic Society of London*, January 1925, pp. 61–80; *Historical Facts for the Arabian Musical Influence* (London, 1926); also Baron R. d'Erlanger, *La Musique arabe*, II; M. Hafny, *Ibn Sina's Musiklehre* (Berlin, 1931); and M. Barkishlī, "Mūsīqī-i Ibn Sīnā," *Livre du millénaire d'Avicenne*, II, 466–477.

75. See *Musica Mensurata* in *Grove's Dictionary of Music and Musicians*.

76. This point is discussed in the introduction of Alain Daniélou, the foremost present-day authority on Oriental music, to the recordings of Persian music issued recently by UNESCO under his direction.

It is even more incorrect to call Persian music Arabic than to call Islamic philosophy Arabic, because Persian and Arabic music are not only distinct from the Greek, but also differ from each other in many fundamental ways although they have influenced each other over the centuries.

77. Concerning Avicenna's psychology, see J. Bakoš, *La Psychologie d'Ibn Sīnā (Avicenna) d'après son oeuvre aš-Šifā*; Ibn Sīnā, *Avicenna's Psychology*, trans. F. Rahman (Oxford, 1959); A. A. Siassi, *La Psychologie d'Avicenne et ses analogies dans la psychologie moderne* (Tehran, 1954); and M. 'Amīd, *Essai sur la psychologie d'Avicenne* (Geneva, 1940).

78. The various faculties of the soul are discussed in E. Gilson, "Les Sources gréco-arabes de l'augustinisme avicennant," *Archives d'Histoire Doctrinale et Littéraire du Moyen Age*, 4:5–149 (1929).

79. We have used the translation of E. G. Browne, *Literary History of Persia* (Cambridge, 1915), II, 111. There is also a good translation of the poem by A. J. Arberry, in Wickens, *Avicenna* . . . , p. 28.

80. Regarding Avicenna's religious ideas, see the masterly study of L. Gardet, *La Pensée religieuse d'Avicenne (Ibn Sīnā)*.

There are many stories in the Islamic world about Avicenna's religious attitude. For example, it is said that one day one of his disciples asked him why he did not claim to be a prophet and start a new religion, seeing that he was the most learned man of his day. Avicenna smiled and said nothing. The next morning at dawn when the call for the morning prayers was made, the disciple arose to go to the pool to make his ablutions before performing his prayers. The weather was quite cold, so Avicenna told him not to go outside to make his ablutions; otherwise he would catch cold and become ill. But the disciple did not heed his advice; rather, he went out, made his ablutions and then performed his prayers. When the prayers were over, Avicenna called him and said, "That is why I do not claim to be a prophet. Here I am, your teacher and master, still alive and the greatest medical authority of the day, telling you not to wash yourself with cold water. You do not heed my advice but follow the directions of a man who lived in Arabia four centuries ago, who was illiterate, and whom you have never met. That is the difference between a prophet and a savant and philosopher."

See also Nasr, "Ibn Sīnā and the Islamic Religion," in *Introduction* . . . , chap. 11.

81. S. H. Barani, "Ibn Sina and Alberuni," in *Avicenna Commemoration Volume*, p. 8.

82. See, for example, A. F. von Mehren, *Traités mystiques d'Avicenne* (Leiden, 1889–1899), vol. III.

83. *Risālah fi'l-'ishq*, trans. E. L. Fackenheim, *Medieval Studies* (Toronto), 7:214 (1945).

84. Concerning prophecy in Islam, especially in the writings of al-Fārābī and Avicenna, see the study of F. Rahman, *Prophecy in Islam — Philosophy and Orthodoxy* (London, 1958) especially pp. 30ff, in which this important question is analyzed in a competent fashion, although the author's interpretation is perhaps too rationalistic and overestimates the Greek precedents of this particularly "Abrahamic" concept. See also L. Gardet, *La Pensée religieuse . . .* , chap. IV.

85. The possible significance of this work and the adjective "Oriental," which in the Arabic script could also be read as "Illuminative," has caused a long series of debates and controversies over the decades, and such famous orientalists as Nallino, Gauthier, Gardet, Goichon, Pines, Corbin, and many others have expressed different views on it. For a summary of these views, see H. Corbin, *Avicenna and the Visionary Recital*, pp. 36ff; Abu'l-'Alā al-'Afīfī, "L'Aspect mystique de la philosophie avicennienne," *Millénaire d'Avicenne*, pp. 399–449; and Nasr, *Introduction . . .* , chap. 11.

86. A far-reaching study of these works and the whole "Oriental Philosophy" of Avicenna has been made by Corbin in his *Avicenna and the Visionary Recital.*

87. Although some good manuscripts of this work exist, it has not as yet been published. Once printed and studied it should bring to light some of the still hidden bonds existing between the Illuminationists and the Avicennian schools.

S. Popper has translated two of Bahmanyār's treatises on metaphysics into German as *Behmenjār ben el-Marzuban, der persische Aristoteliker aus Avicenna's Schule. Zwei metaphysische Abhandlungen von ihm Arabisch und Deutsch mit Anmerkungen* (Leipzig, 1851).

88. Khayyām (d. 526/1132) is one of the few figures in history, or perhaps the only one, to have been a great poet and mathematician at the same time. His poems, however, are often misconstrued, and the attitude of a sage who has realized the "Supreme Identity" and therefore laughs at the whole of the manifested order is mistaken for the doubts of a skeptic and even the sensual joys of an Epicurean. But this is not how Khayyām appeared to contemporaries like Niẓāmī 'Arūḍī, who in his *Chahār maqālah* calls him the "Witness of God" or "of the Truth." Khayyām was not a prolific writer but nearly a dozen of his works on metaphysics and the sciences have survived, including his *Muṣādarāt (Introduction to Researches on Euclid's*

Axioms) in which he indicates that Euclidean geometry depends upon the assumption that two parallel lines never meet, a point which itself cannot be proved by this particular form of geometry.

Regarding Khayyām's works, see Sayyid Sulaimān Nadwī, *Khayyām, ūr uski sawāniḥ wa taṣānīf pur naqīdāna naẓar* ('Aẓamgarh, 1933); and the article on him by V. Minorsky in the *Encyclopaedia of Islam.*

89. Nāṣir-i Khusraw (394/1003 — 452–53/1060 or 1061), who is the most important philosopher immediately following Avicenna, became an Ismā'īlī while in Egypt and later a missionary (*dā'ī*) of this branch of Shī'ism in Khurāsān. His important works include his *Dīwān* in Persian; also, *Jāmi' al-ḥikmatain, Gushāyish wa rahāyish, Zād al-musāfirīn,* and *Rawshanā'ī-nāmah,* as well as his travelogue called *Safar-nāmah.* See H. Corbin's Introduction to *Jāmi' al-ḥikmatain,* ed. Corbin and M. Mo'in (Tehran and Paris, 1953).

90. Ṭūsī was connected directly to Avicenna through five generations of masters and students. He was the student of Farīd al-Dīn al-Dāmād, who was the student of Ṣadr al-Dīn al-Sarakhsī, who in turn was the student of Afḍal al-Dīn al-Ghīlānī. The latter was a disciple of Abu'l-'Abbās al-Lūkarī, and he of the aforementioned Bahmanyār. The chain of masters and disciples in *ḥikmah,* or traditional philosophy, is almost as important as the *silsilah,* or chain, in Sufism because there is always an oral tradition accompanying a written text. Thus, just as in Sufism the chain implies the transmission of the grace, or *barakah,* existing in the brotherhood from one generation to another, so in *ḥikmah* the chain of teacher and student implies the continuation of the oral transmission and all the nuances which permit the student to be able to "read between the lines."

91. See Kāshānī, *Muṣannafāt,* ed. M. Minovi and Y. Mahdavi, (Tehran, 1331–1337).

92. A friend who made a journey through Afghanistan and Pakistan recently to study the traditional *madrasas* in these regions discovered that the only philosophical work which was still being taught in nearly all the independent religious schools in these countries was the *Ḥikmat al-'ain.*

93. Published in three volumes (Tehran, 1335–1337).

94. The influence of Avicenna in the East as well as in the West is also discussed by S. Afnan in his *Avicenna . . . ,* chaps. VIII and IX, although some aspects of his view of the Avicennian tradition in the East is far from that held by those who belong to that tradition and consider its intellectual life to be their own. A very informative account of the Avicennian tradition is the East and its contrast with Latin Avicennianism is given by Corbin in his *Avicenna and the Visionary Recital,* pp. 101ff.

95. Concerning translations of Avicenna into Latin, see M. A. Alonso, "Ibn Sina y sus primera influencias en el Mundo Latino,"

Revista del Instituto Egypcio de Estudios Islámicos, 1:36–57 (1953), and M. T. D'Alverny, "Notes sur les traductions médiévales d'Avicenne," *Archives d'Histoire Doctrinale et Littéraire du Moyen Age*, 27:337–358 (1952). In a footnote on p. 340 of this article, M. T. D'Alverny, who is the foremost authority on this subject and has been preparing for some time a complete edition of Avicenna's works in Latin, has given the name of other works of her own dealing with this subject, as well as articles by H. Bedoret, S. Pines, and M. Alonso.

For a general study of the translation of Arabic texts into Latin, the most authoritative work is still that of M. Steinschneider, *Die europäischen Übersetzungen aus der Arabischen bis Mitte der 17. Jahrhunderts* (Graz, 1956); see also R. Walzer: "Arabic Transmission of Greek Thought to Medieval Europe," *Bulletin of the John Rylands Library*, 29:160–183 (1945–1946).

It is quite significant to note, however, that the writings of Avicenna in which his "esoteric philosophy" was expounded, such as the *Ishārāt* and *Manṭiq al-mashriqīyīn*, were not for the most part translated into Latin, thereby setting the stage for the difference which soon appeared between Eastern and Western interpretations of his philosophy.

96. This treatise was discovered and published by M. T. D'Alverny as "Les Pérégrinations de l'âme dans l'autre monde d'après un anonyme de la fin du XII siècle," *Archives d'Hist. Doct. et Litt. du Moyen Age*, 15–17:239–299 (1940–1942).

97. See R. de Vaux, *Notes et textes sur l'avicennisme latin* (Paris, 1934). The term "Latin Avicennianism" has not been as widely accepted as "Latin Averroism," coined by P. Mandonet in connection with his studies on Siger de Brabant, although even this term has been challenged by such an authority as F. van Steenberghen in his article "Siger of Brabant," *Modern Schoolman*, 29:11–27 (1951). As for Avicenna, many authorities like E. Gilson feel that there was not a school well-enough defined and closely enough associated with his doctrines to deserve being named after him.

For the influence of Avicenna in the Latin world, and schools connected with him, see E. Gilson: "Graeco-Arab Influences" in *History of Christian Philosophy in the Middle Ages*, pt. 6, chap. 1; "Les Sources gréco-arabes de l'augustinisme avicennisant," *Archives d'Hist. Doct. et Litt. du Moyen Age*, 4:5–149 (1929); "Pourquoi saint Thomas a critiqué saint Augustin," *ibid.*, 1:1–127 (1926); *Avicenne et le point de départ de Duns Scotus*. See also K. Foster, O.P., "Avicenna and Western Thought in the 13th Century," in Wickens, ed., *Avicenna . . .* ; and Corbin, *Avicenna . . .* , pp. 102ff.

98. Christian doctors were usually more sympathetic to him than to Averroes, as can be seen by the much milder treatment that he receives in the anonymous *De Erroribus Philosophorum*.

99. For, as Gilson has put it so aptly, "noetics is only a particular

case of cosmology" ("Pourquoi saint Thomas a critiqué saint Augustin," p. 52).

100. P. Duhem, in his monumental study *Le Système du monde* (IV, 317ff), discusses how closely the astronomical revolution already presupposed a change in the spiritual and theological attitude vis-à-vis the cosmos and already implied its "desacralization."

101. With reference to Avicenna's cosmology and angelology, Corbin writes: "But the whole of cosmology was bound up with angelology. To reject the latter was to shake the foundations of the former. Now, this was precisely what perfectly served the interests of the Copernican revolution: so that we witness an alliance between Christian theology and positive science to the end of annihilating the prerogatives of the Angel and of the world of the Angel in the demiurgy of the cosmos. After that, the angelic world will no longer be necessary by metaphysical necessity; it will be a sort of luxury in the Creation; its existence will be more or less probable." *Avicenna* . . . , pp. 101–102.

102. We have dealt fully with this question in our study of Avicenna's cosmology in *Introduction* . . . See also H. A. R. Gibb's preface to that book.

103. Many stories about Avicenna are told in Persia, Central Asia, and the Arab world in a folk language, and he definitely has found a place in the consciousness of even the common people as a folk hero whose science and wisdom dominated over the powers of Nature.

CHAPTER II: SUHRAWARDĪ AND THE ILLUMINATIONISTS

1. Concerning the doctrines and influence of this school see the basic work, L. Gardet and M. M. Anawati, *Introduction à la théologie musulmane* (Paris, 1948), and the monumental study of H. A. Wolfson, *The Philosophy of the Kalām*, which is to be published by the Harvard University Press.

2. Regarding the traditional division of the sciences into the intellectual and transmitted, see Ibn Khaldūn, *Muqaddimah*, trans. F. Rosenthal, vols. II–III (New York, 1958), chap. vi.

3. For the history of this period, see T. W. Arnold, *The Caliphate* (Oxford, 1924), W. Barthold, *Turkestan down to the Mongol Invasion* (London, 1928), M. T. Houtsma, *Recueil de textes retalifs à l'histoire des Seljoucides* (Leiden, 1886–92), vols. I–IV; G. Le Strange, *The Lands of the Eastern Caliphate* (Cambridge, 1930); and J. Sauvaget, *Introduction à l'histoire de l'Orient musulman* (Paris, 1943). As for the particular significance of Shī'ah–Sunnī political domination in the cultivation of the arts and sciences see the prologue to S. H. Nasr, *Introduction to Islamic Cosmological Doctrines*.

4. Numerous studies have been devoted to al-Ghazzālī in European languages so that he is much better known than most of the other

Muslim sages, and for this reason it was decided not to devote a chapter to him in the present volume. Although in some circles too much use is made of al-Ghazzālī as a criterion for the orthodoxy of other Ṣūfīs, there is no doubt that he is one of the most significant figures in Islam, having been placed by the hand of destiny at a decisive moment in Islamic history when the influence of rationalism was to be curtailed and the ground prepared for the sapiental doctrines of Suhrawardī and Ibn 'Arābī.

Regarding the life, doctrines, and influence of al-Ghazzālī, see M. Asin Palacios, *La Espiritualidad de Algazel y su sentido cristiano* (Madrid–Granada, 1934–1941); Carra de Vaux, *Gazali* (Paris, 1902); A. J. Wensinck, *La Pensée de Ghazzali* (Paris, 1940); and F. Jabre, *La Notion de certitude selon Ghazālī dans ses origines psychologiques et historiques* (Paris, 1959).

5. It was because of the translation of this work into Latin that al-Ghazzālī — the Latin Algazel — was identified by St. Thomas and other scholastics as a Peripatetic philosopher. The *Maqāṣid* is actually an almost word-for-word translation of Avicenna's *Dānishnāmah-i 'alā'ī* from Persian into Arabic. But whereas the original is difficult to understand, this being the first attempt to write Aristotelian philosophy in Persian, the Arabic version of al-Ghazzālī is most lucid, which is perhaps the basic reason for its great popularity.

6. Al-Ghazzālī criticizes the philosophers on many points, of which he considers three as cardinal, these being their denial of creation *ex nihilo*, God's knowledge of particulars, and bodily resurrection, all of which are stated clearly in the Quran. See W. Montgomery-Watt, *The Faith and Practice of al-Ghazzali* (London, 1953), pp. 37ff.

7. The Ash'arites, however, benefited from the attack of al-Ghazzālī against the philosophers so that to a certain extent his criticism of them can be considered as a victory for the theologians as well, especially since political and social conditions of the time favored the spread of their teachings.

8. This great theologian, who was one of the most learned men of his time, must be considered after al-Ghazzālī as the most severe critic of the philosophers. He compiled the monumental Quranic commentary, *Tafsīr al-kabīr*, as well as the *Jāmi' al-'ulūm*, on all the sciences of his day of which he had a vast knowledge. His importance in philosophy lies in his detailed analysis and criticism of the *Ishārāt* of Avicenna, to which Khwājah Nāṣir al-Dīn al-Ṭūsī was to reply in his *Sharḥ al-ishārāt* a generation later.

Regarding Imām Fakhr, as he is called in Persia, see M. Horten, *Die spekulative und positive Theologie in Islam nach Razi und Tusi* (Leipzig, 1912); P. Kraus, "The Controversies of Fakhr al-Dīn Rāzī," *Islamic Culture*, 12:131–153 (1938); and S. H. Nasr, "Fakhr al-Dīn al-Rāzī," in *History of Muslim Philosophy*, ed. M. M. Sharif (Wiesbaden, 1963).

9. Shaikh al-ishrāq should not be confused with the series of Ṣūfī masters bearing the name of Suhrawardī, especially Shihāb al-Dīn al-Suhrawardī, the famous Ṣūfī master for whom the founder of the school of Illumination, or *Ishrāq*, has been mistaken even by some Muslim historians.

Concerning the four famous Suhrawardīs, see H. Ritter "Philologika, IX: Die vier Suhrawardī, ihre Werke in Stambuler Handschriften," *Der Islam*, 24:270–286 (1937) and 25:35–86 (1938).

10. Of the writings of H. Corbin on Suhrawardī, mention should be made especially of the translation of some of Suhrawardī's shorter works into French; and also *Suhrawardī d'Alep, fondateur de la doctrine illuminative (ishrāqī)* (Paris, 1939); *Les Motifs zoroastriens dans la philosophie de Suhrawardī* (Tehran, 1946); and Corbin's two prolegomena to Suhrawardī, *Opera Metaphysica et Mystica*, vol. I (Istanbul, 1945); vol. II (Tehran, 1952). Volume I of these two volumes includes the *Metaphysics* of three of Suhrawardī's large treatises, the *Talwīḥāt, Muqāwamāt*, and *Muṭāraḥāt*, and Volume II the complete text of his masterpiece *Ḥikmat al-ishrāq* and two short treatises, *Fī i'tiqād al-ḥukamā'* and *Qiṣṣat al-ghurbat al-gharbīyah*. Volume III, which will be published jointly by Corbin and the present author, will include the complete collection of the Persian works the first part of which is planned for publication during 1963.

11. More recently, some attention has been paid by Arab scholars to Suhrawardī, mostly as a result of the spread of the fruits of Corbin's research in the Arab countries. This is exemplified by Sāmī al-Kiyālī's *al-Suhrawardī* (Cairo, 1955), Aḥmad Amīn's *Ḥayy ibn Yaqẓān li ibn Sīnā wa ibn Ṭufail wa'l-Suhrawardī* (Cairo, 1952) and sections devoted to Suhrawardī in *Fi'l-falsafat al-islāmiyah* by Ibrāhīm Madkour (Cairo, 1947) and *Shakhṣiyāt qaliqah fi'l-islām* of 'Abd al-Raḥmān Badawī (Cairo, 1946), which contains an Arabic translation of Corbin's monograph, *Suhrawardī d'Alep*, mentioned above.

In Persia his *Ḥikmat al-ishrāq* with various commentaries and glosses was lithographed during the last century and has always been a basic text in the *madrasas*, and several of his Persian treatises have been published by Mahdī Bayānī and Muḥsin Ṣabā. There is also the work of 'Alī Akbar Dānāsirisht entitled *Afkār-i Suhrawardī wa Mullā Ṣadrā* (Tehran, 1316), which treats of some of Suhrawardī's basic ideas. See also S. H. Nasr, "Suhrawardī," *History of Muslim Philosophy*, which treats much of the material discussed in this essay.

Before Corbin, the most important works written in European languages on this subject, some of which contain faulty interpretations by otherwise competent scholars, include Carra de Vaux, "La Philosophie illuminative d'après Suhrawardī maqtoul," *Journal Asiatique*,

19:63–94 (1902); M. Horten, *Die Philosophie der Erleuchtung nach Suhrawardī* (Halle, 1912), and the edition and translation into English by O. Spies of several of Suhrawardī's treatises.

12. By theosophy we mean that form of wisdom which is neither philosophy nor theology but a knowledge of the Divine mysteries as the original meaning of this word implied, before it became emptied of meaning by modern pseudo-spiritual movements.

13. The most reliable source for the biography of Suhrawardī is *Nuzhat al-arwāḥ wa rawḍat al-afrāḥ*, a history of philosophy by his disciple and one of the most important commentators on his writings, Shams al-Dīn al-Shahrazūrī. The original Arabic text of this important work has not yet been published but a Persian translation of it by Ḍiā' al-Dīn Durrī appeared in Tehran in 1317 (1938). Accounts of the life of Suhrawardī can be found also in the works of Corbin mentioned above.

14. Corbin has made a similar classification based on four classes of works which we have followed in part but with certain differences. See his prolegomena to the *Opera Metaphysica et Mystica*, I, xvi ff. Pending their complete publication, L. Massignon has also made a provisional classification of Suhrawardī's works in his *Recueil de textes inédits concernant l'histoire de la mystique en pays d'Islam* (Paris, 1929), 113.

15. 'Ain al-Quḍāt, whose career is very similar to those of Ḥallāj and Suhrawardī, since he, too, met with a tragic death at an early age, is one of the important Ṣūfīs of the later period whose doctrines resemble in many ways those of Suhrawardī, although he was not a *ḥakīm*, or theosopher, but a pure Ṣūfī with a background of training in philosophy. His *Zubdat al-ḥaqā'iq* and *Tamhīdāt*, recently published by 'Afīf 'Usairān (Tehran, 1340), are among the most important texts of Ṣūfī doctrine before Ibn 'Arabī.

16. A commentary upon the *Fuṣūṣ* of al-Fārābī has also been attributed to Suhrawardī but no manuscript of the work has yet been discovered.

17. At the beginning of his *Tale of the Occidental Exile*, Suhrawardī writes that Avicenna had reached for the sources of *Ishrāqī* wisdom but had not succeeded in fully discovering them. See H. Corbin, ed. *Opera* . . . , II, 275.

18. See L. Massignon, "Inventaire de l'Hermétisme arabe," in A. J. Festugière and A. D. Nock, *La Révélation d'Hermès Trismégiste* (Paris, 1948), vol. I, and the still authoritative study of D. Chwolsohn, *Die Ssabier und der Ssabismus* (St. Petersburg, 1856).

19. *Kalimat al-taṣawwuf*, MS. Istanbul, Ragip 1480, fol. 407b. Also, see H. Corbin, *Les Motifs zoroastriens dans la philosophie de Suhrawardī* (Tehran, 1948), p. 24.

The *Kalimat al-taṣawwuf* contains many basic doctrines of Suhrawardī and bears close study once its text is critically edited and published. There was, interestingly enough, a commentary upon it written by Muḥammad 'Alī Iṣfahānī, known as 'Alī Ḥazīn, a 12th/18th Persian sage who went to Benares to spend the last part of his life and is buried in that city. Most present-day Ṣūfīs of Benares trace their origin to him. But his commentary, which connects his whole school to that of Suhrawardī, seems to have been lost.

20. Suhrawardī states his belief in the universality of traditional wisdom quite explicitly in the sixth book of the *Physics* of his *Muṭāraḥāt*. See H. Corbin, ed. *Opera* . . . , I, xii.

21. The account of this dream is given in the 55th section of the *Metaphysics* of the *Talwīḥāt* and also by Corbin in *Les Motifs zoroastriens* . . . , pp. 28–29.

22. Ibn Waḥshīyah, *Ancient Alphabet and Hieroglyphic Characters* (London, 1806), p. 100; also, Corbin, *Les Motifs zoroastriens* . . . , p. 18, and *Opera* . . . , vol. I, where Corbin has presented the information that we have summarized here.

23. H. Corbin, ed. *Opera* . . . , II, 10–11.

24. *Ibid.*

25. Henceforth, in Persia, this became the title of a series of sages, Mullā Ṣadrā, the great Safavid *ḥakīm*, being called *Ṣadr al-muta-'allihīn*, the "foremost among the theosophers."

26. The Yemen means also the right hand in Arabic and has the general significance of the Orient of Lights since if one stands facing north, it is the right hand which corresponds to the East. Muslim authors have identified it with the right side of the valley from which Moses heard the voice of God on Sinai, and also with the wisdom of Solomon and therefore a wisdom based on revelation and illumination. Some writers like Mīr Dāmād, the influential Safavid sage, contrast *ḥikmat-i yūnānī*, or Greek philosophy — meaning rationalistic philosophy — with *ḥikmat-i yamānī*, or Yamanī wisdom — that is, a wisdom based on illumination. We may recall at this point, too, that the Yemen played an important role among the Rosicrusians and that their adepts were directed to go "to the Yemen" in their quest after knowledge. Moreover, according to some traditions, Christian Rosenkreutz, the founder of the order, retired to the Yemen when he saw that conditions were not propitious for the continuation of his activities in Europe. See R. Kienast, *Johann Valentin Andreae und die vier echten Rosenkreutzer-Schriften* (Leipzig, 1926), pp. 113ff; H. Corbin, "Le Récit d'initiation et l'Hermétisme en Iran," *Eranos-Jahrbuch*, 17:136–37 (1949).

27. We have dealt fully with this difficult question, which became a central point of contention in later schools in Persia, in the chapter on Suhrawardī in *History of Muslim Philosophy*.

As for Mullā Ṣadrā's position vis-à-vis this question and his own views on the principiality of being, see S. H. Nasr: "Ṣadr al-Dīn Shīrāzī, His Life, Doctrines and Significance," in *Indo-Iranica*, 14:6–16 (December 1961), and Introduction to Mullā Ṣadrā's *Se Aṣl* (Tehran, 1340). See also Sayyid Abu'l Ḥasan Qazwīnī, "The Life of Sadr al-muta'allihīn Shīrāzī and a Discussion of Motion in the Category of Substance"; and Sayyid Muḥammad Ḥusain Ṭabāṭabā'ī, "Ṣadr al-Dīn Muḥammad ibn Ibrāhīm Shīrāzī, the Renewer of Islamic Philosophy in the 11th/17th century," in *Mullā Ṣadrā Commemoration Volume* (Tehran, 1340), pp. 7–21 and 22–34, respectively.

There are certain later masters of the *Ishrāqī* school, like the contemporary Persian *ḥakīm*, Sayyid Muḥammad Kāẓim 'Aṣṣār, who interpret light in the doctrines of Suhrawardī to be the same as *being* in the language of Mullā Ṣadrā and indicate that as such there are no fundamental differences between the two schools on this point. M. Horten had also discovered and discussed this point in his studies on Mullā Ṣadrā and Suhrawardī.

28. This passage from the *Ḥikmat al-ishrāq* is taken from the English translation of M. Smith, *Readings from the Mystics of Islam* (London, 1950), p. 79.

29. This idea is found also in medieval Christianity where the orders of monks were based on those of the angels. There are in fact many correspondances to be drawn between angelology as expounded by Suhrawardī and as expressed in the *Celestial Hierarchies* of Dionysius the Areopagite, whose writings constituted the main source for the study of the angelic world in the Latin Middle Ages.

30. In the present solar Jalālī calendar the name of each month corresponds to that of an angel who according to Zoroastrian beliefs ruled over each month, the lesser deities called *yazatas* dominating over particular days of the month. See A. V. W. Jackson, *Zoroastrian Studies* (New York, 1928), chap. V.

Suhrawardī also employs the name of the Mazdaean angel or celestial fortune and power *khurrah* (Avestic *xvarnah*, *Parsī farrah*) to designate the special glory and light received by the *Ishrāqī* sage. See H. Corbin, ed. *Opera* . . . , II, Prolegomena, pp. 37–38, and *Les Motifs zoroastriens* . . . pp. 36–45.

31. There is in any case a profound similarity between Zoroastrian angelology and that of the Semitic religions to the point that some have thought that Jewish angelology was taken over from the Zoroastrian. As for traditional Islamic angelology, which is derived from the Quran and has similarities to the Jewish scheme, see F. Schuon, *L'Œil du coeur* (Paris, 1950), the chapter entitled "al-nūr."

32. The three aspects mentioned by Avicenna would be the intellection by the intellect of the Necessary Being as necessary, of itself as possible, and of itself as necessary through something other than itself. See the previous chapter on Avicenna.

33. We see that Suhrawardī makes use of Zoroastrian language but correlates it with the traditional Quranic one. .

34. This should not be confused with the term *ummahāt* used by Peripatetic philosophers to mean the four elements — fire, air, water and earth — from which the three kingdoms are "born."

35. Regarding this scheme of angelology see H. Corbin, ed. *Opera . . .*, II, 125ff.

36. This identification becomes crucial in the speculation of some of the later Shī'ah sages who integrated *Ishrāqī* theosophy into Shī'ism.

37. This beautiful concept held by Suhrawardī and by many other Illuminationists and Ṣūfīs corresponds closely to the Mazdaean concept of the host of angels called *farahvashīs* who guide each soul in this world and with one of whom each soul becomes ultimately united. See Jackson, *Zoroastrian Studies*, pp. 59–60, and R. C. Zaehner, *The Dawn and Twilight of Zoroastrianism* (London, 1961), pp. 146–148; also Corbin's *Les Motifs zoroastriens . . .*, pt. III.

It should not be thought, however, that Suhrawardī limits ultimate union to the angelic level rather than considering union with the Divine Self. In his treatise *Ṣafīr-i sīmurgh* (Tehran National Library MS. 1758, pp. 11–12) he divides those who have attained intuitive knowledge into five categories: Those who say *Lā ilāha ill'-allāh*, there is no divinity but the Divine; then the higher stage of those who utter *Lā huwa illā huwa*, there is no "he-ness" but "He"; then *Lā anta illā anta*, there is no "thou-ness" but the (Divine) "Thou"; then *Lā anā illā anā*, there is no "I-ness" but the (Divine) "I"; and finally those who have realized supreme union and say *kullu shai'in hālikun illā wajhahu*, all things perish except His Face.

38. For the discussion on physics see H. Corbin, ed. *Opera . . .*, II, 187ff.

39. Regarding Suhrawardī's psychology see *ibid.*, pp. 203ff.

40. Suhrawardī believes also in the existence of a separate cosmic imagination to which the soul travels to acquire a form which then appears in the human imagination. This intermediary world, which is also called the world of "suspended," or "hanging" forms (*ṣuwar al-mu'allaqah*) or the world of subtle bodies or similitudes (*'ālam al-mithāl*), stands between the sensible world and the world of archetypes and plays an essential role in such questions as creation and eschatology both in the doctrines of Suhrawardī and in those of Ibn 'Arabī and Mullā Ṣadrā. See H. Corbin, *L'Imagination créatrice dans le soufisme d'Ibn Arabī* (Paris, 1958), part II.

41. H. Corbin, ed. *Opera . . .*, II, 225.

42. The eschatology of Suhrawardī as discussed and altered by Mullā Ṣadrā in his glosses upon the last section of *Ḥikmat al-ishrāq* is studied in a long article by H. Corbin scheduled to appear in the

forthcoming *Commemoration Volume* of Mullā Ṣadrā, planned to be published shortly by the Iran Society, Calcutta.

43. I have chosen this particular treatise because there already exists a good translation and commentary upon it in a European language. See H. Corbin and P. Kraus, "Le Bruissement de l'aile de Gabriel," *Journal Asiatique*, July–September 1935, pp. 1–82.

44. See, for example, A. von Kremer, *Geschichte der herrschenden Ideen des Islam* (Leipzig, 1868), pp. 89–100, where he discusses some of Suhrawardī's doctrines in a section entitled "Antiislamische Bestrebungen."

45. L. Massignon, *Salmān Pāk et les prémices spirituelles de l'Islam iranien* (Paris, 1914), p. 11.

46. It was through Quṭb al-Dīn that the *rapprochement* between the schools of Ibn 'Arabī and Suhrawardī gradually began, culminating finally in Mullā Ṣadrā.

It should also be added here that among the followers of the Illuminationist school the study of light and light phenomena occupied an important position, and it is perhaps not accidental that the first correct explanation of the rainbow in the medieval period is to be found in the commentary of Kamāl al-Dīn al-Fārsī upon the *Kitāb al-manāẓir* of Ibn al-Haitham, Kamāl al-Dīn having been a student of Quṭb al-Dīn al-Shīrāzī and, according to his own words, having learned this theory from his teacher.

47. Before the researches of Corbin the only notable studies made of the Safavid school in European languages were those of M. Horten who, besides his study of Suhrawardī mentioned earlier, also published two works on Mullā Ṣadrā, *Die Gottesbeweise bei Schirazi* (Bonn, 1912), and *Das philosophische System von Schirazi (1640)*, (Strassburg, 1913). See also Comte de Gobineau's *La Philosophie et les religions dans l'Asie centrale* (Paris, 1923).There is also the fourth volume of E. G. Browne's *Literary History of Persia* where various authors of this period are mentioned but mostly from the point of view of literature, as is to be expected in such a work. Muḥammad Iqbāl's *Development of Metaphysics in Persia* (London, 1908) is of value despite some errors, including the attributing of the rise of Bābism to the school of Mullā Ṣadrā. In point of fact, the Bāb was a student of the school of Shaikh Aḥmad Aḥsā'ī, who wrote a commentary *against* one of Mullā Ṣadrā's works. See our article in Persian, "Acquaintance with Mullā Ṣadrā in the Occident," *Mullā Ṣadrā Commemoration Volume*, pp. 51–62.

48. Regarding Mīr Dāmād and his disciples, see H. Corbin, "Confessions extatiques de Mīr Dāmād," in *Mélanges Louis Massignon* (Damascus, 1956), pp. 331–378, and S. H. Nasr, "The School of Ispahan," in *History of Muslim Philosophy*.

49. Concerning the importance of *Nahj al-balāghah* in the later

schools of *ḥikmah* and the general relation between philosophy, theosophy, and Sufism with Shī'ism, see Muḥammad Ḥusain Ṭabāṭabā'ī, *Muṣāḥibāt-i ustād Ṭabāṭabā'ī bā professor Henry Corbin dar bārih'i shī'ah, Maktab-i tashayyu'*, yearbook no. 2 (Qum, 1339), pp. 119ff.

50. Concerning Sabziwārī, see M. Iqbāl, *The Development of Metaphysics in Persia*, pp. 175–186, and the chapter on Sabziwārī by S. H. Nasr, in *A History of Muslim Philosophy*.

51. Although the exact way by which Islamic philosophy, and especially these later metaphysical schools, reached India is as yet somewhat uncertain, the extent of the influence of the doctrines of Suhrawardī and Mullā Ṣadrā can be gauged by the number of commentaries and glosses written by Indian Muslims upon their works, the number of manuscripts of their writings existing in such libraries as the Raza Library in Rampur and the Khudā-Bakhsh Library in Patna, and their influence upon such later Indian works of philosophy as *al-Shams al-bāzighah*, which has always been a favorite text of philosophy in traditional schools of the subcontinent. See Tara Chand, "Growth of Islamic Thought in India," in *History of Philosophy East and West*, I, 488–514, and especially p. 507.

The doctrines of Suhrawardī and Mullā Ṣadrā, especially of the latter, continue to be studied in Islamic schools in India, particularly Shī'ah ones like those at Lucknow and Rampur, although since 1947, because of the loss of endowments and lack of availability of Arabic and Persian books, they have lost many of their best teachers. See Abū Maḥfūẓ Ma'ṣūmī, "Ṣadr al-Dīn al-Shīrāzī," *Indo-Iranica*, 14:27 (December 1961).

52. The first chair is presently held by Maḥmūd Shahābī, known to the Western world through his article on Twelve-Imām Shī'ism in Kenneth Morgan's *Islam, the Straight Path*, and the second by Mahdī Ilāhī Qumshahī, whose Quranic commentary, *Dīwān* of Ṣūfī poems, commentary upon the *Fuṣūṣ* of al-Fārābī, and *Ilāhīyāt khāṣṣ wa 'āmm* are well known in the Persian-speaking world.

As for the masters who teach these subjects in the *madrasas*, special mention should be made of Sayyid Muḥammad Kāẓim 'Aṣṣār, professor at both Tehran University and the Sepahsālār *madrasa*; Sayyid Abu'l-Ḥasan Qazwīnī, perhaps the greatest living teacher of traditional philosophy, who resides in Qazwīn where he is training a small group of disciples; and Sayyid Muḥammad Ḥusain Ṭabāṭabā'ī, the most important master of the intellectual sciences in Qum, the present center of Shī'ah studies and the most prolific of the contemporary *ḥakīms* in Persia. His writings include the three-volume *Principles of Philosophy* (*Uṣūl-i falsafah*) with the commentary of Murtiḍā Mutahharī; a twenty-volume commentary of the Quran, *al-Mīzān*, of which eleven volumes have been published already; answers to questions posed to him by Henry Corbin, published as the second yearbook of *Maktab-i tashayyu'*. He is also editing the new edition of Mullā Ṣadrā's *Asfār* with his own commentary, which is being currently published in Tehran.

CHAPTER III: IBN 'ARABĪ AND THE ṢŪFĪS

1. It is the refusal by the vast majority of orientalists to accept this fundamental aspect of Islam as a part of the Islamic tradition and an intrinsic element of its orthodoxy that has made the picture of Islam in most Western eyes such a dry and sterile one, devoid of any spirituality or beauty. Among the few well-known Western scholars who have conceded the Quranic origin of Sufism one can name Margoliouth, and especially Massignon and Corbin, whereas most of the other famous scholars, like Horten, Nicholson, Asin Palacios, and, more recently, Zaehner and Arberry, have posited a Hindu, Neoplatonic, Christian, or even Zoroastrian, origin for Sufism, mistaking too often the borrowed formulations of the Ṣūfīs with the inner experience and realization which is based absolutely on the grace, or *barakah*, issuing from the Prophet.

For the view of Sufism as the inner dimension of Islam, see the illuminating work of F. Schuon, *The Transcendent Unity of Religions*, trans. P. Townsend, especially chap. III, and his *Comprendre l'Islam* (Paris, 1961), Chap. IV; also R. Guénon, "L'Esotérisme islamique," in *L'Islam et l'Occident*, Cahiers du Sud (Paris, 1947), pp. 153–159.

2. See Abu Bakr Siraj al-Din, "The Origins of Sufism," *The Islamic Quarterly*, 3:53–64 (April 1956); also Mir Valiuddin, *The Quranic Sufism* (Delhi, 1959).

3. The followers of Sufism are never called Ṣūfīs in the Islamic languages, this being considered as lack of courtesy; for a Ṣūfī is one who has already realized the goal and achieved the state of "Supreme Identity." A follower of the Ṣūfī Path is usually called a *faqīr* ("poor in spirit," from which the English "fakir" originates), or *mutaṣawwif, that* is, one who participates in Sufism (*taṣawwuf*); or in Persian, *darwīsh* (the English "dervish"), as well as several other names connected with various aspects of the "Way" or "Path."

4. Since the spiritual life presents itself essentially as a "way," as can be seen, too, in Taoism, the Ṣūfī order is called a *ṭarīqah*, a way (pl., *ṭuruq*) and the adept is often designated as "one who follows a way" (*ahl al-ṭarīqah*). Concerning the Ṣūfī orders, see the article on "tarīḳa" in the *Encyclopaedia of Islam* by Massignon, and the classical works of O. Dupont and X. Cappolani, *Les Confréries religieuses musulmanes* (Alger, 1879), and L. Rinn, *Marabouts et Khouanes* (Alger, 1884).

5. This saying is quoted in the famous *Risālat al-qushairīyah* (Cairo,

1940), p. 20. See also "The Origins of Sufism," in the *Islamic Quarterly* (April 1956), p. 58.

There has been much debate among traditional Muslim scholars as well as among Western students of Sufism on the derivation of the word *ṣūfī*. Opinions have differed as to whether it comes from *ṣūf*, meaning wool which the early Ṣūfīs wore, or *ṣafā'*, meaning purity, or *ṣaff*, meaning the line of prayer, since the Ṣūfīs occupied the first line of prayer behind the *imām*; or even from the Greek *sophia* (this being the most unlikely derivation because *sophia* in Arabic would be with an *s* rather than an *ṣ*). There has also been the view expressed by certain masters that the term *ṣūfī* is too exalted to be derived from anything else and that its basic significance is indicated by the fact that *taṣawwuf* is numerically equivalent to Divine Wisdom (*al-ḥikmat al-ilāhīyah*) according to the traditional calculation of *Jafr*. See the article by R. Guénon, "L'Esotérisme islamique" (n. 1 above).

Concerning the various meanings given to the term *ṣūfī*, see R. A. Nicholson, "An historical inquiry concerning the origin and development of Sufism, with a list of definitions of the terms *ṣūfī* and *taṣawwuf* arranged chronologically," *Journal of the Royal Asiatic Society of London* (1906), pp. 303–348.

7. Although there is no complete "history of Sufism," there have been several attempts made to study various Ṣūfī schools over the centuries and to correlate their doctrines and practices. Of these the most important in European languages are the numerous studies of Massignon, especially his *Essai sur les origines du lexique technique de la mystique musulmane* (Paris, 1954), especially chaps. III-V; also *La Passion d'al-Hosayn Ibn Mansour al-Hallaj, martyr mystique de l'Islam* (Paris, 1922), which contains a wealth of information on the spiritual life of the first three centuries of Islam; and his article on *taṣawwuf* in the *Encyclopaedia of Islam*. Also, the first section of the recent study by G. C. Anawati and L. Gardet, *La Mystique musulmane* (Paris, 1961), is devoted to the history of Sufism. In this connection may also be mentioned the work of famous scholars like R. A. Nicholson, especially his article cited in n. 6 above; *Studies in Islamic Mysticism* (Cambridge, 1921); *The Mystics of Islam* (London, 1914); *The Idea of Personality in Sufism* (Cambridge, 1923); and his annotated translation of Hujwīrī's *Kashf al-maḥjūb* (Leyden, 1911). See also M. Asin Palacios, *El Islam cristianizado, estudio del sufismo a través de las obras de Abenarabi de Murcia* (Madrid, 1931); E. Dermenghem, *Les Saints musulmans* (Alger, 1944); and M. Smith, *Studies in Early Mysticism in the Near and Middle East* (London, 1931).

There are several important histories of the Ṣūfīs, or rather accounts of the lives and sayings of the saints of Islam written by the Ṣūfīs themselves, of which the most famous are *Ṭabaqāt al-ṣūfīyah* of al-Sulamī, *Ḥilyat al-awliyā'* of Abū Nu'aim al-Iṣbahānī; *Tadhkirat al-*

awliyā' of Farīd al-Dīn al-'Aṭṭār; and *Nafaḥāt al-uns* of 'Abd al-Raḥmān Jāmī.

In Arabic and Persian there have been several studies devoted to the history of Sufism. Among those in Arabic are: A. al-Ṭībāwī, *al-Taṣawwuf al-islāmī al-'arabī* (Cairo, 1928); J. 'Abd al-Nūr, *al-Taṣawwuf 'ind al-'arab* (Beirut, 1938); Zakī Mubārak, *al-Taṣawwuf al-islāmī*, 2 vols. (Cairo, 1954), and A. N. Nādir, *al-Taṣawwuf al-islāmī* (Beirut, 1960). Among the Persian studies are: Q. Ghanī, *Tārīkh-i taṣawwuf dar islām* (Tehran, 1952), and many by Badī' al-Zamān Furūzānfar and Jalāl Homā'ī on Rūmī, 'Aṭṭār, and other well-known Ṣūfīs.

8. This period is amply treated by Massignon in his *Essai sur les origines* . . . , chap. IV.

9. This work, nearly unknown in the West, has always been considered in the Shī'ah world as one of the basic testaments of the esoteric teachings of Islam. Many Ṣūfīs who followed the teachings of Ibn 'Arabī studied and wrote a commentary on this work.

10. Muḥāsibī is the author of some of the earliest works on Sufism, such as *Kitāb al-tawahhum* (*The Book of Apprehension*), ed. A. J. Arberry (Cairo, 1937), and *Kitāb al-ri'āyah* (*The Book of Consideration*), ed. M. Smith (London, 1940). He is also well known for his method of examining the conscience. See M. Smith, *An Early Mystic of Baghdad; a Study of the Life and Teaching of Ḥārith b. Asad al-Muḥāsibī* (London, 1935).

11. The similarity between some of the locutions (*shaṭḥīyāt*) of Basṭāmī (his name is usually written as Bisṭāmī, but he comes from a town which in Persian is pronounced Basṭām) and certain Vedantic formulations have led R. C. Zaehner to posit a Hindu origin for the school of Sufism propagated by Basṭāmī. See his *Mysticism Sacred and Profane* (Oxford, 1957), pp. 166ff, and especially his *Hindu and Muslim Mysticism* (London, 1960), pp. 93ff. But such formulations as "that art thou" (*takūnu anta dhāka*) of Basṭāmī, or the Sanskrit *tat tvam asi*, are so universal and so deeply rooted in the texture of reality that they do not need to point to any historical borrowing whatsoever.

There are of course many other famous Ṣūfīs of this age, like Rābi'ah, Ibn Karrām, Ḥakīm al-Tirmidhī, and Abū Sahl al-Tustarī, who are also worthy of special mention. They are treated by both Massignon in the *Essai* . . . , chap. V, and Anawati and Gardet in their *La Mystique musulmane*, pp. 26ff.

12. For a discussion of Islamic arts and sciences, see Chapter I above.

13. This important source book of early Sufism was edited by R. A. Nicholson (London, 1941).

14. Edited and translated by A. J. Arberry under this title (Cambridge, England, 1935).

15. The quatrains have been rendered into English by R. A. Nicholson in his *Studies in Islamic Mysticism.*

16. See Sardar Sir Jogendra Singh, *The Persian Mystics. The Invocations of Shaikh 'Abdullāh Ansāri of Herat* (London, 1939).

17. The study of Asin Palacios, *Abenmasarra y su escuela* (Madrid, 1914), reveals the basic cosmological ideas of Ibn Masarrah which were influential in some of the formulations of Ibn 'Arabī.

18. See W. H. T. Gairdner's translation of the work (London, 1924).

19. This beautiful treatise of the *fedeli d'amore* in Islam has been edited by H. Ritter (Istanbul, 1942).

20. This work is one of the best-known treatments of the spiritual virtues considered from the Ṣūfī point of view. A translation of it has been made with commentaries by Asin Palacios (Paris, 1933).

21. Najm al-Dīn, entitled "the maker of saints," had twelve major disciples all of whom became famous Ṣūfīs themselves. He was the founder of the Central Asiatic school of Sufism with which the names of Simnānī, Sa'd al-Dīn al-Ḥammūyah, and Najm al-Dīn al-Dāyah are connected, and which is especially noted for the interest it showed in the symbolism of light which it used to express various inner experiences of the soul. See H. Corbin, "L'Intériorisation du sens en herméneutique soufie iranienne," *Eranos Jahrbuch,* 26:57–187 (1957).

One of the most widespread and best preserved Ṣūfī orders in Persia today, the *Dhahabīyah,* whose center is in Shīrāz, is a branch of the Kubrawīyah.

22. His function can be compared in many ways to that of Shankara in Hinduism.

23. Ibn 'Arabī's life has been described in nearly all the traditional histories and biographies of the later centuries, such as *Nafḥ al-tibb* of al-Maqqārī; *Bustān al-'ārifīn* of al-Nawawī; *Ta'rīkh al-islām* of al-Dhahabī; *al-Wāfī bi'l-wafayāt* of al-Ṣafadī; *Mir'āt al-jinān* of al-Yāfi'ī; *al-Bidāyah wa'l-nihāyah* of Ibn Kathīr; *al-Ṭabaqāt al-kubrā* of al-Sha'rānī; *Shadharāt al-dhahab* of Ibn al-'Imād; and *Ṭarā'iq al-ḥaqā'iq* of Ma'ṣūm 'Alī Shāh. There have also been many biographies of Ibn 'Arabī written by disciples who have tried to defend their master from accusations made against him by some of the jurists. Of these one of the oldest is *Manāqib ibn 'Arabī* by Ibrāhīm al-Baghdādī, ed. S. Munajjid (Beirut, 1955) with a list of sources on Ibn 'Arabī given by the editor in his preface.

As for works in European languages on his life, there is the notable book by Asin Palacios, *El Islam cristianizado,* which is confined to a study of Muḥyī al-Dīn's life and spiritual method, in which the author has assembled the pertinent details from various traditional sources. See also H. Corbin, *L'Imagination créatrice dans le soufisme d'Ibn 'Arabī* pp. 32ff; and R. A. Nicholson, "The lives of Umar Ibnul-Farid and Ibnul Arabi," *Journal of the Royal Asiatic Society* (1906), pp. 797–

824, which includes the original Arabic text of *Shadharāt al-dhahab* concerning these two Ṣūfī masters. Asin Palacios also translated Ibn 'Arabī's *Risālat al-quds* under the title *Vidas de Santones Andaluces* (Madrid, 1933), in which the spiritual life of the master is described in his own words, revealing an aspect of him which is often forgotten when one studies only his metaphysical writings.

There have also been some recent works in Arabic on Ibn 'Arabī, such as T. 'Abd al-Bāqī Surūr, *Ibn 'Arabī* (Cairo, 1955), and 'Umar Farrukh, *al-Taṣawwuf fi'l-islām* (Beirut, 1947), an important chapter of which is devoted to Muḥyī al-Dīn.

24. *Al-Futūḥāt al-makkīyah* (Cairo, 1329 A.H.), I, pp. 153–154. This passage has been translated into Spanish by Asin Palacios in *El Islam cristianizado*, pp. 39–40, and into French by Corbin in *L'Imagination créatrice . . .* , pp. 34–36.

25. This is in reference to the Quranic verse (20:12) in which Moses is ordered to take off his sandal. Ibn 'Arabī's interest in this work of definite Shī'ah origin is significant in the light of the immense influence that he was to have later in the Shī'ah world and the rapidity with which his doctrines were assimilated into Shī'ah gnosis.

26. There must have been a basic relation between Ibn 'Arabī and Ibn al-'Arīf, and, through the latter, with Ibn Masarrah, although one cannot by any means "reduce" all of Ibn 'Arabī's doctrine to that of these predecessors. It is known in any case that he befriended 'Abdallāh ibn Ghazzāl, Ibn al-'Arīf's disciple, and had a definite affinity with the various Ṣūfī schools connected with Almeria.

27. See Asin Palacios, *El Islam cristianizado*, p. 41, n. 2, and H. Corbin, *L'Imagination créatrice*, p. 37, n. 15.

28. It was also here, in the city of his birth, before his departure, that Ibn 'Arabī composed what is most likely his first book, *Mawāqi' al-nujūm* (*The Setting Place of the Stars*) in which he expounded the various levels of meaning contained in religious rites.

29. The figure of Khiḍr (Al-Khadir) is a very important one in the spiritual hierarchy of Islam and is closely tied to that of Elie, the prophet who was taken to heaven, and the whole complex of myths and tales associated with him. See L. Massignon, "Elie et son rôle transhistorique, Khadirīya, en Islam," *Etudes carmélitaines*: *Elie le prophète* (Paris, 1956), II, 269–290, and his numerous studies that have appeared in the *Revue des études islamiques* over the years; see also the articles, "al-Khaḍir" and "Ilyas," by A. J. Wensinck in *Encyclopaedia of Islam.*

For an iconographic study of Khiḍr, see A. K. Coomaraswamy, "Khawāja Khadir and the fountain of life, in the tradition of Persian and Mughal art," *Ars Islamica*, 1:173–182 (1934).

30. Ibn 'Arabī had contact with many of the well-known figures of his day, some of whom, like Suhrawardī and the Persian poet Awḥad

al-Dīn al-Kirmānī, he had encountered personally and others, like Ibn al-Fāriḍ, Sa'd al-Dīn al-Ḥammūyah, and Fakhr al-Dīn al-Rāzī with whom he corresponded. (Ibn 'Arabī's letter to Fakhr al-Dīn advising him to put aside formal learning and seek after gnosis has been recently translated into French by M. Vâlsan, in "Epître adressée à l'Imām Ar-rāzī," *Etudes Traditionnelles,* 62:242–253 (July–August and September–October 1961).

31. The Syrian scholar Osman Yahya has been carrying on intensive research on the works of Ibn 'Arabī over the past few years and has made some remarkable discoveries in some of the libraries of Turkey. His forthcoming *L'Histoire et la classification des oeuvres d'Ibn 'Arabī* should be of great value in shedding light upon a subject that has remained obscure until now.

32. Al-Sha'rānī, *Kitāb al-yawāqīt* (Cairo, 1305), based on chaps. 89 and 348 of the *Futūḥāt.* See Corbin, *L'Imagination créatrice . . . ,* p. 59, where this and other passages pertaining to how the work was inspired are translated from Ibn 'Arabī's own words.

33. In this connection, see T. Burckhardt, *Die Alchemie* (Olten, Switzerland, 1960) and his *Clé spirituelle de l'astrologie musulmane d'après Mohyiddin ibn Arabi* (Paris, 1950), which demonstrate how the Alexandrian cosmological sciences became integrated into the perspective of Islamic gnosis and how the Universe in which the Muslims lived also partook of the Revelation and became "Muslimized."

34. The *Fuṣūṣ* has been printed many times in the original Arabic, the most critical one (to which I shall henceforth refer) being that of Abu'l-'Alā 'Afīfī (Cairo, 1946) in which the editor has assembled many valuable sections of the well-known commentaries on the work to elucidate the text. It has been translated with remarkable clarity by T. Burckhardt as *La Sagesse des prophètes* (Paris, 1955), with very helpful explanations. There is also a somewhat free translation of the work in English under the title *The Wisdom of the Prophets* (Madras, 1929), made by Khaja Khan.

Numerous commentaries have been written on the *Fuṣūṣ,* the most famous being those of Ṣadr al-Dīn al-Qunawī, 'Abd al-Razzāq al-Kāshānī, Dāwūd al-Qaiṣarī, 'Abd al-Ghanī al-Nablusī, Bālī Afandī, and 'Abd al-Raḥmān Jāmī, all well-known Ṣūfīs of later centuries. It continues to be studied in the Islamic world wherever Sufism flourishes and must be considered as the foremost authoritative text on gnosis (*'irfān*).

The *Lawā'iḥ* of Jāmī, trans. E. H. Whinfield and M. M. Ḳazvīnī (London, 1914), is also a commentary upon the *Fuṣūṣ* and a summary of its basic themes.

35. See *Fuṣūṣ,* p. 47.

36. The profound symbolism of the title of this work is fully de-

veloped by Burckhardt in his introduction to *La Sagesse des prophètes*, pp. 6ff.

37. These three works have been edited with an introduction and summary translation into German by H. S. Nyberg in his *Kleinere Schriften des Ibn al-'Arabi* (Leiden, 1919).

38. The Quranic commentary published in Cairo in his name, however, is by his disciple 'Abd al-Razzāq al-Kāshānī.

39. Ibn 'Arabī has so many works on each subject that it is not possible to give even an intimation of the dimension of his writings without devoting a separate study to them.

40. This work was translated into English by R. A. Nicholson (London, 1911).

41. Ibn al-Fāriḍ, the author of the famous *Khamrīyah* (see E. Dermenghem, *L'Eloge du vin*, Paris, 1931), and the greatest of Ṣūfī poets in the Arabic language, was a contemporary and friend of Ibn 'Arabī. It is said that on one occasion Ibn 'Arabī wrote a letter to Ibn al-Fāriḍ asking his permission to write a commentary upon his *Tā'īyah*. Ibn al-Fāriḍ answered that the *Futūḥāt* was itself a commentary and that its author did not need to write another.

42. This is true to such an extent that several of the followers of the school of Ibn 'Arabī wrote dictionaries of his terminology, which also became the terminology of the later Ṣūfīs. Of these the *Iṣṭilāḥāt al-ṣūfīyah* of al-Kāshānī, his well-known commentator, and the *Ta'rīfāt* of al-Jurjānī are particularly famous. See al-Jurjānī, *Definitiones: Accendunt Definitiones theosophi Mohji ed-din Mohammed Ben Ali vulgo Ibn Arabi dicti*, ed. G. Flügel (Leipzig, 1845). See also Burckhardt, *La Sagesse des prophètes*, pp. 207–223, where a glossary of technical Ṣūfī terms is given with an explanation of their meaning, as well as their translation into French.

43. The "sources" of Ibn 'Arabī are discussed in the second part ("Doctrina Espiritual de Abenarabi") of Asin Palacios' *El Islam cristianizado*; in Nyberg's introduction to his *Kleinere Schriften* . . . ; in the notes and appendices of Corbin's *L'Imagination créatrice* . . . and in the Appendix of A. E. Affifi, *The Mystical Philosophy of Muhyid Dīn-Ibnul 'Arabī* (Cambridge, 1939).

44. See T. Burckhardt, "Nature sait surmonter nature," *Etudes Traditionnelles*, 51:10–24 (January–February 1950).

45. There are very few studies in the European languages concerning Ibn 'Arabī's doctrines, considering his importance and influence. One may mention the well-known study of Affifi, *The Mystical Philosophy of Muhyid Dīn-Ibnul 'Arabī*, which has some good translations but which applies notions taken from modern European philosophy where they do not actually apply; R. Landau, *The Philosophy of Ibn 'Arabī* (London, 1959), which deals briefly with some of Ibn 'Arabī's doctrines and also has a few selections from his writings; and Corbin,

L'Imagination créatrice . . . , which is an important study devoted to the Shaikh's doctrine of creative imagination, the "sympathy" existing between man, the Universe, and God, and related questions. There are also the few works cited above and other studies which are enumerated in the Bibliography.

Of paramount importance for the study of the doctrines of Ibn 'Arabī is T. Burckhardt's *Introduction to Sufi Doctrine*, trans. D. M. Matheson (Lahore, 1959), which is in reality an introduction to the *Fuṣūṣ* as well as to Sufism in general; and also his introduction to and translation of *al-Insān al-kāmil* (*De l'homme universel*) of 'Abd al-Karīm al-Jīlī (Lyon, 1953), which is a more systematic treatment of the doctrines of Ibn 'Arabī by one of the greatest Ṣūfīs of the later centuries. There are also several studies of Ibn 'Arabī with translations of his works by M. Vâlsan which have appeared in the *Etudes Traditionnelles* from 1948 onward.

46. Ibn 'Arabī writes of his *Futūḥāt*: "This work, as all of my other works, does not follow the method current in works of others . . . In reality, all authors write under the authority of their own free will, whatever they may say about their freedom being subordinated to the Divine Decree, or under the inspiration of science they possess as their specialty . . . On the other hand, the author who writes under the edict of Divine inspiration, often records things which are without (apparent) relation to the subject matter of the chapter that he is treating. They appear to the profane reader as an incoherent interpolation, whereas according to me they belong to the very heart of the chapter even if it is by virtue of a reason which others ignore." *Futūḥāt*, I, p. 24; Asin Palacios, *El Islam cristianizado*, p. 102, and H. Corbin, *L'Imagination créatrice* . . . , p. 59.

47. "Such a distinction [between metaphysics and philosophy] may appear unwarrantable to those who are accustomed to regard metaphysics as a branch of philosophy . . . In order to define clearly the difference between the two modes in question, it may be said that philosophy proceeds from reason (which is a purely individual faculty), whereas metaphysics proceeds exclusively from the Intellect." F. Schuon, *The Transcendent Unity of Religions*, p. 9.

"A metaphysical doctrine is the incarnation in the mind of a universal truth . . . A philosophical system is a rational attempt to resolve certain questions which are put to ourselves. A concept is a 'problem' only in relation to a particular ignorance." F. Schuon, *Spiritual Perspectives and Human Facts*, trans. D. M. Matheson (London, 1954) p. 11.

48. For the study of this question in a quite different traditional background, that of Tibetan Buddhism, see M. Pallis, "The Marriage of Wisdom and Method," *France-Asie*, 17:1601–1620 (January–February 1961).

49. "To live in thoughts is continually to replace one set of concepts by another. In ratiocination concepts are worn threadbare without any possibility of their being replaced, on this level by something better. Nothing is more harmful than this wearing out of truth by the mind; it is as though true ideas took their revenge on anyone who limits himself to a thinking of them. . .

"Mental virtuosity, which endlessly plays with concepts without having either the ability or the desire to reach a definite result, has nothing whatsoever in common with speculative genius; moreover, the formulae of speculative genius [such as that of Ibn 'Arabī] will appear 'naïve' to such virtuosity, which is indeed opposed to intellectual intuition even as Lucifer is opposed to God." F. Schuon, *Spiritual Perspectives and Human Facts*, pp. 11–12.

"The Divine Reality is at the same time Knowledge and Being. He who seeks to approach that Reality must overcome not only ignorance and lack of consciousness but also the grip which purely theoretical learning and other 'unreal' things of the same kind exert on him. It is for this reason that many Ṣufis, including the most outstanding representatives of gnosis such as Muḥyi-d-Dīn Ibn 'Arabī and 'Omar al-Khayyām, affirmed the primacy of virtue and concentration over doctrinal learning. It is the truly intellectual who have been the first to recognize the relative nature of all theoretical expressions. The intellectual aspects of the Way include both the study of the doctrine and getting beyond this by intuition. If error is always strictly excluded, the mind, which is both a vehicle for truth and at the same time in a certain sense limits it, must itself also be eliminated in unitive contemplation." T. Burckhardt, in *Introduction to Sufi Doctrine*, p. 103.

50. It is only with the realization of the significance of the science of symbols that so much of traditional art and science that seems outmoded to the modern mind can be revivified and made to convey the meaning contained in traditional forms.

51. The profound study of various symbols of the traditions of the East, of the medieval West, as well as of prehistoric people, by such scholars as A. K. Coomaraswamy and, in more recent years, M. Eliade, have shown the indisputable truth of this assertion.

52. As H. A. Wolfson has demonstrated so clearly in his works, especially in *Philosophy of Spinoza, Unfolding the Latent Processes of His Reasoning* (Cambridge, Mass., 1948), vol. I, chaps. 3 and 4, the medieval philosophers were unanimous in placing God, or Pure Being, above substance. How, then, could the Ṣūfīs, who consider the Divine Essence (*dhāt*) to transcend even Being, believe in God having a substance which he shares with the Universe? See T. Burckhardt, *Introduction to Sufi Doctrine*, chap. 3. See also A. K. Coomaraswamy, "Pantheism,' Indian and Neo-Platonic," *Journal of Indian History*, 16:249–

252 (1937), in which the arguments advanced by the author would apply to Sufism as well.

53. The idea of natural mysticism has been discussed by J. Maritain in "L'Expérience mystique naturelle et le vide," in *Quatre essais sur l'esprit dans sa condition charnelle* (Paris, 1956), chap. 3; and by O. Lacombe in several studies devoted to Hinduism such as, "La Mystique naturelle dans l'Inde," in *Revue Thomiste*, 51:134–153 (1951). It has been applied specifically to Sufism by R. C. Zaehner, and by L. Gardet, especially in *La Mystique musulmane*, pp. 90ff.

54. For a profound discussion of this question, see F. Schuon, "Is There a Natural Mysticism?" in *Gnosis, Divine Wisdom*, trans. G. E. H. Palmer (London, 1957), chap. 3.

55. We generally avoid using the term *mysticism* because of the ambiguous meaning of this term in English. If used in its original sense as "understanding of the mysteries" and distinguished from its other connotations (as in German one distinguishes between *Mystik* and *Mysticismus*), then it would be appropriate to call Sufism Islamic mysticism.

56. This very important Ṣūfī treatise, also called *Kitāb al-ajwibah* and *Kitāb al-alif*, has occasionally been attributed to other Ṣūfīs, among them al-Balbānī and al-Suyūṭī; but it is in any case a synopsis of Ibn 'Arabī's views and belongs definitely to his school. Although the original Arabic text of the work has not yet been published, there is an excellent translation of it into French by Abdul Hadi in *Le Voile d'Isis*, 34:15–17 (January 1933) and 34:55–72 (February 1933) and a translation into English by T. H. Weir, "Translation of an Arabic Manuscript in the Hunterian Collection, Glasgow University," *Journal of the Royal Asiatic Society*, 809–825 (1901).

57. T. H. Weir, "Translation of an Arabic Manuscript . . . ," pp. 809–810. Regarding the independent existence of creatures, Ibn 'Arabī writes: "And the existence of the created things and their non-existence are the same thing. And, if it were not so, there would of necessity be an origination of something fresh which was not (before) in His oneness, and that would be a defect, and His Oneness is too sublime for that!" (*ibid.*, pp. 817–818).

58. This is the main theme of the *Fuṣūṣ*, as can be seen in the first two chapters which summarize the doctrines of Ibn 'Arabī.

59. Burckhardt has explained this concept fully in his introduction to *La Sagesse des prophètes*, pp. 9–11. The use of antinomian formulations and discontinuous expositions, which is closely related to the nomadic spirit of the Arabs, in its emphasis on the discontinuous aspects of things, recurs over and over again in Ibn 'Arabī's writings.

60. In the Quran (57:3) Allah is called the Exterior and the Interior, the First and the Last.

61. The terms *aḥadīyah*, *wāḥidīyah*, and others used by Ibn 'Arabī

are systematized and expanded to describe all the degrees of the "descent" or "determination" of the Principle from the Transcendent Essence to the world of corporeal forms by such later Ṣūfīs of this school as al-Jīlī and Jāmī.

62. See T. Burckhardt, *Introduction to Sufi Doctrine*, p. 62.

63. The *Shahādah* in this second aspect has the function of transforming all positive qualities *in divinis;* thus "there is no beauty but The Beauty"; "there is no goodness but The Goodness"; and so on. See F. Schuon, "Shadādah et Fātiḥah" in *Le Voile d'Isis*, 34:486–498 (December 1933).

64. "As for the Divine Names, they are necessarily limited in number, being nothing other than the Qualities summarized in certain fundamental types and 'promulgated' by Sacred Scriptures as 'means of grace' which can be invoked." T. Burckhardt, *Introduction to Sufi Doctrine*, p. 63.

65. Anawati and Gardet, *La Mystique musulmane*, p. 54.

66. The various aspects of the Universal Man are discussed in nearly every work of Ibn 'Arabī, and the *Fuṣūṣ* is essentially based on this concept. Also, his *Shajarat al-kawn*, or *The Tree of Being*, trans. with notes by A. Jeffrey in *Studia Islamica* (Leiden), 10:43–77 and 11:113–160 (1959), is specifically concerned with the idea of the Universal Man and is a basic source for the study of Ibn 'Arabī's "logos doctrine."

67. The sacred *ḥadīth*, "I was a hidden treasure; I wanted to be known, so I created the world," summarizes the Ṣūfī conception of creation and its purpose. By sacred saying (*ḥadīth qudsī*) in Islam is meant that body of utterances of the Prophet which are of direct Divine inspiration and in which God speaks in the first person through the mouth of the Prophet. This kind of tradition, or *ḥadīth*, is thus somewhat similar to the Quran although not a part of the Sacred Book.

68. The symbol of mirrors combined with that of the Universal Man is synthesized by Maḥmūd Shabistarī in his *Gulshan-i rāz*, that inspired poem which summarizes in the following verses these doctrines in the most explicit and clear formulation of them that can be found in Ṣūfī writings:

Non-being is the mirror, the world the image [of the Universal Man], and man
As the eye of the image in which the Person is hidden.
Thou art the eye of the image and He the light of the eye,
Who has ever been able to see with the eye that by which things are seen [namely, the eye itself].
The world has become man and man a world.
There is no clearer explanation than this.

A somewhat different translation is given by E. H. Whinfield in his translation called the *Gulshan-i Rāz, the Mystic Rose Garden* (London, 1880), verses 140–142.

69. For Ibn 'Arabī and other Ṣūfīs the letters of the Arabic alphabet, that is, the letters of the sacred language of the Quran, symbolize the celestial essences, or possibilities, which are manifested in the Universe as well as in the Quran. See M. A. Aïni, "Du mystère des lettres," in *La Quintessence de la philosophie de Ibn-i Arabi* (Paris, 1926), chap. II.

70. *Lā takrār fi'l-tajallī.*

Concerning the renewal of creation at every instant, which is closely connected to the process of realization and the "themes of meditation" accompanying the incantatory rites of the Ṣūfīs, see Burckhardt, "The 'renewing of creation at each instant,'" in *Introduction to Sufi Doctrine*, chap. IV; and Corbin, *L'Imagination créatrice . . .* , pp. 149ff.

71. A graphic design synthesizing the cosmological scheme described in the *Futūḥāt* is given by Burckhardt in his *La Sagesse des prophètes*, p. 108. The Quranic cosmological scheme of Ibn 'Arabī and other Ṣūfīs is based essentially on the "Throne Verse" (*āyat al-kursī*), 2:254.

72. Many Ṣūfīs have expounded cosmology in terms of the symbolism of the letters of the Arabic alphabet as well as in terms of the Divine Names whose inner meaning is closely tied to their very shape when written in the Arabic script. For example, in the *Futūḥāt*, Ibn 'Arabī combines astrological symbolism with the science of names and letters by making each of the 28 stations of the moon correspond to one of the 28 letters of the Arabic alphabet, each planet to one of the prophets, and each sign of the Zodiac to one of the Divine Qualities, so that the Universe is thus "Muslimized," and the revolution of the heavens appears as a process by which the light of Being is disseminated throughout the Universe by the various Qualities which "polarize" its light. This marriage of Islamic and Hermetic cosmologies by Ibn 'Arabī is studied in an illuminating fashion by Burckhardt in his *Clé spirituelle de l'astrologie musulmane d'après Mohiddin Ibn Arabi.*

73. See Anawati and Gardet, *La Mystique musulmane*, pp. 232–233, where these determinations are connected to states of contemplation gained through the practice of invocation as outlined by Ibn 'Aṭā'allāh al-Iskandarī; see also Burckhardt, *Introduction to Sufi Doctrine*, p. 96.

74. T. H. Weir, "Translation of an Arabic Manuscript . . . ," p. 811.

75. This famous saying is one of forty sacred *ḥadīths* upon which much of the theory and practice of Sufism is based and which contain the epitome of the esoteric teachings of the Prophet.

Concerning Ibn 'Arabī's doctrine of union, see Burckhardt, *Introduction to Sufi Doctrine*, chap. VII, especially p. 94, where this *ḥadīth* is quoted and discussed.

76. *Fuṣūṣ*, p. 104, and *La Sagesse des prophètes*, pp. 103–104.

77. The gradual interiorization of prayer until it becomes the prayer of the heart, and in its realized state a prayer possessing creative power, is essential to Sufism. The "theophanic prayer" of the Ṣūfīs and the creative power of the heart, as well as that of the imaginative faculty, is discussed in detail by Corbin, in *L'Imagination créatrice . . .*, chaps. II and III. In this short study we have had to omit a discussion of the meaning of imagination and other elements of Ibn 'Arabī's doctrines concerned with psychology. This aspect of his teaching, besides being discussed in the works of Burckhardt and Corbin, has been studied by Asin Palacios in his "La Psicología según Mohidin Abenarabi," *Actes du XIV Congrès Inter. des Orient.* (Alger, 1905), vol. III (Paris, 1907), and in several of his other studies devoted to Ibn 'Arabī.

78. The significance of prayer in all of its modes and in its theophanic function should make it clear that whatever Ibn 'Arabī's doctrine of the "transcendent unity of Being" may mean it has nothing to do with the philosophical monism with which it is often identified.

79. *Fuṣūṣ*, p. 62, and *La Sagesse des prophètes*, pp. 45–46. Ibn 'Arabī also writes in this chapter on the "word of Seth" — that in looking at a physical mirror one realizes that one can either look at the surface of the mirror and not see his own image or look at his image and not see the surface. This also is true of contemplating God: either the gnostic contemplates God, in which case he does not "see" his own essence, or he contemplates his own essence *in divinis* but does not "see" God separately. He also adds that the mirror is the most perfect symbol of the relation between the world and God, as well as of man's contemplation of God, and that God created the mirror specifically in order to enable man to have the means of envisaging these otherwise inexpressible relationships.

80. Jalāl al-Dīn Rūmī also refers often to the unity of religions and has many stories in the *Fīhi mā fīhi* (*The Discourses*), as well as in the *Mathnawī*, which demonstrate the unity of the inner content of all revelations above the formal plane.

81. Since at that time Islam, like other religions, lived in a separate world which for it was *the* world, there was no need, as there is today, to apply the principle of the universality of revelation to specific comparisons and the study of details. See F. Schuon, *The Transcendent Unity of Religions*, where this question has been studied in all its aspects.

82. *Tarjumān al-ashwāq*, trans. R. A. Nicholson, p. 67.

The use of love in this and similar contexts must be understood as the realized aspect of gnosis. Islamic spirituality is essentially gnostic, but it is a gnosis which is always combined with love and filled with its fragrance. When the Ṣūfīs oppose love to knowledge, they mean by the first realized wisdom and by the second only theoretical knowledge which has not become operative.

83. For example, the school of *waḥdat al-shuhūd* (The Unity of witness) was opposed to Ibn 'Arabī's *waḥdat al-wujūd*, but even the members of this school were influenced by the Andalusian sage. See Mir Valiuddin, "Reconciliation between Ibn Arabi's *Wahdat al-Wujud* and the Mujaddid's *Wahdat al-Shuhud*," *Islamic Culture*, 25:43–51 (1951).

84. The influence of Ibn 'Arabī in the East and the significance of such figures as Ṣadr al-Dīn have been discussed by Corbin in his "Notes et Appendices" to *L'Imagination créatrice* . . . See also S. H. Nasr, Introduction to the *Se Aṣl* of Mullā Ṣadrā.

85. This correspondence will be published shortly for the first time by Sidi Sulaimān Boukhshem in the series of the Institut Franco-Iranien in Tehran.

86. These little-known figures, who are of some significance in the later intellectual and spiritual life of Persia, have been studied for the first time in the West by Corbin in such works as "L'Intériorization du sens en herméneutique soufie iranienne," and in several other studies of his on Shī'ism that have appeared over the years in the *Eranos Jahrbuch*, as well as in his works cited in Chapter II above and in his latest essay on Ḥaidar Āmulī to be published soon in the *Mélanges Massé*.

87. The rapid integration of Ibn 'Arabī's doctrine into Twelve-Imām Shī'ism poses the interesting question of his possible relation with Shī'ism, one on which many Shī'ah figures have pondered over the centuries. Muḥyī al-Dīn is known to have been a Sunnī from the Sharī'ite point of view; yet he wrote a treatise on the Twelve *Imāms* that is highly valued by Shī'ah gnostics, and in the *Futūḥāt* (Chap. 366) speaks of the Mahdī and the conditions of his return in terms which coincide with those of traditional Shī'ah sources. Sufism stands essentially above the Shī'ah-Sunnī division in Islam but with Ibn 'Arabī there are, in addition to these universal principles accepted by both Shī'ah and Sunnī esotericists, doctrines of a specifically Shī'ah character regarding the imamate and other related matters which make the question of his possible relations with Shī'ism a difficult one to solve.

88. The influence of Islam, and particularly Ibn 'Arabī, on Dante was studied by Asin Palacios, *Islam and the Divine Comedy*, trans. H. Sunderland (London, 1926); and later E. Cerrulli, *Il 'Libro della Scala' e la questione delle fonti arabo-spagnole della Divina Commedia* (Vatican City, 1949) which affirms for the most part Asin's theses.

89. For example, glosses upon the *Fuṣūṣ* were published several years ago by one of the well-known *ḥakīms* of present-day Persia,

Fāḍil Tūnī, under the title of *Ta'līqah bar sharḥ-i fuṣūṣ* (Tehran, 1316).

90. Regarding Shaikh al-Tādilī, see Muḥammed at-Tādilī, "Lā ilāha illā Allah," trans. Abd al-Rahīm at-Tādilī and R. Maridort, in *Etudes Traditionnelles*, 53:344–350 (December 1952); and "La Vie traditionnelle c'est la sincérité," trans. with notes by A. Broudier, *Etudes Traditionnelles*, 59:212–227 (August–October 1958); 59:263–271 (November–December 1958); 60:84–89 (March–April 1959).

91. Shaikh Aḥmad al-'Alawī, known to his disciples as Shaikh Bin 'Alīwā, was one of the great saints of this century. His influence, even in his own lifetime, spread far beyond the borders of his native Algeria and has today reached the whole of the Muslim world and even the Occident, where several studies have been made of his life and doctrines. See A. Berque, "Un mystique moderniste," *Revue Africaine*, 79:691–776 (1936); and the excellent study of M. Lings, *A Moslem Saint of the Twentieth Century* (London, 1961). Particularly worthy of mention is Shaikh al-'Alawī's interest in the study of other religions and desire for a *rapprochement* between Islam and other traditions against materialism and modernism which he considered as their common foe.

INDEX

Abbasid, 4, 6, 10, 11, 14, 52, 53, 132
'Abd al-Bāqī Surūr, T., 160
'Abd al-Nūr, J., 158
'Abd al-Qādir, 97
'Abd al-Qādir al-Jīlānī, 89
'Abd al-Raḥīm al-Tādilī, 170
'Abd al-Rāziq, Muṣṭafā, 131, 132
abdāl (substitutes), 95
'Abdallāh al-Anṣārī, Khwājah, 87
Al-Abharī, Athīr al-Dīn, 47
abjad, 31, 141
Abrahamic Tradition, 15, 25
Absolute Reality, 106
Abū 'Alī Sīnā. See Avicenna
Abū Bakr, 84
Abu Bakr Siraj al-Din, 156
Abū Dharr, 84
Abū Ḥayyān al-Tawḥīdī, 18 19, 88
Abū Madyan, 89
Abū Naṣr al-Sarrāj, 87
Abū Nu'aim al-Iṣbahānī, 157
Abū Rīdah, 131–133
Abū Sa'īd ibn Abi'l-Khair, 21, 87
Abū Sahl al-Kūhī, 18
Abū Ṭālib al-Makkī, 87
Abu'l-Barakāt al-Baghdādī, 18, 36, 137
Abu'l-Ḥakam 'Amr ibn Sarrāj, 94
Abu'l-Ḥusain Muḥammad ibn Jubair, 94
Abu'l-Wafā', 18
"Adamic Word," 99
Ādhar Kaiwān, 82
Afḍal al-Dīn al-Kāshānī, 46, 145
Affifi, A., 144, 162
Afghanistan, 120, 145
'Afīfī. See Affifi
Afkār-i Suhrawardī wa Mullā Ṣadrā, 149
Afnan, S., 138, 145
Agathedemon, 62
aḥadīyah (unconditional unity), 108, 165
ahl al-ṭarīqah (one who follows a way), 156
Aḥmad al-Rifā'ī, 89
Aḥsā'ī, Shaikh Aḥmad, 81, 154
Ahūrāmazdā, 72
Al-Ahwāzī, 'Alī ibn 'Abbās, 34
'Ain al-Quḍāt al-Hamadānī, 58, 89, 150
Aïni, M. A., 167
ākhir (Last), 108, 165
'Alā, al-Dawlah, 22
'ālam al-mithāl (the world of similitudes), 113, 153
Al-'Alawī, Sayyid Aḥmad, 47
Al-'Alawī, Shaikh Aḥmad, 120, 170
Albertus Magnus, 49
Albumasar. *See* al-Balkhī, Abū Ma-'shar
Alchemy, 35, 132
Aleppo, 14, 57
Alexander Aphrodisias, 9, 38, 132
Alexandria, 3, 60
Alexandrian commentators, 9, 38
Alexandrian Hermeticism, 101
Algarbes, "Monastic state" in, 89
Algazel. *See* al-Ghazzālī, Abū Ḥāmid
Algeria, 170
Alhazen. *See* Ibn al-Haitham
'Alī al-Riḍā (*Imām*), 86
'Alī Ḥazīn. *See* Muḥammad 'Alī Iṣfahānī
'Alī ibn Abī Ṭālib, 6, 44, 81, 83–85
'Alī ibn Jāmi', 96
Allah, 107, 165
'Allāmah Ḥillī, 80
Almeria, 95, 160
Almohade, 94
Alonso, M. A., 145, 146
Alpharabius. *See* al-Fārābī
Al-Alwāḥ al-'imādīyah (*Tablets dedicated to 'Imād al-Dīn*), 58
Al-Amad 'ala'l-abad (*Time within Eternity*), 19
Amesha spentas, 72
'Amīd, M., 140, 143
Amīn, A., 149
Amīn, O., 134

Al-'Āmirī, Abu'l-Ḥasan, 18, 19, 134, 138
Amshaspands, 72
ana'l-ḥaqq (I am the Truth), 86
Anatolia, 57, 80, 96, 120
Andalusia, 1, 54, 92, 95
Andalusian philosophers, 46, 54
Andalusian sage. *See* Ibn 'Arabī
Andrea Alpago, 48
Angelology, 29–30, 45, 49, 50, 60, 69–71, 113, 140, 147, 152, 153; *see also* Angels
Angels, role of, 27, 29, 30, 45, 49–51, 68, 70–75 passim, 77, 78, 140, 147, 152, 153; *see also* Angelology
Antioch, 3
al-anwār al-mudabbirah (regent lights), 73
'āqil (intellect), 108
'aql (intelligence), 28
'Aql-i surkh (*The Red Archangel*), 59
Ārā' ahl al-madīnat al-fāḍilah (*Treatise on the Opinons of the Citizens of the Ideal State*), 15
Arabia, 1, 143
Arabic alphabet, 31, 167
Arabic language, 2, 4–6, 14, 17; Avicenna's use of, 23, 24, 37, 48; Suhrawardī's use of, 58–59; in Ibn 'Arabī's writings, 100, 113
Arabs, 149; and Suhrawardī, 165
arbāb al-anwā' (masters of the species), 72
arbāb al-ṭilism (masters of the theurgies), 72
Arberry, A. J., 133, 137, 139, 143, 156, 158
Archangel, 65, 71–73, 79
Archimedes, 133
Aristotle, 11, 12, 14, 17, 36, 38, 61, 67, 93, 131–135, 138
Aristotelian philosophy. *See* Peripatetic philosophy
Aristotelian logic, 5, 14
Armenia, 96
Arnold, T. W., 147
Asclepius, 62
Asfār (*The Four Journeys*), 19, 156
al-Ash'arī, Abu'l-Ḥasan, 52
Ash'arite theology 52, 53, 148; See also *Kalām*
Ashi'at al-lama'āt (*Rays of Divine Gleams*), 119
'āshiq (Lover), 108
ashqiyā' (the evil and ignorant), 77
Asia, 1, 37, 52
aṣīl (principial), 26
Asin Palacios, M., 95, 148, 156, 157, 159, 160, 162, 163, 168, 169
'Aṣṣār, Sayyid Muḥammad Kāẓim, 152, 155
Astrology, 11, 132, 133
Astronomical tables, 4
Astronomy, 22, 32, 33, 71, 132, 133, 140
Athenian, 11
'Aṭṭār, Farīd al-Dīn, 87, 90, 158
Augustinian Platonism, 55
Avendeuth. *See* Joannes Hispalensis.
Averroes, 15, 46, 48, 49, 54–56, 93, 94, 133, 140, 141, 146
Avicenna, 6, 9, 11, 12, 14–51, 52, 54, 56, 59–61, 64–67, 71, 75, 80, 87, 88, 101
Avicennianism, 145
"Avicennizing Augustinianism," 49
Āwāz-i par-i Jibra'īl (*The Chant of the Wing of Gabriel*), 59, 78
Awḥad al-Dīn al-Kirmānī, 160
awtād (pillars), 95
awwal (First), 108, 165
āyāt (portents), 104

Bāb, the, 154
Bābism, 154
Babylonian, 3, 4, 61
Bacon, Roger, 35, 49
Badawī, 'Abd al-Raḥmān, 149
Baghdād, 5, 10, 14, 18, 19, 52, 53, 86, 96, 134
Bahman, 71
Bahmanyār, Abu'l-Ḥasan, 45, 52, 144, 145
al-Baihaqī, Abu'l-Ḥasan, 18
Bakoš, J., 126, 139, 143
al-Balbānī, 165
Bālī Afandī, 119, 161

al-Balkhī, Abū Ma'shar, 13, 133, 134
al-Balkhī, Abū Zaid, 13, 19, 134
baqā' (subsistence), 114
al-Bāqillānī, Abū Bakr, 52
barakah ("grace"), 101, 106, 145, 156
Barani, S. H., 144
Barkishlī, M., 142
Barthold, W., 147
barzakh (isthmus or purgatory), 72, 75
Baṣra, 3, 10
al-Basṭāmī (Bāyazīd), 62, 64, 86, 90, 101, 158
bāṭin (Interior), 103, 108, 165
Bayānī, M., 149
Beatrice, 45, 96
Bedoret, H., 146
Being, 25–27, 41, 111, 112, 139, 164, 167
al-Bidāyah wa'l-nihāyah, 159
Bilāl, 84
al-Bīrūnī, 10, 17, 18, 46, 131, 133, 137, 144
al-Bitrūjī, 36
Blaise (*Poem on Medicine*), 48
Books of the Hours, 59
Botany, 24, 32
Boukhshem, Sidi Sulaimān, 169
Browne, E. G., 142, 143, 154
Bukhārā, 20, 21
Burckhardt, T., 161–168
Buridan, John, 36
Būstān al-'ārifīn, 159
Būstān al-qulūb (*The Garden of the Heart*), 58
Būzarjumihr, 63
Byzantium, 3, 4, 62

Canon (of Avicenna), 24, 32, 34, 35, 48, 139
Cardanus, 11, 133
Carra de Vaux, B., 131, 136, 138, 148, 149
Categories (of Aristotle), 14, 28
Central Asia, 3, 16, 21, 87, 147, 159
Chahār maqālah, 144
Chain of being, 38
Chemistry, 17, 35
China, 37
Christian philosophers, 5, 25, 54, 120
Christianity, 3, 4, 93, 147; and mysticism, 106
Companions of the Prophet, 85
Coomaraswamy, A. K., 160, 164
Copernican revolution, 50, 147
Corbin, H., 55, 138, 140, 144, 145, 149, 150, 153–156, 159–163, 167–169
Cordova, 92, 94
Cosmogony, 49
Cosmology, 17, 23, 28–31, 49–51, 97, 99, 111, 113, 140, 147, 167
Crombie, A. C., 142
Crusaders, 57

Dabīrān al-Kātibī al-Qazwīnī, 47
dā'ī (missionary), 145
D'Alverny, M., 139, 146
Damascus, 5, 57, 96, 97, 120
Dānāsirisht, A., 149
Daniélou, A., 143
Dānishnāmah-i 'alā'ī (*Book of Science dedicated to 'Alā' al-Dawlah*), 23, 32, 37, 139, 148
Dante, 32, 59, 96, 120, 169
Dar ḥaqīqat wa kaifiyat-i silsilah-i mawjūdāt (*On the Chain of Being*), 140
darwīsh, 156
al-Dawānī, Jalāl al-Dīn, 47, 80
Dāwūd al-Anṭākī, 139
Dāwūd al-Qaiṣarī, 161
De Anima, 34, 132
De Caelo, 14
De causis primis et secundis et defluxu qui consequitur eas (Avicenna) 48
De Intellectu, 11
De Mineralibus, 35
De Scientiis, 133, 134
De Subtilitate, 133
Definitions (*al-Jurjānī*), 62
Dermenghem, E., 157, 162
al-dhāt. *See* Divine Essence
dhikr (invocation), 84
Dhu'l-Nūn al-Miṣrī, 62, 86
Dieterici, F., 134, 135
Dionysius the Areopagite, 152
Dioscorides, 34

Divine Beauty, in Sufism, 114
Divine Being, 114
Divine Comedy, 45
Divine Essence, 69, 105, 108, 110, 112, 113, 139, 164
Divine Intellect, 43
Divine Names, 100, 110–112, 116, 117, 121, 166, 167
Divine Origin, 79
Divine Qualities, 100, 109, 111, 112, 115, 116, 166, 167
Divine Reality, 107–109
Divine Self, Union with, 153
Dīwān (of Ibn 'Arabī), 100
Dīwān (of Ilāhī Qumshahī), 155
Dīwān (of Nāṣir-i Khusraw), 145
Duhem, P., 134, 142, 147
Dunlop, D. M., 134, 135
Duns Scotus, 49, 139
Durrat al-tāj, 47
Durrī, Ḍiā' al-Dīn, 150

East, the: Avicenna's influence in, 32, 35, 49, 50, 138, 145; Ibn 'Arabī's doctrines in, 80, 96, 118, 120; *see also* Orient
Edessa, 3, 4
Egypt, 3, 61, 120, 145
Elements of Theology, 9
Eliade, M., 164
Empedocles, 62
Enneads, 9, 135
Epistles (of the Ikhwān al-Ṣafā'), 88, 101
d'Erlanger, Baron R., 135, 139, 142
Eschatology, 69, 76, 139, 153
"Esoteric philosophy," 40, 43, 44, 50, 146
Euclid, 132, 133, 141, 145
Europe, 32, 48, 97, 140, 146, 151

"Face of the Beloved," 113
Fackenheim, E. L., 144
Faddegon, M., 134
Fāḍil Tūnī, 170
Failasūf al-'arab wa'l-mu'allim al-thānī, 131
Fakhr al-Dawlah, 21
Fakhr al-Dīn al-'Arāqī, 119
Fakhr al-Dīn al-Rāzī, 36, 46, 54, 57, 148, 161
fanā' (annihilation), 114
fann al-samā' al-ṭabī'ī (principles of natural philosophy), 141
faqīr (a follower of Sufism), 156
Fārāb, 14
al-Fārābī, Abū Naṣr, 9, 11, 12, 13, 14–20, 24, 37, 39, 54, 61, 64, 71, 131, 132, 134–136, 144, 150, 155
farahvashī (host of angels), 153
al-Fārānī, Ismā'īl al-Ḥusainī, 17, 137
Farīd al-Dīn al-Dāmād, 145
Farīdūn, 62
Farmer, H. G., 142
farrah (see *khurrah*)
Farrukh, 'U., 160
Farshādshūr, 63
Fate, 24, 40
Fāṭimah of Cordova, 92
Fedeli d'amore, 119, 120
Festugière, A. J., 150
Fī ithbāt al-mufāraqāt, 46
Fī i'tiqād al-ḥukamā' (*Symbol of Faith of the Philosophers*), 58, 149
Fī ma'ānī'l-ḥurūf al-hijā'iya . . ., 140
Fīhi mā fīhi (*The Discourses*), 168
al-Fihrist, 10, 18
Fi'l-falsafat al-islāmīyah, 149
Firdaws al-ḥikmah (*The Paradise of Wisdom*), 34
First Intellect, 24, 110
First Teacher (The). *See* Aristotle
Flügel, G., 162
Foster, K., 146
Free will, 24
Furūzānfar, B., 158
Fuṣūṣ al-ḥikam (*Bezels of Wisdom*) of al-Fārābī, 16, 136, 137, 150, 155
Fuṣūṣ al-hikam (*Bezels of Wisdom*) of Ibn 'Arabī, 62, 98, 99, 110, 115, 119, 161, 163, 165, 168, 169
al-Futūḥāt al-makkīyah (*The Meccan Revelations*), 96–98, 118, 161–163, 167, 169

Gabriel, 42, 73, 78, 79
Gabrieli, F., 135
Gairdner, W. H. T., 159
Galen, 32, 34, 39, 49, 141
Galenic medicine, 22
Galileo, 33, 36
Gardet, L., 131, 138–140, 143, 144, 147, 158, 165–167
Gautama the Buddha, 86
Gauthier, L., 131, 144
Gawhar murād, 47
Gawharīn, S. S., 138
Gemistos Plethon, 62
Geography, 13, 132, 133
Geography (of Ptolemy), 132
Geology, 24, 32, 33, 35, 133
Geometry, 32
Gerard of Cremona, 48
Ghanī, Q., 158
ghasaq (obscurity), 70
al-Ghazzālī, Abū Ḥāmid, 46, 53–55, 60, 88, 89, 101, 147, 148
al-Ghazzālī, Aḥmad, 89
al-Ghīlānī, Afḍal al-Dīn, 145
Ghiyāth al-Dīn Manṣūr al-Shīrāzī, 47
Gibb, H. A. R., 147
Gilson, E., 49, 131, 135, 138, 139, 143, 146
Gnosis, 16, 17, 24, 50, 51, 55, 56, 64, 76, 81, 83, 86, 87, 90, 97, 105, 121, 160, 161, 164, 168
Gnosticism, 17
Gobineau, Comte de, 154
God: in metaphysics of Avicenna, 25–51 passim; Suhrawardī's concept of, 69, 70, 78; in teachings of Prophet, 84; Ibn'Arabī's view of, 98, 99, 107–117 passim
de Goeje, M. J., 134
Georr, Kh., 136
Goethe, 88
Goichon, A. M., 138–141, 144
"Golden Chain of Philosophers, The," 15
Greece, 61, 134
Greek alphabet, 141
Greek philosophy, 6, 25, 60–61, 132, 144, 151
"Green Prophet". *See* al-Khaḍir
Grosseteste, Robert, 35, 49
Gruner, O. C., 139
Guénon, R., 156
Guido, M., 131
Gundissalvus, Dominicus, 48
Gulshan-i rāz (Secret Rose Garden), 119, 166, 167
Gurkan, Ḳ I., 142
Gushāyish wa rahāyish, 145

ḥadīth (tradition), 2, 59, 85, 100, 115, 166, 167
ḥadīth qudsī (sacred tradition), 166
Ḥāfiẓ, 87
Hafny, M., 142
al-hāhūt (the world of the Divine Nature), 113
hai'ah (form), 70
Ḥaidar Āmulī, Sayyid, 119, 169
ḥakīm (sage), 51, 64, 81, 137, 150–152, 155, 169
al-Ḥallāj, Manṣūr, 58, 60, 62, 64, 86, 101, 150
Haly Abbas (see al-Ahwāzī)
Hamadān, 21, 22
al-ḥaqīqat al-muḥammadīyah (Reality of Muḥammad), 111
ḥaqq (Truth), 108
Ḥarrān, 3, 4, 14, 60
Hartner, W., 133
Hārūn al-Rashīd, 4
Ḥasan al-Baṣrī, 85
Hayākil al-nūr (The Temples of Light), 58, 80
Ḥayy ibn Yaqẓān (The Living Son of the Awake), 23, 44, 46, 149
Hellenistic influence, 3, 4, 12, 133–134
Herder, 88
Hermeneutics (of Aristotle), 14
Hermes, 3, 60, 61, 63
Hermetic sources, 101
Hermetic symbolism, 79
Hermeticism, 4, 12, 59, 60, 63, 83, 98, 101, 113
ḥikmah (wisdom), 145, 155
Ḥikmat al-'ain, 47, 145
al-ḥikmat al-'atīqah (ancient wisdom), 61
al-ḥikmat al-ilāhīyah (Divine Wisdom), 157

Ḥikmat al-ishrāq (*The Theosophy of the Orient of Light*), 58, 61, 66, 76, 77, 79, 80, 119, 149, 152, 153
al-ḥikmat al-ladunīyah (Divine Wisdom), 61
Ḥikmat-i Bū 'Alī, 47
ḥikmat-i yamānī (Yamanī wisdom), 151
ḥikmat-i yūnānī (Greek philosophy), 151
Ḥilyat al-awliyā', 157
Hindu wisdom, 4, 61; as source of Sufism, 156, 158
Hinduism, 165
Hippocrates, 32, 34, 141
Holmyard, E. J., 142
Holy Spirit (*rūḥ al-qudus*), 66, 73
Homā'ī, J., 158
von Horten, M., 137, 141, 148, 150, 152, 154, 156
Houtsma, M. T., 147
Ḥujjat al-ḥaqq. *See* Avicenna
Hujwīrī, 87, 157
Hulagu (Mongol conqueror), 56
Ḥunain ibn Isḥāq, 5, 132

Ibn Abī Jumhūr, 119
Ibn Abī Uṣaibi'ah, 19, 138
Ibn al-'Arīf, 89, 95, 160
Ibn al-Fāriḍ, 100, 161, 162
Ibn al-Haitham, 46, 154
Ibn al-Nadīm, 10, 18
Ibn al-Qifṭī, 138
Ibn 'Arabī, 6, 51, 55, 56, 59, 68, 80, 81, 82–121, 136, 137, 148, 153, 154, 156–170
Ibn 'Atā'allāh al-Iskandarī, 167
Ibn Bājjah, 54
Ibn Dāwūd. *See* Joannes Hispalensis
Ibn Ghazzāl, 'Abdallāh, 160
Ibn Ḥawqal, 13
Ibn 'Imad, 159
Ibn Jawzī, 54
Ibn Kammūnah, 80
Ibn Karrām, 158
Ibn Kathīr, 159
Ibn Khaldūn, 55, 147
Ibn Masarrah, 88, 90, 95, 101, 159, 160
Ibn Miskawaih, 18, 20
Ibn Muqaffa', 5
Ibn Qasyī, 89, 95
Ibn Rushd. *See* Averroes
Ibn Sīnā. *See* Avicenna
Ibn Taimīyah, 54
Ibn Ṭufail, 54
Ibn Turkah, 119
Ibn Waḥshīyah, 63, 151
Ibn Yūnus, 18
Ibn Zailah, 45
Ibrāhīm al-Baghdādī, 159
Ibrāhīm ibn Adham, 86
Idrīs, 3, 60, 61; *see also* Hermes
Ikhwān al-Ṣafā' (Brethren of Purity), 18, 24, 31, 88, 101, 137
Ilāhī Qumshahī, Mahdī, 137, 155
Ilāhīyāt, 140
Ilāhīyāt khāṣṣ wa 'āmm, 155
al-I'lām bi manāqib al-islām (*Declaration of the Virtues of Islam*), 19
Illumination, 89, 149 (see also *Ishrāq*)
Illuminationist, 6, 40, 45, 47, 51, 52, 55, 80, 144, 153, 154 (see also *Ishrāqī*)
"Illuminationist theosophy," 45
Imām, 15, 60, 63, 64, 85, 86, 95, 118, 157, 169
Impeto (of Galileo), 36
al-Imtā' wa'l-mu'ānasah, 18, 137
India, 47, 56, 80–82, 87, 120, 131, 155
Indian philosophy, 6
Indus Valley, 1
al-insān al-kāmil (Universal Man), concept of, 91, 110, 112, 166
al-Insān al-kāmil (*Universal Man*), 119, 163
Inshā' al-dawā'ir (*The Creation of the Spheres*), 99
Intellect, Avicenna's concept of, 28
Intellectual substance, *See* Angels
intellectus adeptus, 39
intellectus in actu, 39
intellectus in habitu, 39
intellectus materialis, 39
Intelligences, The, 38, 45
Iqbāl, M., 154, 155
Iran, 79

Iranian learning, 4, 19, 33
Īrānshahrī, Abu'l-'Abbās, 9, 131
'irfān, 16, 137; *see also* Gnosis
iṣālat al-māhīyah (principiality of essence), 67
iṣālat al-wujūd (principiality of being), 67
Isḥāq ibn Ḥunain, 5
ishārah (directive), 91
al-Ishārāt wa'l-tanbīhāt (The Book of Directives and Remarks), 23, 43, 46, 47, 59, 80, 146, 148
Ishrāq, 55, 60, 62, 64, 68, 149
Ishrāqī, 24, 56, 58–67, 69–71, 77–81, 150, 152, 153
Islam, arts and sciences of, 22, 24, 98; Avicenna's influence on, 51; philosophy of, 9–10, 12–15, 17–20, 30, 31, 40–41, 50, 53–56, 59, 63, 64, 101; universality of, 79; and Sufism, 83–89, 93, 103, 106, 118
Islamic Revelation, 1, 83, 91, 109
"Islam of 'Alī," 85
Ismā'īlī, 20, 31, 46, 137, 145
Ismā'īlism (see Ismā'īlī)
Ispahān, 21–23, 33, 56, 81, 96
al-Istakhrī, 13, 134
Iṣṭilāḥāt al-ṣūfīyah, 162

al-jabarūt (the world of spiritual existence), 113
Jābir ibn Ḥayyān, 31, 79, 88, 141
Jābirian corpus, 88, 101
Ja'far al-Ṣādiq (*Imām*), 85
Jafr, 31, 78, 98, 141, 157
Jalālī calendar, 152
Jāmāsp, 63
Jāmī, 'Abd al-Raḥmān, 158, 161, 166
Jāmi' al-ḥikmatain, 145
Java, 87
Jeffrey, A., 166
Jesus Christ, 86
Jewish culture, 3–5, 25
Jews, the, 31
al-Jīlī, 'Abd al-Karīm, 80, 119, 163, 166
al-Jīlī, Majd al-Dīn, 56
jism (body), 28
Joannes Hispalensis, 48
Jones, E. R., 131
Junaid, 86
Judaism, 31
Jundīshāpūr, 4, 10
Jurjān, 21
al-Jurjānī, Sayyid Sharīf, 58, 62, 139, 162
Jurjānīyah, 21
al-Juzjānī, Abū 'Ubaid, 20, 45, 48, 138

Ka'ba, 118
Kabbala, 31
Kai Khusraw, 62
Kalābādhī, 87
Kalām, 47, 52, 147
kalimah, 99; *see also* Word
Kalimat al-taṣawwuf, 150
Kamāl al-Dīn al-Fārsī, 154
Kāmil al-ṣinā'ah, 34
al-Kāshānī, 'Abd al-Razzāq, 80, 119, 161, 162
Kashf al-maḥjūb (The Unveiling of the Hidden), 87, 157
Kayūmarth, 62
Ḳazvīnī, M. M., 137, 161
al-Khaḍir, 96, 160
Khaja Khan, 161
Khal' al-na'lain (Taking off of the Sandals), 95
Khālid ibn Yazīd, 2
khalq (creature), 108
khalwah (spiritual retreat), 84
Khamrīyah, 162
al-Kharraqānī, Abu'l-Ḥasan, 62
Khatm al-awliyā' (The Seal of Sanctity), 101
Khayyām, 'Umar, 46, 144, 164
Khiḍr (see al-Khaḍir)
khirqah (mantle), 96
Khudā-Bakhsh Library, 155
al-khulafā' al-rāshidūn, 2
Khurāsān, 14, 19, 21, 86, 145
Khurdād (archetype of water), 72
khurrah, 152
Khwārazm, 33
al-Khwārazmī, 18
Kindah, tribe of, 10

al-Kindī, Abū Ya'qūb, 9–13, 17, 24, 39, 131–134
al-Kindī wa falsafatuhu, 131
Kitāb al-adwār, 135
Kitāb al-ajwibah, 165
Kitāb al-alif, 165
Kitāb al-ḥāwī (*Continens*), 17, 34
Kitāb al-hidāyah, 47
Kitāb al-ḥujjah, 45
Kitāb al-jam' bain ra'yai al-ḥakīmain Aflāṭūn al-ilāhī wa Arisṭū (*The Book of Argument between the Ideas of the Two Sages, the Divine Plato and Aristotle*), 15
Kitāb al-luma' (*The Book of Flashes*), 87
Kitāb al-malikī. See *Kāmil al-ṣinā'-ah*
Kitāb al-manāẓir, 154
Kitāb al-manṣūrī (*Liber Almansoris*), 34
Kitāb al-masālik wa'l-mamālik, 13, 133
Kitāb al-mūsīqa'l-kabīr (*The Grand Book of Music*), 16
Kitāb al-ri'āyah (*The Book of Consideration*), 158
Kitāb al-siyāsat al-madanīyah (*On the Government of the City State*), 15
Kitāb al-ta'arruf (*Doctrine of the Ṣūfīs*), 87
Kitāb al-taḥṣīl (of Bahmanyār), 45
Kitāb al-tawahhum (*The Book of Apprehension*), 158
Kitāb al-yawāqīt, 161
Koran. See Quran
Koyré, A., 142
Kraus, P., 137, 141, 148, 154
Kremers, E., 142
Kubrawīyah order, 89, 159
Kūfa, 3, 10

al-Lāhījī, 'Abd al-Razzāq, 47, 80
al-lāhūt (the world of the Divine Nature), 113
Lama'āt (*Divine Gleams*), 119
al-Lamaḥāt (*The Flashes of Light*), 58
"Latin Averroism," 54, 146
"Latin Avicennianism," 49, 139, 146
Law. See *Sharī'ah*
Lawā'iḥ, 161
Laws (of Plato), 15
Liber der Causis, 9
Liber regius, regalis disposito. See *Kāmil al-ṣinā'ah*
Logic, 10, 11, 14, 16, 17, 20, 23, 24, 48, 56, 66, 67, 135, 138
Logos. See Word
Lucknow, India, 155
Lughat-i mūrān (*The Language of Termites*), 59
al-Lūkarī, Abu'l-'Abbās, 52, 145
Lull, Raymond, 120

Macrocosm, Universe as, 32
"Macrocosmic Quran," 104
al-Madkhal al-kabīr, 134
Madkour, I., 134, 135, 138, 149
madrasas (religious schools) 16, 54, 56, 80, 81, 145, 149, 155
Mafātīḥ al-'ulūm, 18
Maghrib, the, 89
maḥabbah (love), 72
Maḥāsin al-majālis (*The Virtues of Ṣūfī Gatherings*), 89
Mahdī, 44, 169
māhīyah (quiddity, or essence), 25
Maḥmūd of Ghazna, 21, 22
al-Maibudī, Ḥusain, 47
al-malakūt (the world of psychic substance), 113
Malik Ẓāhir, 57, 96
al-Ma'mūn, 4, 5, 10
Manāqib ibn 'Arabī, 159
Manāzil al-sā'irīn (*The Stations of the Travelers*), 87
Manichaeanism, 17
Manṭiq al-mashriqīyīn (*The Logic of the Orientals*), 23, 43, 146
Maqāṣid al-falāsifah (*The Purposes of the Philosophers*), 53, 148
al-Maqqārī, 159
ma'qūl (intelligible), 108
Marāghah, 47, 56
marbūb (servant), 116
Margoliouth, D. S., 156
Maritain, J., 165
Marrākush, 94

mashshā'ī, 9, 16; *see also* Peripatetic philosophy
ma'shūq (Beloved), 108
al-Masīḥī, Abū Sahl, 20
Massignon, L., 79, 86, 132, 141, 150, 154, 156–158, 160
Master of Illumination. *See* Suhrawardī
Master of *Ishrāq*. *See* Suhrawardī
Mas'ūd (of Ghazna), 22
al-Mas'ūdī, 133
Ma'ṣūm 'Alī Shāh, 159
al-Ma'ṣūmī, Abū 'Abdallāh, 46
Ma'ṣūmī, Abū Maḥfūẓ, 155
Mathematics: in writings of Avicenna, 24, 32, 37; in works of al-Kindī, 32
Mathnawī, 118, 168
Mattā ibn Yūnus, 14, 18
Mawāqi' al-nujūm (*The Setting Place of the Stars*), 160
Mazdaean, 71, 72, 153
Mecca, 95, 96
Medicine, 4, 11, 17, 18, 20, 21, 24, 31, 33–35, 48–50, 133
Medina, 1, 84
"Mensural music," 37
Metaphysics: of Avicenna, 23, 24, 28–29, 47, 48; of al-Fārābī, 14; of al-Kindī, 10, 11; of Ibn 'Arabī, 90, 97, 98, 100; of Peripatetics, 16
Metaphysics (of Aristotle), 14, 20
Metaphysics, Treatise on (al-Kindī), 11
Meteorology, 23, 32, 33, 133
Meteorology (of Aristotle), 14
Meyerhof, M., 137, 142
Microcosm, Man as, 32
Middle Ages, 13, 35, 48, 59, 61, 68, 152
Middle East, 1
Mineralogy, 32, 35
Minorsky, V., 134, 145
Mīr Dāmād, 24, 26, 47, 67, 81, 134, 151, 154
Mir Valiuddin, 156, 169
Mir'āt al-jinān, 159
Mīrzā Ṣāliḥ Ḥā'irī Māzandarānī, 47
Mishkāt al-anwār (*The Niche for Lights*), 60, 89
al-Mīzān, 155
Mongol invasion, 1
Monophysites, 3
Montpelier, 48
Morocco, 89
Moses, 151, 160
Mount Ḥirā', 84
Mount Qāsiyūn, 97
Muḥākamāt (*Trials*), 47
Muḥammad, 1, 2, 6, 83–85, 90, 101, 107, 111, 156, 166, 167
Muḥammad al-Tādilī, Shaikh, 120, 170
Muḥammad 'Alī Iṣfahānī, 151
al-Muḥāsibī, 86, 158
Muḥyī al-Dīn (see Ibn 'Arabī)
Mullā Ṣadrā, 19, 24, 26, 47, 67, 80, 81, 119, 132, 151–156, 169
mumkin (possible), 26
mumtani' (impossible), 26
Munājāt (*Supplications*), 87
al-Munqidh min al-ḍalāl (*Our Deliverance from Error*), 53
Muqābasāt, 18, 137
Muqaddimah, 147
Muqāwamāt (*The Book of Oppositions*), 58, 149
Murcia, 92, 95, 119
Murdād (archetype of the plants), 72
Murīdīn, the, "Monastic State" of, 89
Muṣādarāt (*Introduction to Researches on Euclid's Axioms*), 144
Muṣannafāt (of Kāshānī), 145
Music, 11, 15, 32, 37, 133, 139, 142
Muslim community, 1, 2, 52; culture in, 4–6; Iranian influence on, 19; and Sufism, 88
Muslim philosophy, 9, 26, 36, 53, 59, 62–63, 67, 81, 93, 119–120, 132; symbolism in, 31; *see also* Peripatetic philosophy
Muslims. *See* Muslim community
al-Mu'taḍid, 13
Muṭahharī, M., 155
Muṭāraḥāt (*The Book of Conversations*), 58, 149, 151
al-Mu'taṣim, 4, 10

Mu'tazilites, 12, 95
muta'allih (theosopher), 64, 77
muta'allihīn (see *muta'allih*)
mutaṣawwif (follower of Sufism), 156
al-Mutawakkil, 10

nā kujā ābād, 78
al-Nāblusī, 'Abd al-Ghanī, 119, 161
Nādir, A. N., 158
Nadwī, Sayyid Sulaimān, 145
Nafaḥāt al-uns, 158
nafas al-raḥmān (Breath of the Compassionate), 112
Nafḥ al-ṭibb, 159
nafs (soul), 28
al-nafs al-nāṭiqah (rational soul), 76
Nagy, A., 131, 132
Nahj al-balāghah, 81, 86, 154
Naishāpūr, 19
Najāt (*The Book of Deliverance*), 23, 32, 37, 43, 48, 66, 139, 140
Najm al-Dīn al-Dāyah, 159
Najm al-Dīn al-Kubrā, 89, 159
Nallino, C. A., 132, 144
Naṣīr al-Dīn al-Ṭūsī, Khwājah, 36, 37, 46, 47, 56, 80, 119, 145, 148
Nāṣir-i Khusraw, 46, 145
Nasr, S. H., 137–140, 143, 144, 147–149, 152, 154, 155, 169
al-nāsūt (the world of bodily forms), 113
al-Nātilī, Abū 'Abdallāh, 20
al-Nawawī, 159
Near East, 60, 141
Necessary Being, 27, 29, 38, 140, 152
"Neo-Empedoclean," 101
Neoplatonism, 9, 11, 12, 62, 67, 83, 98, 156
Neoplatonist, 11, 12, 15, 101
Neopythagoreanism, 4, 101, 132
Nestorians, 3
Nicholson, R. A., 105, 156, 159, 162, 168
Nichomachean Ethics, 14
Nisibis, 3, 4
Niẓāmī 'Arūḍī, 144
Noetics, 50, 146
North Africa, 1, 95, 120
nujabā' (nobles), 95
nuqabā' (chiefs), 95
nūr al-anwār (Light of Lights), 69–71, 73, 75
al-nūr al-aqrab (Most Proximate Light), 71
al-nūr al-a'ẓam (Greatest Light), 71
al-nūr al-isfahbadī (lordly or signeural light), 73, 76
al-nūr al-qāhir (victorial light), 71
nūr 'araḍī (accidental light), 70
nūr mujarrad (incorporeal light), 70
Nūrī, 86
Nuzhat al-arwāḥ wa rawḍat al-afrāḥ, 150

Occident, the, 11, 44, 48, 65, 79, 135, 170
"Occidental exile," 68
Occult sciences, 12, 132
Ontology, 24–26, 69
Optics (of Euclid), 132
Orient, the, 44, 50, 65, 79, 89, 95, 151
"Orient of Light," 66, 151
"Oriental Philosophy," 23, 43, 45, 50, 141, 143, 144
Olivi, Peter, 36
Osman Yahya, 161
Oxford University, 48

Pahlavi writings, 4, 5
Pakistan, 120, 145; Scholars of, 55
Pallis, M., 163
Palmer, G. E. H., 165
Paracelsus, 49
Paris, University of, 48
Parsifal, 78
Partaw-nāmah (*Treatise on Illumination*), 58
Path, the, 84, 100, 156; followers of, 8; *see also* Sufism
Peripatetic philosophy, 9, 16, 23, 24, 31–33, 36, 38, 40, 43–47, 52–56, 58, 60, 61, 63, 65–69, 71, 74, 75, 80, 81, 88, 102, 131, 135–137, 148, 152
Persia, 4, 17, 21, 35, 37, 46, 47, 55–57, 61, 79–81, 87, 89, 119, 120,

134, 137, 143, 147, 149, 151, 155, 159, 169
Persian culture, 4, 56, 60, 81, 135
Persian language, writings in, 23, 37, 46, 58–63, 66, 71, 87, 89, 118, 119, 140, 150–156 passim, 158
Persian philosophy, 4, 9, 58, 59, 60–63, 80, 141, 145; *see also* Sufism
Peter of Spain (Pope John XXI), 49
Philo, 101
Philoponos, John, 36
"Philosopher of the Arabs," 9, 132; *see also* al-Kindī, Abu Ya'qub
philosophia perennis, 61
Physics, 14, 20, 23, 33, 36, 37, 48, 66, 69, 74, 133, 138, 151, 153
Pines, S., 136, 137, 142, 144, 146
Plato, 12, 14, 15, 17, 61–64, 67, 135
"Platonic ideas," 67, 72, 110
Platonism, 17, 55, 59, 60
Plotinian, 29
Plotinus, 61
Poem on Medicine, (see Urjūzah fi'l-ṭibb)
Poetics (of Aristotle), 14
Political philosophy, 15, 16
Porphyry, 14, 28, 67
Portugal, 89
Posterior Analytics, 14
Pre-Aristotelian Philosophy, 63
Pre-Islamic learning, 4–6, 59, 60
primum mobile, 65, 140
"Prince of Physicians." *See* Avicenna
Prior Analytics, 14
Proclus, 9, 11, 15
Prophecy, 42, 144
Prophet, the. *See* Muḥammad
Psychology, 23, 24, 32–34, 38, 40, 69, 74, 97, 139, 153, 168
Ptolemy, 33, 132, 141
Pure Being, 164
Pythagoras, 62, 64
Pythagorean. *See* Pythagoreanism
Pythagoreanism, 12, 15, 37, 59, 60, 137

Qābūs ibn Wushmgīr, 21
Qādirīyah order, 89
qahr (domination), 72
Qairawān, 65
Qajar, 80, 81
Qānūn. See *Canon*
al-Qaṣīdat al-'ainīyah (*Ode on the Soul*), 24, 40
al-Qayṣarī, 119
Qazvīnī, M. Muḥammad Khān. *See* Ḳazvīnī, M. M.
Qazwīn, 155
Qazwīnī, Sayyid Abu'l-Ḥasan, 152, 155
Qiṣṣat al-ghurbat al-gharbīyah (*Tale of the Occidental Exile*), 59, 65, 149, 150
Quadri, G., 131
Quadrivium, 15, 37
Qum, 155
Quniyah, 96
Quran, 2, 20, 24, 42, 51, 59, 71, 83, 84, 99, 104, 109, 113, 117, 118, 133, 140, 148, 152, 155, 160, 165–167
Quranic commentary, 40, 97, 148, 155, 156, 162; *see also* Quran
Qūt al-qulūb (*The Nourishment of the Heart*), 87
quṭb (Pole), 64, 95, 111
Quṭb al-Dīn al-Rāzī, 47
Quṭb al-Dīn al-Shīrāzī, 46, 80, 119, 154

rabb (The Lord), 116
rabb al-naw' al-insānī (archetype of humanity), 73
Rābi'ah, 158
Rahman, F., 143, 144
Rampur (India), 155
ramz (inner meaning), 104
Rasā'il. See *Epistles* of the Ikhwān al-Ṣafā'
Rasā'il al-Kindī al-falsafīyah, 131, 133
Rawshanā'ī-nāmah, 145
al-Rāzī. Muḥammad Zakarīyā, 17, 34, 137
Renaissance, 11, 13, 35, 48, 55, 133
Republic (of Plato), 15
Rhazes. *See* al-Rāzī
Rhetoric (of Aristotle), 14
Rifā'īyah order, 89

Risālah fī ḥālat al-ṭufūlīyah (Treatise on the State of Childhood), 59
Risālah fī ḥaqīqat al-'ishq, 59
Risālah fi'l-'ishq (Treatise on Love), 23, 41, 43, 59, 144
Risālah fi'l-mi'rāj (Treatise on the Nocturnal Journey), 59
Risālat al-aḍḥawīyah (Treatise on the Day of Splendor), 139
Risālat al-aḥadīyah (Treatise on Unity), 107, 114
Risālat al-khalwah (Treatise on the Spiritual Retreat), 99
al-Risālat al-ladunīyah (Treatise on Divine Knowledge), 89
Risālat al-nairūzīyah, 31
Risālat al-quds, 160
Risālat al-qushairīyah (The Treatise of Qushairī), 87, 156
Risālat al-ṭair (Treatise of the Bird), 23, 44, 59
Ritter, H., 131, 149, 159
Rosenthal, E. I. J., 135
Rosenthal, F., 133, 135, 138, 147
Rosicrusians, 151
Rūmī, Jalāl al-Dīn, 87, 117–119, 136, 158, 168
Rūzī bā jamā'at-i ṣūfiyān (A Day with the Community of Sūfis), 59

al-Sa'ādah wa'l-is'ād (On Seeking and Causing Happiness), 19
Ṣabaeans, 3, 60
Sabziwārī, Ḥājjī Mullā Hādī, 81, 132, 155
Sachau, E., 131
Sacred Book, 24, 166
Sacred Scripture, 32, 60, 166
Sa'd al-Dīn al-Ḥammūyah, 159, 161
Sa'dī, 87
Ṣadr al-Dīn al-Dashtakī, 47
Ṣadr al-Dīn al-Qunawī, 80, 96, 118, 119, 137, 161
Ṣadr al-Dīn al-Shīrāzī. *See* Mullā Ṣadrā
Ṣadr al-muta'allihīn. *See* Mullā Ṣadrā
ṣafā' (purity), 157
al-Ṣafadī, 159
Safar-nāmah, 145
Safavid, 47, 80, 82, 134, 151, 154
Ṣafī al-Dīn al-Urmawī, 135
Ṣafīr-i sīmurgh (The Song of the Griffin), 59, 153
Ṣaḥīfat al-sajjādīyah, 86
Saif al-Dawlah al-Ḥamdānī, 14
Saints: role of, 77, 111; in Sufism, 86, 89, 90, 92, 159; prayer of, 116
St. Bernard, 45
St. Thomas Aquinas, 49, 140, 148
Saladin, 57
Ṣalāḥ al-Dīn al-Ayyūbī, 57
Salāmān wa Absāl, 23, 44
Salerno, 48
Saliba, Dj., 139
Ṣāliḥīyah, 97
Salmān (al-Fārsī), 84
samā' (spiritual concert), 16
Sāmī al-Kiyālī, 149
Sanā'ī, 87
ṣanam ("icon"), 72
Sanskrit, 4, 5
al-Sarakhsī, Aḥmad ibn Ṭayyib, 13, 133
al-Sarakhsī, Ṣadr al-Dīn, 145
Sardar Sir Jogendra Singh, 159
Sareshel, Alfred, 35
Sarton, G., 131, 134
Sassanid, 19
Sawāniḥ al-'ushshāq (Auspices of Divine Lovers), 89
Sayili, A., 141
Sayyid Abū Sa'īd, 94
Scholasticism, 55
Scholastics, Latin, 26, 139
Schuon, F., 140, 152, 156, 163–166, 168
Sciences, classification of, 10
Se aṣl, 152, 169
Second Intellect, 29
"Second Teacher." *See* al-Fārābī
Seljuq, 52, 88
Semite. *See* Semitic
Semitic, 31, 141, 152
sensus communis, 39, 68, 76
Sepahsālār madrasa, 155
Seth, 62, 63, 168
Seville, Spain, 92
Shabistarī, Maḥmūd, 87, 119, 137, 166

Shadharāt al-dhahab, 159, 160
al-Shādhilī, Abu'l-Ḥasan, 136
Shādhilīyah order, 136
Shāh 'Abbās, 81
Shahādah, 106, 109, 166
al-Shahrazūrī, Sham al-Dīn, 59, 79, 80, 150
Shahrīwar (archetype of minerals), 72
al-Shaikh al-akbar (Doctor Maximus). *See* Ibn 'Arabī
Shaikh al-ishrāq (see Suhrawardī)
al-Shaikh al-ra'īs. *See* Avicenna
Shaikhī, 81
Shajarat al-kawn (*The Tree of Being*), 166
Shakhṣīyāt qaliqah fi'l-islām, 149
al-Shams al-bāzighah, 155
Shams al-Dawlah, 21
Shankara, 159
al-Sha'rānī, 159, 161
Sharḥ al-ishārāt, 148
Sharī'ite, 169
Sharī'ah, 2, 5, 41, 83, 84
shaṭaḥīyāt (theophonic locutions), 158
Shawāriq, 47
Sherwani, H. K., 135
Shī'ah, 13, 44, 52, 56, 79, 81, 85, 103, 119, 134, 147, 155, 158, 169
Shiblī, 86
al-Shifā' (*The Book of Remedy*), 23, 32, 35–37, 43, 46–48, 66, 138–141, 143
Shī'ism, 56, 80–82, 85, 119, 136, 145, 153, 155
Shīrāz, 82, 159
shirk (polytheism), 106
Siassi, A. A., 143
Siger de Brabant, 146
Sign of the Balance, 66
al-Sijistānī, Abū Sulaimān, 10, 18, 19
al-Sijzī, 'Abd al-Jalīl, 18
silsilah (spiritual chain), 85, 145
Simnānī, 'Alā' al-Dawlah, 159
Sirr al-asrār (*Secret of Secrets*), 17
Smith, M., 152, 157, 158
Ṣiwān al-ḥikmah, 18
sophia, 96, 157
Sophistics (of Aristotle), 14
Soul, Avicenna's concept of, 28
Souls (of the heavens), 38, 41, 45
Spies, O., 138, 150
Spirit. *See* Universal Man
Spirit of the Prophet Muḥammad, 73
Stagirite, 14, 15, 54; *see also* Aristotle
van Steenberghen, F., 146
Steinschneider, M., 134, 146
Stoics, 12, 101
su'adā' (the pure), 76
Sufficientia, 23
Ṣūfī, 6, 16, 21, 43, 51–53, 57, 58, 61, 62, 83–121, 136, 139, 148–151, 153, 155, 156–170
Sufism, 16, 50, 53, 54, 57, 60, 83–121, 145, 155, 156–170
Suhraward, 56
Suhrawardī, Shaikh al-ishrāq, 6, 9, 24, 26, 45, 50, 51–82, 89, 119, 147–156, 160
al-Suhrawardī, Shihab al-Dīn 'Umar, 96, 149
Sultan Selim II, 97
Sumatra, 87
Sunnī, 52, 56, 79, 85, 147, 169
Supreme archangel, 29
Supreme Deity, 25
"Supreme Identity," 144, 156
Supreme Light, 69, 70, 74, 76, 77
Supreme Logos, 117
Supreme Pole, 95
Supreme Word, 78, 99
ṣūrat al-ḥaqq (Divine Qualities), 115
Ṣuwar al-aqālīm (*The Figure of the Climes*), 13
ṣuwar al-mu'allaqah (the world of "suspended" forms), 153
al-Suyūṭī, 165
Syria, 57, 120
Syriac language, 2, 5

ta'ayyun (determination), 113
al-Ṭabaqāt al-kubrā, 159
al-Ṭabarī, Abu'l-Ḥasan, 34
Ṭabaqāt al-ṣūfīyah, 157

Ṭabāṭabā'ī, Sayyid Muḥammad Ḥusain, 152, 155
al-Tadbīrāt al-ilāhīyah (*The Divine Directions*), 99
Tadhkirat al-awliyā', 157
Tafsīr al-kabīr, 148
Tahāfut al-falāsafah (*The Incoherence of the Philosophers*), 53
Tahāfut al-tahāfut, 54
Taḥṣīl al-sa'ādah (*On Attaining Happiness*), 15
Ṭā'ī, 92
Ṭā'īyah, 162
Ta'līqah bar sharḥ-i fuṣūṣ, 170
Talwīḥāt (*The Book of Intimations*), 57, 58, 80, 149, 151
Tamhīdāt, 150
tanzīh (transcendence), 109
Taoism, 156
Ṭarā'iq al-ḥaqā'iq, 159
Ta'rīfāt (*Definitions*), 62, 162
Ta'rīkh al-islām, 159
Tārīkh-i taṣawwuf dar islām, 158
Ṭarīqah, 83, 156
Tarjumān al-ashwāq (*The Interpreter of Desires*), 100, 168
taṣawwuf, 16, 136, 156, 157
al-Taṣawwuf al-islāmī, 158
al-Taṣawwuf al-islāmī al-'arabī, 158
al-Taṣawwuf fi'l-islām, 160
al-Taṣawwuf 'ind al-'arab, 158
tashbīh (comparison or "anthropomorphism"), 109
tat tvam asi, 158
Tatimmah ṣiwān al-ḥikmah, 18
ta'wīl (spiritual exegesis), 103, 104
Tehran University, 81, 155
Tenth Intellect, 29, 30, 42
Tenth Intelligence (see Tenth Intellect)
Thābit ibn Qurrah, 5
Themistius, 9, 38
Theology, 3, 11–13, 52, 53
Theology of Aristotle, 9, 61, 132, 135, 139
theoria, 102
Theosophy, 56, 58, 61, 80, 81, 101, 153, 155
"Theurgy," 72, 75
Third Intellect, 29
"Third Teacher," the, 134
Thomistic system, 49
al-Ṭībāwī, A., 158
Tibetan Buddhism, 163
ṭilism (*see* "Theurgy")
Timaeus, 17
al-Tirmidhī, Ḥakīm, 90, 101, 158
Toledo, Spain, 48
Torah, the, 118
Treatise on Metaphysics (of al-Kindī), 11
"Tree of Being," 110
Trivium, 15
ṭūlī (longitudinal), 71
Tunis, 95
Turkey, 161
ṭuruq (see *Ṭarīqah*)
al-Tustarī, Abū Sahl, 62, 64, 158
Twelve-Imām Shī'ism, 155, 169

Udang, G., 142
'ulamā' (doctors of the law), 57
al-'ulūm al-'aqlīyah (intellectual sciences), 52
al-'ulūm al-naqlīyah (transmitted sciences), 52
Umayyads, 2
ummahāt, 71, 153
Universal Existence, 110
Universal Intellect, 31, 40, 42; *see also* Active Intellect
Universal Man, the, 110
Universal Soul, 31, 39
Universe, the, 28, 32
'Uqlat al-mustawfiz (*The Spell of the Obedient Servant*), 99
Urdībihisht (archetype of fire), 72
Ukhnūkh, 60
Urjūzah fi'l-ṭibb (*Poem on Medicine*), 24, 48
'Usairān, 'A., 150
Uṣūl-i falsafah (*Principles of Philosophy*), 155
'Uyūn al-anbā', 19
'Uyūn al-ḥikmah (Fountains of Wisdom), 23

de Vaux, R., 49, 146
de Vinci, Leonardo, 142
Vohūmen, 71